The Coppolas

THE COPPOLAS

A Family Business

VINCENT LOBRUTTO AND HARRIET R. MORRISON

Modern Filmmakers
Vincent LoBrutto, Series Editor

 PRAEGER

AN IMPRINT OF ABC-CLIO, LLC
Santa Barbara, California • Denver, Colorado • Oxford, England

Library of Congress Cataloging-in-Publication Data

LoBrutto, Vincent.
  The Coppolas : a family business / Vincent LoBrutto and Harriet R. Morrison
     p. cm. — (Modern filmmakers)
  Includes bibliographical references and index.
  ISBN 978–0–313–39161–3 (hard copy : alk. paper) — ISBN 978–0–313–39162–0
(ebook)
1. Coppola, Francis Ford, 1939– —Criticism and interpretation. 2. Coppola, Sofia,
1971– —Criticism and interpretation. 3. Coppola, Roman—Criticism and
interpretation. I. Morrison, Harriet R. II. Title.

PN1998.3.C67L53   2012
791.4302′33092—dc23   2012018352

ISBN: 978–0–313–39161–3
EISBN: 978–0–313–39162–0

16 15 14 13 12   1 2 3 4 5

This book is also available on the World Wide Web as an eBook.
Visit www.abc-clio.com for details.

Praeger
An Imprint of ABC-CLIO, LLC

ABC-CLIO, LLC
130 Cremona Drive, P.O. Box 1911
Santa Barbara, California 93116-1911

This book is printed on acid-free paper ∞

Manufactured in the United States of America

For Lawrence (Larry) Virgilio
Firefighter, physical therapist, actor, marathon runner,
winemaker, first responder
—Perished at the World Trade Center, September 11, 2001

Contents

Series Foreword

The Modern Filmmakers series focuses on a diverse group of motion picture directors who collectively demonstrate how the filmmaking process has become *the* definitive art and craft of the 20th century. As we advance into the 21st century we begin to examine the impact these artists have had on this influential medium.

What is a modern filmmaker? The phrase connotes a motion picture maker who is *au courant*—they make movies currently. The choices in this series are also varied to reflect the enormous potential of the cinema. Some of the directors make action movies, some entertain, some are on the cutting edge, others are political, some make us think, some are fantasists. The motion picture directors in this collection will range from highly commercial, mega-budget blockbuster directors to those who toil in the independent low-budget field.

Gus Van Sant, Tim Burton, Charlie Kaufman, and Terry Gilliam are here, and so are Clint Eastwood and Steven Spielberg—all for many and for various reasons, but primarily because their directing skills have transitioned from the 20th century to the first decade of the 21st century. Eastwood and Spielberg worked during the sixties and seventies and have grown and matured as the medium transitioned from mechanical to digital. The younger directors here may not have experienced all of those cinematic epochs themselves, but nonetheless they remained concerned with the limits of filmmaking: Charlie Kaufman disintegrates personal and narrative boundaries in the course of his scripts, for example, while Tim Burton probes the limits of technology to find the most successful way of bringing his intensely visual fantasies and nightmares to life.

The Modern Filmmakers series will celebrate modernity and postmodernism through each creator's vision, style of storytelling, and character presentation. The directors' personal beliefs and worldviews will be revealed through in-depth examinations of the art they have created, but brief biographies will also be provided where they appear especially relevant. These books are intended to open up new ways of thinking about some of our favorite and most important artists and entertainers.

Vincent LoBrutto
Series Editor
Modern Filmmakers

Acknowledgments

We would like to thank many individuals who helped us bring this project to fruition in various ways.

To Alex Morrison, San Franciscan, sommelier, and wine specialist, much appreciation for your insights into Francis Ford Coppola's industry outside of film. Our respect and gratitude to Dr. Wendy Doniger, Mircea Eliade Distinguished Service Professor of Religions in the Divinity School of the University of Chicago, for her knowledge about *Youth without Youth* and other Francis Coppola projects.

We especially thank Daniel Harmon, the first editor of this project, for his warmth, compassion, and professionalism. To Jane Messah, we are grateful for her patience and perseverance in working with us to shepherd this book to completion.

To Susan Stodolsky for her assistance; to Harry Northup and Holly Prado, and to Randy Weinstein, we are indebted to you for your friendship. As always, our affection to Rebecca Roes for her unconditional support. Vincent LoBrutto acknowledges: at the School of Visual Arts (SVA), thanks to Reeves Lehmann, chair of the Department of Film, Video and Animation for his constant support; and to Sal Petrosino, director of operations, for his friendship and encouragement. And to all SVA students—past and present—thanks for their motivation. To Edgar Burcksen, former editor-in-chief of *American CinemaEditor*, to Jenni McCormick, American Cinema Editors' production manager; and to President Randy Roberts and Vice President Alan Heim of the ACE Board, my gratitude for keeping me in the fold.

To all interview subjects: Richard Marks, Walter Murch, Gordon Willis, the late William Reynolds, and the late Rudi Fehr—much gratitude for your expertise and contribution to the world of film.

We would like to acknowledge the following authors whose works on Francis Ford Coppola preceded this book: Gene D. Phillips, Rodney Hill, Peter Cowie, Michael Goodwin and Naomi Wise, Michael Schumacher, and

Jon Lewis. Their books are listed in the Bibliography, and where citations have been used they are in the notes.

Finally, with warm appreciation we acknowledge the passion and enthusiasm of film director, screenwriter, and producer Francis Ford Coppola. We were privileged to be part of the audience at a sold-out viewing of *Apocalypse Now* at New York City's Ziegfeld Theater before its official opening. We watched in amazement the Francis Ford Coppola Presents Hans-Jürgen Syberberg's *Our Hitler* event at Hunter College auditorium in New York City and witnessed Abel Gance's *Napoleon* with live orchestra conducted by Carmine Coppola at Radio City Music Hall. These experiences and so many more cinematic gifts have enriched our lives.

We are grateful to have had the opportunity to delve into the artistry of the Coppola dynasty and to apply the belief of President John F. Kennedy to them: "If art is to nourish the roots of our culture, society must set the artist free to follow his vision wherever it takes him."

Introduction

Undeniably Francis Ford Coppola has been an artistic force to be reckoned with throughout his bombastic five-decade career. Since his UCLA days when he assisted Roger Corman on "B" movies and leveraged that experience into his first professional screenwriter/director credit, *Dementia 13*, Coppola, father-figure of the American New Wave of the 1970s, has alternately embraced, rejected, manipulated, and been manipulated by Hollywood.

Instilled in Coppola's Italian roots is a deep and abiding imaginative sensibility he has cherished and nurtured as a constant in his creative life. Equally significant is the participation of family members from three generations in virtually all his endeavors. Coppola has kept his relatives close at hand, blending their talents and abilities with his own. His immediate family, wife Eleanor and children Gian-Carlo (1963–1986), Roman, and Sofia, have been a continual support system, often physically present during production. Most notably, they were with him for most of a three-year production experience in the Philippines and environs during the making of *Apocalypse Now*.

Coppola has been a Hollywood journeyman and a risk-taking entrepreneur. Throughout, he has maintained a fierce commitment to a highly personal way of life, a unique artistic integrity, and a profound credo that his existence is sustained by an unshakable relationship with the blood of his blood and a relationship with a community of artists and artisans who are of like mind and spirit.

Coppola's passage in the development of art, craft, and human discourse is unique. His worldview and legacy from his generation to the next personifies an artist's gift.

Coppola has been the subject of many journalistic volumes. There are number of full biographies on Coppola, as well as countless analyses and critiques of his major works. The primary purpose of *The Coppolas: A Family Business* is to illuminate Coppola's career and life in the context of *family*. Coppola was and is intimately involved with three generations of his biological family, and almost all have played a part in his creativity. Conversely, his influences are expressed in the unique artistry of many of his relatives. In this volume, the focus is especially on Sofia Coppola, as her career for over the past decade is closest to the screenwriting/film-directing path of her father. Also of import are the many extended family relationships and loyalties Coppola has developed with actors and crew. Such relationships are not exclusive to this filmmaker; nevertheless, they are striking and have produced some of the finest collaborations and most respected actors of the past four decades. In the view of the authors, Francis Coppola has earned a place in the pantheon of great film artists and has done so with his forebears and descendants imbued in his creations.

Roots

Francis Ford Coppola was born on April 7, 1939, in Detroit, Michigan, the second child to Carmine and Italia Coppola. His middle name, "Ford," is attributed to Henry Ford, the automobile icon who put Detroit on the map. The family had no deep roots in Detroit, but Carmine, a Juilliard-trained flautist and composer, followed the work. He was first flautist with the Detroit Symphony Orchestra and arranger for the Ford Sunday Evening Hour until the early 1940s.

Carmine, New York City–born, was offered the opportunity to play with Arturo Toscanini and the NBC Symphony Orchestra, and Francis and his older brother August were transplanted to the suburbs of New York City, where their younger sister Talia was born in 1946. Francis did not thrive in the neighborhoods where the family lived. Moving from place to place, he spent much of his youth in Woodside, Queens, uncomfortable with the roughness of the environment, not doing well in school, and not fitting in. There were, however, compensations. Carmine brought the children to Manhattan and to the backstage of the Radio City Music Hall to watch their uncle Anton conduct the orchestra there. They saw Broadway musicals, and at home the family enclave was filled with song, storytelling, toys, games, and art supplies.

In 1949 Coppola's preadolescence was shaken when he contracted polio. He suffered paralysis and remained in his bedroom for over a year with the disease. Coppola remembers that during this solitary convalescence he occupied himself with the family television set, puppets, a 16mm projector given to him by his maternal grandfather, and a tape recorder.[1]

Carmine Coppola sought help for his son's condition from the March of Dimes, and through physiotherapy Francis regained the use of his limbs and was able to return to school. His days at school were not happy ones, and he felt many of his teachers hated him. He says he thought the New York City public schools were like penitentiaries.[2] Francis was not considered a good-looking child. His ears stuck out, he wore glasses because of poor eyesight, and his name was a source of ridicule—spelled as Frances, it was a girl's name, and *Francis the Talking Mule* was a popular movie series starting in 1950 that invited teasing and embarrassment.

A significant outlet for Francis and his brother "Augie" was the time they spent at the movies. Francis and August took full advantage of New York City and the movie theaters in Queens; they educated themselves about movies, enticed by the film fare of the day. Francis revered his brother August, who was five years his senior. August was handsome and self-assured and unflaggingly protective of his younger brother. While August intended to be a writer and won writing prizes in high school, Francis was obsessed with all things mechanical and scientific. As a teenager Francis began to play the tuba and was proficient enough to enter the New York Military Academy at Cornwall-on-Hudson, a residential school where he could be housed while Carmine was on the road conducting musicals with Italia and little Talia in tow. The Academy was not a good match for Francis with its emphasis on sports and strict regimens. In Peter Cowie's biography, *Coppola*, he claims Francis made pocket money writing love letters for his fellow cadets.[3] A fish out of water, Coppola abandoned the Academy and ran off to New York City. August, who by then was studying English at the University of California–Los Angeles (UCLA), invited him out for the summer and exposed him to the writings of prominent authors of the day such as Aldous Huxley and James Joyce.

Returning to Great Neck, New York for high school in the fall, Francis continued playing his tuba and began developing an interest in theater. The mechanics of theater production intrigued him, and soon he was working the light board, acting, directing, and developing scripts. When it was time to attend college, Francis tried out for Hofstra University (then Hofstra College) at his brother's suggestion. His successful audition piece was *Cyrano de Bergerac*, and Francis Coppola entered Hofstra's Theater Arts Department on scholarship. His years at Hofstra were filled with artistic experimentation and success. Francis Coppola had found his footing. He wrote, produced, and directed dramas and musicals and was recognized as a major imaginative force. As he approached his final year at Hofstra he gravitated toward film (he had been making shorts all the while) and became overwhelmed with the revolutionary work of Russian filmmaker Sergei Eisenstein when he attended a screening of *Ten Days That Shook the World*. He spent his waking hours screening films at the Museum of Modern Art and devoured writings on film theory and technique. Francis started a film club that met on Tuesday evenings. His passions diverged. "On Monday I was in the theater and on Tuesday I wanted to be a filmmaker."[4]

The die was cast. In the fall of 1960 he entered the master's program at UCLA film school.

2

Francis Ford Coppola in Hollywood: A Big Boy Now

There were two major film schools in Los Angeles when Francis Coppola entered UCLA in 1960. Along with UCLA, the University of Southern California (USC) had a burgeoning film department. Of the two, USC was more hands-on, with an emphasis on student filmmaking. Coppola had entered the more academic master's program, and although Coppola was proving a competent screenwriter, he wanted practicum and collaboration. There was a prestigious faculty. In particular, he had one teacher who encouraged him greatly. This was Dorothy Arzner, the only female director in Hollywood. By then in her 60s, she was the first female member of the Directors Guild of America (DGA).

Roger Corman, the king of the "B's," combed the film school looking for an assistant; Coppola jumped at the chance. He soon proved a jack-of-all-trades and fulfilled any Corman request. Coppola was industrious and willing. One Corman assignment eventually led Coppola to England to shoot a Grand Prix sequence for Corman's *The Young Racers*. More than anxious to shoot a film of his own, Coppola pitched an idea he could accomplish with the equipment already at hand; he would go to Ireland and mount a low-budget horror film. Corman often used the technique of shooting two films back-to-back in the same general location—a sound economic strategy. Coppola would apply the same approach when he made *The Outsiders* and *Rumble Fish* back-to-back in Tulsa. Director Oliver Stone also employed this method when his production of *Talk Radio* took him to Texas. While Stone was in postproduction on *Talk Radio*, *Born on the Fourth of July* was being mounted, and Stone's production designer Bruno Rubeo dressed Texas to look like the streets of Massapequa, Long Island.[1]

In 1963 Coppola was able to write and direct *Dementia 13* through the graces of maverick producer Corman. Bankrolled with more than $20,000 from Corman, Coppola hastily crafted a script. *Dementia 13* is generally considered Coppola's first feature film. The thin plot deals with a dysfunctional family, a mysterious murderer, an old family secret, and an elaborate decaying castle as the main location; in the mix was the required Corman sex quotient. Coppola sold the idea to Roger Corman by describing it as a *Psycho*-like theme. Coppola was able to obtain some additional funds from a producer at a Dublin studio. His cast and crew were spillovers from *The Young Racers* and some of Coppola's own friends. As producer, Corman tinkered with Coppola's version, adding some additional elements: an axe murder and some narration for storyline clarity. The debut film was shown on a double bill with Corman's *X—The Man with the X-Ray Eyes* and opened to mixed reviews and a decent box office. Coppola was on the map. Most significantly, a young assistant art director, Eleanor "Ellie" Neil, was also on the set. A designer attending UCLA's master's program, the two quickly became a couple. After the film wrapped, Neil went back to Los Angeles to complete her degree and Coppola continued working with Corman. Several months later they worked together for Corman on *The Terror*.

On February 2, 1963, Neil and Coppola were married in Las Vegas. The marriage was spontaneous, and Eleanor had not even met any of Francis's family. Eleanor was the oldest of three children and the only girl. Her father died when she was 10 years old. The Coppolas set up housekeeping in Los Angeles, and Francis was offered a job almost immediately as a contract screenwriter for Seven Arts. Soon the family expanded with the birth of the Coppolas' first child, Gian-Carlo, on September 17, 1963.

Coppola's eventual impact as a director is so powerful that his sizable credits as a screenwriter are often overlooked. He developed a substantial catalog of adapted screenplays for Seven Arts. As is often the case, some of these products never saw the light of day or were reworked before eventually reaching the screen, with credit redounding to other writers. Conversely, Coppola was the recipient of credit for screenplays he doctored for Seven Arts. Among the scripts he wrote under contract for Seven Arts are *Reflections of a Golden Eye* and *Is Paris Burning?*, cowritten with Gore Vidal. Coppola's second son, Roman, was born in Neuilly-sur-Seine on April 22, 1965, while Coppola continued crafting the script under difficult circumstances. The original screenwriter, Anthony Veiller, was ill, and Seven Arts sent Coppola to provide assistance—although Veiller thought Francis was only there to learn the ropes from him. Veiller passed away, and Coppola was left with the arduous task of completing a complex script. It was at this point that Gore Vidal was called in. Vidal, the more experienced of the two, worked compatibly with Coppola to complete the task.

Coppola is credited as screenwriter for *This Property Is Condemned*, which ultimately was a flop after many failed business machinations, and he cowrote a version of *Patton* with Edmund North. The *Patton* screenplay had gone through several incarnations. The Coppola version eventually reached the screen, and the Academy Award–winning film yielded the Best Original

Screenplay Oscar for Coppola and North. In 1970, a 30-year-old Coppola, father of two, won his first of many Academy Awards, highlighting one of his multiple gifts: screenwriting.

Coppola was a bundle of energy and was not restricting his time to writing for Screen Arts. Unbeknownst to them, he was developing a screenplay he wanted to direct on his own. His desire to direct was fierce, and he pressed to make it happen. The clandestine script was *You're a Big Boy Now*, loosely adapted from a British novel.[2] Coppola intended to finance the project through independent sources, but Seven Arts got wind of the plan and insisted it was their property because it was written while he was still under contract. Warner-Seven Arts stated the budget as $1.5 million, but Coppola asserts the film cost $800,000 all told.[3] Still, Coppola would embark on his first mainstream film as screenwriter/director. Because of financial constraints, the film was cast with an admixture of unknown actors and established actors selected for lesser roles. Coppola was persuasive in personally hyping the script to well-known actors Julie Harris, Geraldine Page, and Rip Torn, who would appear alongside Peter Kastner, Karen Black, and Elizabeth Hartman, all of whom had barely any experience.

You're a Big Boy Now is essentially a coming-of-age story about a somewhat lovable, inept 19-year-old with overbearing parents who has yet to learn the ways of the world. Set in New York City with the "big boy" (Kastner) working in the stacks of the New York Public Library, the plot involves the foibles Kastner experiences, including sexual high jinks, on the road to manhood. Coppola made the city another character, utilizing high-tech equipment (with resistance from the traditional crew) that was flexible enough to allow him to maneuver through the actual public library (thanks to Mayor John Lindsay) and the streets and stores of New York. This infused the film with a vitality, almost a frenetic quality. For the score, Coppola used the jaunty rock songs of the Lovin' Spoonfuls. In addition to breaking out of the studio-set mode, Coppola exercised another methodology he would use throughout his film-directing career. Comfortable as a theater director, Coppola believed in the value of rehearsal and spent the first few weeks of production preparing the cast through improvisation and character study. When the cast began working with the script they were well acquainted with their own characters and the characters with whom they would interact and were free to focus on line readings in a more informed manner. This is not a typical film director's approach. An exception was the late Sidney Lumet, who was known for this ritual; he came out of the Jewish theater and live television and saw the benefit of these preliminary activities and their cost-saving value; he maintained the director would need less takes.

Overall, the movie's dynamic communicated youth at a time when the lines were being sharply drawn between the older generation and the Beatles culture. Coppola has acknowledged an equivocal debt to director Richard Lester's *A Hard Day's Night* (1964), stating, "it was definitely influenced by

A Hard Day's Night. But it was all there already before I even saw *Hard Day's Night.*"[4] *You're a Big Boy Now* received a mixed critical reaction, but the reality that Coppola was given attention as a director was of major significance. Rex Reed described him as "the Orson Welles of the hand-held camera."[5] The film also served to satisfy his master's thesis, and Coppola was now a graduate of the UCLA master's program. He was seen as a transitional figure, leaving old Hollywood and touting the birth of a new American filmic transition. He told a respected film critic of the *Los Angeles Times*, Charles Champlin, "I want to make films in Denver, Hartford, Seattle, places nobody ever makes films. Give me $400,000 and six guys who love to make films and I'll do it." Champlin wrote, "It is one of those rare American things, what the Europeans call an *auteur* film."[6] What Coppola at the time was expressing was an evolving dimension of his artistic credo; it came to be known as the American New Wave.

3

Journeyman/One for Francis

You're a Big Boy Now was concrete proof that Francis Coppola was a bona fide director. The film was screened at the Cannes Film Festival where Coppola was nominated for the coveted Palme d'Or. Geraldine Page was nominated for a best supporting actress Oscar for her role as the overbearing mother. Despite the reality that the film was a low-budget, studio-controlled vehicle, Francis considered he had paid his dues. He envisioned his filmmaking future as independent. He would fashion his own deals and create projects that met his artistic standards. He had been conceiving an idea for a film called *The Conversation*. Prepared to move full speed ahead, his professional life took an unplanned detour. Coppola told Peter Cowie in *Coppola*, "I had made a promise to myself—the one I didn't keep—a vow that somehow what could make me exceptional was the fact that I could write original screen material—write the screenplay, and then execute it as producer and director."[1]

The year was 1968, and a declining old Hollywood was producing musicals to piggyback on the success of The *Sound of Music*. *Funny Girl* was in production, and the newly managed Seven Arts (merged with deteriorating Warner) had the property *Finian's Rainbow*. The 1947 Broadway musical with a whimsical, well-intentioned, antibigotry fantastical theme had not aged well but had a magnificent score. Warner-Seven Arts did not intend to pay for a high-budget blockbuster but banked on a youthful Francis Coppola to breathe air into the old chestnut. Seven Arts knew that Coppola had a background directing musicals in college and, coming off the youthful enthusiasm of *Big Boy*, Coppola seemed like a promising and prudent choice. This final project under Jack Warner's banner already had a commitment from the incomparable Fred Astaire to play Finian. The budget was set at $3.5 million with a 12-week shooting schedule, meager figures for a Hollywood musical. Francis wanted to refuse but convinced himself to consent based on the beauty of the score and the chance to involve his father Carmine as an orchestrator on the production. It would be Coppola's first opportunity to engage a family member in a Coppola picture, and the possibility that his father could be part of a film production at this stage of his professional life was heartening. Carmine had many unfulfilled years without a major breakthrough. His passion was not to play the flute, although he played masterfully, but to be a serious composer. Francis approached Carmine, who enthusiastically agreed to participate in *Finian's Rainbow*.

Coppola began production with a rehearsal period as he had with *Big Boy*. The cast was a mismatched conglomeration. British pop sensation Petula Clark played Astaire's daughter, the choice calculated to attract a hip, young audience (she was also under contract to Warner's record division). This notion was also applied to British crooner Tommy Steele and Canadian night-club singer and TV star Don Francks, both playing love interests in the musical but with no acting chops. Keenan Wynn played a blustery segregationist sena-tor. Coppola quickly concluded that the beauty of the Harburg/Saidy/Lane score was in no way supported by the screenplay. He tried to modernize cer-tain details, but it didn't really have an impact on the storyline. He knew he would have to find a way to make it work. Fred Astaire, at 68, was a veteran of countless Hollywood musicals created in controlled studio environments with meticulously choreographed production numbers. In addition to being a superb choreographer in his own right, the legendary Hermes Pan had been hired to design the choreography for *Finian's Rainbow*. Pan and Astaire had collaborated on 17 Hollywood film musicals. From the outset there was fric-tion. No studio sets with proper dance flooring were available for the film. Warner-Seven Arts wanted the existing back lot set originally used for *Camelot* to double for the countrified environment of *Finian's Rainbow*. Pan complained the set was not suitable for dancing and requested additional rehearsal time to iron it out. Coppola was pressed; there was no time. Pan was fired, and Coppola absorbed responsibility for the choreography. Francis Coppola was an artist with multiple gifts, but choreography was not among them. He tried, instead, to let the camera infuse the musical numbers with energy. He wangled eight days of location shooting, and for the rest, in essence, he fudged it. At best, the results were mixed. Coppola hired his UCLA buddy Carroll Ballard to shoot the second unit, and the result is a super-scenic Americana opening sequence. Other scenes survive through the sheer beauty of the song lyrics, but the film's overall impression is not compel-ling. To add insult to injury, Warner-Seven Arts decided to blow up the 35mm print to 70mm in first-run screenings in the old roadshow style. In changing the film's aspect ratio,[2] the top and bottom of the frames were lost! If there were any acceptably choreographed sequences, the audience couldn't see those dancing feet. The box office was not particularly good, and Coppola learned another painful classic Hollywood lesson: decisions were made in the front office, after the fact, and without consultation with the director.

There were a few bright spots during the *Rainbow* experience. In produc-tion on the desolate Warner lot, Coppola noticed a young man quietly observ-ing the shoot. Coppola approached him and asked his business. The young observer was a USC film student named George Lucas. Lucas had already won first prize at the third National Student Film Festival for his short film *Electronic Labyrinth THX 1138 4EB* and then a Warner Bros. scholarship affording him six months at Warner's studio. Unfortunately, the studio was in decline, and *Finian's Rainbow* was the only action on the lot. From the sidelines, Lucas watched Francis Coppola's work-in-progress. Lucas knew Coppola by reputation. Coppola was five years his senior, but the two were part of the young film school generation and ecstatic to have that bond. The two became fast friends although their personalities were polar opposites. Lucas was a slender, bearded young man in white shirt and chinos, reserved, cautious, and pragmatic; Coppola also had a beard but was extroverted, emotional, and a risk taker. Lucas came to the set every day, and Francis asked him to take Polaroids of the action. They talked about their futures, and Coppola told Lucas he envisioned a new era of filmmaking: low budget location shoots with the moviemaker in control from script through edit. With this in mind, he asked Lucas to join him as documentarian and production associate on his next venture. Setting aside an unfinished script of *The Conversation*, Coppola decided to approach Warner-Seven Arts for an advance on another project he had been developing—he was now titling it *The Rain People*.

Coppola began organizing *The Rain People* with the intent of fulfilling his independent filmmaker concept. He chose as producers Ron Colby, with whom he had worked on *Big Boy* and *Finian's Rainbow*, and Bart Patton, a classmate from UCLA. To cast the film he looked to young actors from the theater community who were just crossing over to film and television: the three lead actors, Shirley Knight, James Caan, and Robert Duvall, all fit the criteria. The lead actress was Knight, whom Coppola had met at Cannes when *Big Boy* was screened there in 1967. Knight was confronted by a hostile press reacting to her role as a racist prostitute in LeRoi Jones's film *The Dutchman*.[3] An unnerved Knight was in tears, and Coppola comforted her by remarking that he would write a film for her. James Caan had been at Hofstra when Coppola was there and then studied at the Neighborhood Playhouse under the esteemed acting teacher Sanford Meisner.[4] A year after *The Rain People* he would have his break-out role as Brian Piccolo in the made-for-television movie *Brian's Song*. Robert Duvall also studied in New York under Sanford Meisner and had a small but pivotal role in *To Kill a Mockingbird* (1962).

The Rain People was a road picture that followed a young married and pregnant woman on a personal journey of self-discovery. Unsure of her status as wife and mother-to-be, she takes off in her station wagon to find out what she wants in life. Coppola took the entire cast and crew across the United States, formulating much of the story as they proceeded from location to location. Hitchhiker James Caan becomes Knight's companion on the road; the character is a brain-damaged ex-football player injured during a game. Caan becomes a kind of surrogate son as Knight sorts out her maternal feelings. Caan meets a violent end when Knight has a romantic encounter with

Duvall, playing a widowed motorcycle policeman. Much of *The Rain People*'s script was improvised and written as Coppola took advantage of settings and circumstances while the caravan journeyed cross country. Although tempers flared from time to time and living conditions were barely adequate, most of the young cast and crew rolled with the punches. They knew they were participants in a guerilla filmmaking experience that was on the cusp of a revolution in filmmaking; at the helm was a passionate and astute trailblazer. Of the lead actors, Shirley Knight had the most difficulty with the experience. She and Coppola argued creatively, and it probably didn't help that, in fact, she was pregnant like her character.

Coppola had invested in equipment he could utilize on the fly. The tools of the trade were transported along with the troupe. Coppola displayed solid working knowledge of the camera and editing concepts and had the respect of his crew.

Cinematographer Bill Butler, who would also shoot *The Conversation*, recalls in the interview book *Masters of Light*, "I love working with Coppola because Coppola is heavy. The things that he's putting on the screen are heavyweight ideas. He gives you lots of freedom. He lets your creativity work for him. I like that a lot."[5] Editor Barry Malkin, who was also raised in Woodside, Queens, sat at a Steenbeck (then state-of-the-art as opposed to the Moviolas still in use in Hollywood) in the kitchenette of a trailer cutting material as it was processed. At a certain point he needed to catch up with the mounting footage, and the group holed up in Ogallala, Nebraska, for five weeks while he assembled the material. George Lucas, the film's documentarian (*filmmaker: a diary by george lucas*) suggested his girlfriend Marcia Griffin (who later became Marcia Lucas) become assistant editor and support Barry Malkin's editing process. Lucas's documentary was a 16mm cinéma vérité chronicle of the production. George Lucas shot, edited, and recorded it; it has become a classic accompaniment to *The Rain People* adventure. Lastly, after the show was in the final edit stages, Coppola needed sound work to round out its technical elements. George Lucas had a sound guru friend at USC and approached him on Coppola's behalf. Working with no sound library material (he was afraid of being caught since he was nonunion), Walter Murch became another addition to the expanding crew of young upstarts who eventually would be icons of the American New Wave of the 1970s. Murch, like Butler, observed in *On the Edge: The Life & Times of Francis Coppola*, "Francis had a tendency to hire people and give them a great deal of freedom to do what they were doing and authority over their domain. So in a sense you feel an upwelling of responsibility for *him*."[6]

The Rain People opened in New York City in August 1969, about a year after the cavalcade had begun its journey. Coppola's family—Eleanor, Gio, and Roman—had been along for the ride. Throughout his career, Francis's family would travel with him whenever filming was away from home and lasted more than two weeks. He often involved family members. On *The Rain*

People, Ellie's brother Bill Neil participated as production assistant. The final product received a lukewarm response, but Coppola made true on his investment with Warner, completing the film on time and under the $750,000 allowance. Most consequential for Francis Coppola was the moniker at the end credits—"Produced by American Zoetrope, San Francisco," the name Francis Coppola had chosen for his production company.

And so the Zoetrope adventure began.

Zoetrope—Wheel of Life:
The Godfather, The Conversation, The Godfather Part II

At age 30, Francis Coppola had completed a largely independent film, *The Rain People*, which met many of the objectives he had striven for as a developing artist. He had taken his own script from start to finish, cast the film with actors of his choosing without interference, used locations for authenticity, and surrounded himself with a dedicated crew. His team used state-of-the-art equipment Coppola purchased in Europe where the French New Wave (*nouvelle vague*) and other independent artistic movements were flourishing. To boot, the project came in on time and on budget. Thus motivated, Coppola began conceptualizing an independent company where he could build on his theory of a community of artists and artisans crafting films outside of the old rules and regulations of the classic Hollywood studio system.

The Rain People wrapped in San Francisco, where Walter Murch did the sound mix. The early American Zoetrope participants agreed they did not want to locate their filmmaking commune in Los Angeles. San Francisco seemed to be the consensus. The first American Zoetrope location was on Folsom Street in a warehouse converted into a three-story loft. Coppola was the owner and George Lucas was vice president. Mona Skager, who assisted Coppola on projects from early on, was treasurer and secretary. Young filmmakers were eager to come on board. American Zoetrope was buzzing with activity as a new breed of filmmakers made use of the high-tech equipment all housed in one facility.

Coppola was committed to providing George Lucas with the opportunity to expand his *THX-1138* short into a fully realized feature. When it was clear that Lucas needed assistance writing the screenplay, Lucas ultimately turned to Walter Murch to fashion a script that would allow them to go into production.

It was then Coppola's task to obtain financing. As he had in the past, he approached Warner-Seven Arts, but there was little enthusiasm for Lucas's oddball script, and Coppola could not persuade them. Eventually a deal was struck, but not for *THX* alone. Instead Coppola had to agree to a seven-picture deal to be accomplished using the various American Zoetrope properties in development. Among them were *Apocalypse Now*, with a script by John Milius slated for direction by George Lucas, and *Vesuvia*, a project originated by his UCLA classmate Carroll Ballard. This placed a heavy burden on the fledgling company to deliver a number of profitable products. *THX-1138* began production in September 1969, and was completed in 10 weeks for $800,000.[1] That was the good news, but not the only news.

Coppola screened the film for its backers, and enthusiasm was low. Expressing a lack of trust in American Zoetrope and the marketability of Lucas's first feature, the film fell into Warner Bros.'s hands, where venerable Rudi Fehr (who had been Jack Warner's right-hand man and head of production) tried a light re-edit. The film was distributed by Warner-Seven Arts, but the fallout was devastating. Warner-Seven Arts severed its relationship with American Zoetrope, cancelling its seven-project deal and demanding repayment for the Lucas venture. The whole experience embittered Lucas and placed pressure on the Lucas-Coppola relationship. This was one of many examples of Coppola's disconnect between finances and artistry. There would be more. The dream of American Zoetrope was turning nightmarish.

Francis Coppola was hundreds of thousands of dollars in debt with no silver lining in sight. The American Zoetrope site became an equipment rental and postproduction house, which managed to keep it afloat. Coppola's only claim to fame toward the end of 1970 was as co-screenwriter of *Patton*, which was a box-office bonanza.

Because of the success of *Patton*, all was not lost. Coppola's reputation as a screenwriter still kept him in the game. He was receiving low-level directing offers, and among them was a property owned by Paramount Studios. The novel *The Godfather* by Mario Puzo was selling very well as a popular page-turner about a mafia family and its intrigues. Paramount thought it would attract an audience and brought Puzo out to Hollywood to create the script. Paramount had suffered reversals with several high-budget films that did not do well, including *Catch-22*, *Paint Your Wagon*, and *Darling Lili*. As a result they were in the hole for billions of dollars. Their strategy was to develop multiple low-budget vehicles and begin recouping the losses they had incurred. Robert Evans was the West Coast head of operations with Frank Yablans as his East Coast counterpart. Other directors had turned down the gangster film property, and when Coppola was approached he was reluctant after reading less than 100 pages of the novel. When Paramount asked again, Lucas gave him a push, reminding him of the debt hanging over his head. Coppola consented, and Albert Ruddy was assigned as line producer. Ruddy's key responsibility was to keep the production within the parameters that were established and, most of all, to keep Coppola on the straight and narrow.

A meeting was set with the president of Paramount studios, Stanley Jaffe, Robert Evans, Ruddy, and Coppola. Ruddy had prepped Coppola to adhere to the party line so his superiors would feel comfortable; when it was Francis's turn to speak, he held court on the theory of filmmaking and what his approach to *The Godfather* would be. After 25 minutes it was unclear if his audience understood his oration; nevertheless it was persuasive enough that the job was his. This was vintage Coppola, and it worked. Coppola was hired to direct and work with Puzo on the script. His salary was a purported $150,000 and a purported $7\frac{1}{2}$ percent of net profits.[2]

Conflicts began to surface immediately when the studio wanted to update the timeframe of the story and set it in St. Louis, claiming a New York shoot would be too expensive. Coppola stood pat, allowing Ruddy to present Coppola's objections to Robert Evans and Frank Yablans; $1 million was added to the budget for the New York location, and the timeframe was retained as post–World War II. Coppola wanted the Sicilian part of the story photographed in Sicily; Coppola was nearly fired, but in the end the studio acceded to this demand.

To develop the script Coppola used an approach that was successful when he directed theater pieces. He took the entire novel page by page and framed each page in a workbook, writing copious notes on the framed margin. He eliminated portions he didn't think would work on screen and developed dialogue, blocking directions, individual scenes, and visualizations. He and Puzo collaborated by sending versions back and forth. That method served *The Godfather* well. Puzo readily understood that Francis was the director and in command. Puzo told Coppola biographer Michael Schumacher, "The great thing about Francis is he never criticized my work. If I sent him a draft and he didn't use some of it, I knew he didn't like it. He never criticized it or said, 'Gee, this is shit.' He just didn't use it."[3]

The next challenge was to cast the picture and determine the crew. For the cast, Coppola was eager to use actors with whom he had worked successfully. James Caan and Robert Duvall immediately came to mind. For the key role of Don Corleone, Puzo himself envisioned Marlon Brando and had sent him the book. Coppola, who had approached Brando the year before about *The Conversation*, welcomed Puzo's idea. Jaffe was vehemently opposed, and Evans was right behind him. Brando's reputation was at a low point. He was overweight and unreliable. He had been off the radar for years. Well-established actors were considered for the role, and others pursued it. It was a star turn. Coppola grew increasingly adamant that Brando, the ultimate American actor of the second half of the twentieth century, *was* the Don. Jaffe relented only to a point. He wanted Brando to do a screen test.

Coppola found a way to make it happen without Marlon knowing that a taping they did was a screen test. After Jaffe and Evans saw the tape they immediately came on board. During the brief scene Coppola devised, Brando morphed into Don Corleone. As noted in Patricia Bosworth's book on Marlon Brando, Coppola advised Brando: "The Godfather could be played as a sweet little old man. Powerful people don't need to shout." About Brando, Coppola observed, "Before we started, I thought Marlon was this strange, moody titan, but he turned out to be very simple, very direct."[4]

Paramount wanted Caan for the role of Michael Corleone, the heir apparent, but Francis disagreed. He was intrigued by a young New York theater actor with a maturing off-Broadway career—Al Pacino. Virtually unknown in Hollywood, Pacino had been compelling the previous year in one of his first films, *The Panic in Needle Park*, directed by Jerry Schatzberg, who was part of the so-called New York School of directors—East Coast directors such as Arthur Penn and Sidney Lumet known for their gritty, naturalistic style. In 1973 Schatzberg would direct Pacino again, this time with Gene Hackman as his costar. Resistance to casting Pacino was fierce, as he appeared too diminutive for the role. He did not test well for the part, forgetting his lines. In Schumacher's biography, Pacino is quoted as saying he did not think he was right for the part—but Francis did. Coppola had seen him perform off-Broadway and thought he was a great actor. Having won the Brando battle, Coppola prevailed, and the rest is history.

Robert Duvall, who had appeared in *The Rain People* and Lucas's *THX 1138*, was cast as Tom Hagen, the adopted son and consigliore to the Don, and James Caan was to play the hot-headed Sonny Corleone. John Cazale, also a young theater actor who worked with Pacino, was cast as the ineffectual oldest son Fredo. For the role of Connie Corleone, Fred Roos, casting director, recommended Talia Shire. Shire, who attended Yale School of Drama, asked her brother for an audition. He said no. Roos was Talia's agent, and he pressed Coppola for an audition. Coppola relented. Evans thought the audition was wonderful, and Talia was cast. At the time, Evans and the studio did not know she was Coppola's sister; she was married to composer David Shire, and that was her professional name. In an online interview with Alex Simon (*The Hollywood Interview*), Shire reflects, "After I was picked, Francis and I had a long talk, because he was very concerned about the politics that go on in studios." In retrospect, Shire recognized the burden her presence placed on Francis as a fledgling director. Rounding out the actors who would all become stars after *The Godfather* was Diane Keaton. Mario Puzo had seen her in a popular television commercial airing at the time and suggested her for the role of Kay.

There was another incredibly significant New York choice. Cinematographer Gordon Willis was an East Coast director of photography with a solid career in commercials who was virtually unknown in Hollywood. His first feature film, *The End of the Road*, was shot in New York in 1970 and directed by Aram Avakian. *The Landlord*, directed by Hal Ashby, Irvin Kirshner's *Loving*, and *Klute*, directed by Alan J. Pakula, quickly followed.

Willis's contribution to *The Godfather* is incalculable. Willis is considered the master of low-key lighting and was dubbed "The Prince of Darkness" by his friend and fellow cinematographer the late Conrad Hall, but his lighting approach baffled the Hollywood suits at Paramount. In an author's interview he recalls, "Paramount was giving Francis a terrible time while he was shooting the movie. They almost fired him, and I don't think they were too happy with some of the things I was doing." Willis continues, "*The Godfather* changed moviemaking completely. The whole approach was different. People saw visuals in *The Godfather* that made it possible to do things today they were never allowed to do."[5]

Albert Ruddy chose Dean Tavoularis as production designer. Tavoularis's contribution to the visual look of the film created the perfect trinity of director, cinematographer, and production designer. Tavoularis continued collaborating with Coppola for the majority of his career.

Aram Avakian was the supervising editor of record and was dismayed at the voluminous footage Coppola amassed. Two prestigious Hollywood film editors, William Reynolds and Peter Zinner, finessed the abundant footage. In an author's interview, William Reynolds explained how they coedited:

> Francis said, "Bill, I want you to take the first half of the picture, and Peter, you take the last half." We had a real wealth of material to work with . . . there was lots and lots of editing to do to get a first cut. The picture was very long, well over three hours. Francis said to us editors, "I just can't show the picture at this length to Bob Evans" . . . so we did some really drastic surgery under Francis' direction. At that point we brought it to Bob Evans for the first time. When the screening was finished Bob said, "Well, this looks good, but I remember lots of wonderful material that isn't in the film; where is it?" Francis was very upfront about it. He said flat out that he didn't think the studio would buy a picture at an excessive length and Bob, bless his heart, said, "I don't care how long the picture is, put that material back. It's that good, so let's have it that long." It was because of Bob Evans and the clout that he carried at Paramount at that time that they brought the picture at that length.[6]

William Reynolds, a gentleman through and through, may have cleaned up the actual exchange between Coppola and Evans a bit, but Evans did instruct Coppola to make the picture longer to retain the many nuances of the storyline.

Volumes have been written about *The Godfather*. Invariably it appears on 10-best lists. It is number three on the American Film Institute's 100 Years—100 Films list with only *Citizen Kane* and *Casablanca* above it, and is number two of all Oscar-winning films since 1929. *Casablanca* is number one.

Before *The Godfather* went into production the studio needed to contend with another issue. The Italian-American Civil Rights League opposed the film, asserting it would defame Italian Americans. After strenuous negotiations, Paramount agreed to refrain from using the terms *mafia* and *la Cosa*

Nostra in the script. Understandably, the debate about glorifying the mafia and its effect on Italian Americans as an ethnic group has never gone away, just as it existed in the blockbuster television series *The Sopranos.*

The production was grueling, especially after the in-fighting about casting had sapped so much of Coppola's energy. Paramount continued to display mistrust and, rightfully, Coppola felt he was always on the verge of being fired. In truth, Coppola was not an experienced director, and some mechanics were beyond him. His direction was artistic and operatic to a flaw, but the crew had to do a lot of mop up. Ultimately, it was the actors who gave Coppola the capacity to reach the heights. Although they could be temperamental, they functioned as an extended family. And Coppola had the opportunity to involve his real family. Shire proved to be an unconditional support system. Shire described the Coppolas as a circus family. Shire remarks in *The Hollywood Interview*, "I've always said that we're in the tradition of a circus family. . . . We may be competitive, but as in great circus families, we never drop the other members, so we can do what I call the dangerous tricks."[7] Still, to the very end Francis believed the film was a massive failure and that his career was in jeopardy.

Coppola also had his father Carmine write incidental music for the film, and Gio, Roman, and Eleanor were extras in the church sequence. Baby Sofia Coppola, born on May 14, 1971, debuted as Connie Corleone's son in the pivotal baptism scene that intercuts with the film's bloody, dramatic conclusion. To Coppola, the kernel of *The Godfather* is about family and succession. • It has been described as Shakespearian in theme and proportion. *The Godfather* opened on March 11, 1972, to huge public success. It has amassed millions and millions of dollars over the past four decades. *The Godfather* was nominated for 11 Academy Awards and won three—Best Picture, Best Actor (Brando), and Best Adapted Screenplay (Coppola shared with Puzo). Coppola won the Golden Globes Best Director Award. Most noteworthy for Coppola was recognition from his peers. At age 33 he won the prestigious DGA award as best director. For the foreseeable future Francis Ford Coppola could write his own ticket.

When reality set in and Coppola finally could be assured *The Godfather* was a hit, he still took on a rush assignment at Evans's request. Paramount was developing *The Great Gatsby* as an "A-list" production, and the studio was not pleased with the Truman Capote screenplay. Time was of the essence, and Evans implored Coppola to redo a script in a month's turnaround. Coppola agreed and began writing in a North Beach café, spending many hours a day for five weeks. He applied the cut-and-paste notebook approach he had used successfully for *The Godfather*. Despite the pressure, he enjoyed the challenge of adapting such a prestigious novel. When he had completed the script, Evans labeled it "a brilliant adaptation."[8] It was a source of pride for Francis. He could not know then that director Jack Clayton would tinker with the script during production delays; the majority of Coppola's material was eliminated. Coppola had only disdain for the finished product.

Also following the release of *The Godfather*, Lucas approached Coppola about a project Lucas was trying to realize with little success. The film was *American Graffiti*. Coppola agreed to produce the film, and with his emerging bankability *Graffiti* was launched. The film is a reverie of West Coast cruising and rock-and-roll in the early 1960s. To everyone's amazement, it was a colossal hit. Although the project caused tension between Lucas and Coppola, mostly over financial disputes, where Coppola believed he ultimately came up short, *Graffiti* jump-started Lucas's career and allowed *Star Wars* to be more than just a twinkle in his eye. The unparalleled *Star Wars* franchise made Lucas a very wealthy man.

Coppola contemplated his next film project. He returned to *The Conversation*, a story he conceived in the late 1960s that had been put on the back burner. The storyline's text is about eavesdropping and surveillance; its subtext is loneliness. The film's subject was only heightened by the national paranoia of the Watergate bugging. The lead character, a renowned sound surveillance expert, Harry Caul, played by Gene Hackman, is undone when he becomes personally obsessed by a love-triangle assignment that results in murder. Coppola and Hackman worked very precisely on the details of the character of Harry Caul and the technology of eavesdropping, knowing that Harry Caul, for the first time in his career, is confronted with taking responsibility in a personal way for the principals of the eavesdropping.

The Conversation was made under the auspices of a newly formed unit—the Directors' Company—comprised of William Friedkin, Peter Bogdanovich, and Coppola, all successful new-generation filmmakers who wanted to exert some additional clout over their projects. It was financed by Paramount. The studio believed the three directors were settling into a more mature stage and traded backing for the directors' loyalty, foreseeing a good cash return in the end. With each director coming off of a big success—Friedkin, *The Exorcist*; Bogdanovich, *The Last Picture Show*; and Coppola, *The Godfather*—the studio indulged them. When *The Conversation*, perceived as an art-house film by Paramount, became Coppola's first offering, Paramount was irritated. In addition, Friedkin and Bogdanovich did not really like *The Conversation*, so there was dissension within the ranks. Bogdanovich came through with *Paper Moon* but quickly announced he was planning *Daisy Miller* as a showcase for his girlfriend Cybill Shepherd. By this time Paramount was prepared to reject this extra layer of authority and kiboshed the whole arrangement. Before it was disbanded, *The Conversation*, *Paper Moon*, and *Daisy Miller* were the sum total work products, and only *Paper Moon* was profitable. Once again, a conflicted Coppola was not able to totally gain the upper hand with the studios nor was he totally able to walk away.

About *The Conversation* Coppola has often referred to this moody film as his personal favorite and the most personal to him. He acknowledges several influences in *The Conversation*. He references Italian director Michelangelo Antonioni's *Blow-Up* and Hermann Hesse's iconic novel *Steppenwolf*.

Coppola, always fascinated with electronics, was able to develop a story that worked on many levels, including sound itself as an integral character. To shoot the film Coppola had hired Haskell Wexler, who was the visual consultant on *American Graffiti*. A conflict developed between him and trusted production designer Tavoularis, and Coppola replaced Wexler with Bill Butler, who had shot *The Rain People*. Along with Francis, Roos and Mona Skager coproduced the film. Coppola cast John Cazale, who had played Fredo in *The Godfather*, as an employee of Harry Caul's who is fascinated by his extraordinary abilities but frustrated by his withholding character. Gene Hackman described Harry as an "uptight, right-wing eccentric, secretive, but with no axes to grind."[9] Other cast members were Frederic Forrest, with whom Coppola would make many pictures; Cindy Williams; and Harrison Ford, who acted in *American Graffiti*. Robert Duvall appears uncredited. As would be the case in every subsequent film until *Twixt* was released in 2011, Coppola employed family members. His oldest son Gian-Carlo appears uncredited. To score the film, Coppola selected his brother-in-law, David Shire, and gave him the script well before production. Although not typical, it was fortuitous as Shire could begin to develop musical themes early on. The schedule for the film was tight because *The Godfather Part II* was already on the docket.

Perhaps the most crucial crew member on *The Conversation* was Walter Murch, who is a film editor, sound editor, and sound designer. Murch was responsible for the aural aspects of a film where sound is a key element. In an author's interview, Murch explains the electronic component of the film's opening sequence.

> You start to be aware of this electronic component element, but you don't know what it is. So that peaks your curiosity. There's nothing you are looking at that has anything to do with this sound. Of course, in three or four minutes you discover it. We had to invent some logic. This film was made in 1973, but we said: "There's going to be digital sound. Let's pretend somehow that Harry Caul has his hands on some prototype digital processing equipment, and when he's recording these people's voices, he's recording some kind of digital interference matrixing. When they're in focus it's fine. When you get off focus, are the digital underpinnings of the sound. So you start to hear the code itself rather than words. One of the hardest things to do in film is to intentionally do bad sound, but that's what we had to do. We had to intentionally imply that it's drifting away, otherwise it just sounds like bad mixing.[10]

Murch goes on to discuss the decisive phrase that is central to the plot of *The Conversation*: "He'd kill us if he got the chance." Throughout the film the phrase has been interpreted by Caul as "He'd *kill* us if he got the chance." When Caul listens to the phrase for the last time, he hears "He'd kill *us* if he got the chance." This shift in emphasis haunts him because he cannot decipher who is in danger in the love triangle. Murch talks about this change in the phrasing.

> "He'd kill *us* if he got the chance" was something Fred Forrest came up with spontaneously in one of those recording sessions in Pacific Heights Park. When I was putting the film together, I didn't use that take. I set it aside because it was not the right reading. So the film got put together; it was locked . . . and we were still having story problems . . . the film is an intensively subjective single point of view . . . You see everything through Harry's eyes. So I thought, "Harry is a lonely guy and without him knowing it, he is falling in love with this attractive woman (Cindy Williams) who he thinks is the victim . . . He's very adept at getting rid of filters on the tape but . . . Harry is forced to realize that the most powerful filter of all is the one that's in his head."[11]

In the film there is a dream sequence where Harry tries to make an emotional connection with the girl. He tells her about his sickly childhood, a clear recollection of Francis's own boyhood. "I was very sick when I was a boy. I was paralyzed in my left leg. I couldn't walk for six months. One doctor said I'd probably never walk again . . . " Harry then tries to warn her, yelling, "He'll kill you if he gets the chance." In the end, Harry is prey to his own devices. Now he knows the tables are turned and he is being bugged by his employer. He strips his apartment bare layer by layer trying to find the bug. The final scene is a poignant Harry Caul alone in his demolished apartment playing his saxophone for solace and refuge.

The Conversation was an art film and was well received critically. At Cannes Coppola won the coveted Palme d'Or, which Roman Coppola proudly carried for his father. The film was nominated for Academy Awards for best picture, best sound, and best original screenplay, competing against frontrunner *The Godfather Part II*. Of utmost significance, Francis felt deeply rewarded by the recognition *The Conversation* received—a film that was so special to him.

Coppola began principal photography on *The Godfather Part II* on October 1, 1973—redefining the term *sequel* in twentieth-century motion pictures. The atmosphere surrounding the production was markedly different from Coppola's anxiety-driven experience on the first film. It was clear he had carte blanche. As he stated in a *Playboy* interview in 1975, "I had to fight a lot of wars the first time around. In *Godfather II* I had no interference. Paramount backed me up in every decision. The film was my baby and they left it in my hands."[12] In Coppola's vision, there were several stated intentions for *Part II*. He mapped out a story that was intrinsically tied to *The Godfather* so he could eventually weave the material from the two films into one epic. While providing deep biography of Vito Corleone's roots, he also took pains to underscore Michael's deterioration into a vengeance-filled, isolated existence, so that by the film's conclusion the audience would understand the true evils of the mafia lifestyle. As Coppola articulates it in *Playboy*, "I didn't want Michael to die. I didn't want Michael to be put in prison. I didn't want him to be assassinated by his rivals. But in a bigger sense, I also wanted to destroy Michael. There's no doubt that, by the end of the picture, Michael Corleone, having beaten everyone, is sitting there alone, a living corpse."[13]

Much of the crew carried over from the original *Godfather* production. Barry Malkin and Richard Marks joined the editing staff with Zinner. Carmine Coppola took on additional composing responsibilities. Tavoularis and Willis returned to complete the remarkable production designer–director of photography–director triumvirate. All lead cast members returned. Robert De Niro as the young Vito Corleone was the significant new player in the cast. Of the returning actors, Talia Shire observes, "We were a family at that point. The second one was so stunning, which rarely happens with a sequel, but Mario and Francis were always working to up the ante. Now you have Greek literature, because you have the death of a mother, and a brother killing a brother."[14]

As always, Coppola brought his family. Eleanor and the three children can be seen in the sequence when young Vito Corleone comes to America. Roman also has a brief turn as a young Sonny. It was Francis's joy to include family members, meshing his work and his family. Even his mother Italia helps out, subbing as Mama Corleone in her coffin because Morgana King, the actress who played her, was spooked by the idea. This is not to say that there was no strain on Eleanor Coppola, who had dutifully accompanied Francis on all productions that took him out of the San Francisco area, where they had a sumptuous Pacific Heights mansion overlooking the Golden Gate. At every location in *Part II* (Santo Domingo, New York City, and Lake Tahoe) the weather was awful. Constant rain, even when it should have been sunny in the Caribbean, left Eleanor crying and depressed.

Early shooting was at the Lake Tahoe location where Michael Corleone has his compound. The production design of Michael's house on the lake is in stark contrast to Vito Corleone's cloistered but warm suburban environment. It was particularly cold and dank during this part of the schedule, and it wore everyone down. Al Pacino was especially affected. Between his performance as Michael in *The Godfather* and this production, Pacino had developed into a New York screen sensation with performances in Jerry Schatzberg's *Scarecrow* (costarring Gene Hackman) and Sidney Lumet's *Serpico*. Pacino was now able to compare directorial work methods and was irritated by Coppola's pace.

Coppola continued to maintain his own rhythm but understood that Pacino was under great stress. In the *Playboy* interview Coppola observes that, "The role of Michael is a very strange and difficult one and it put a terrific strain on him. It was like being caught in a kind of vise. In the first picture, he went from being a young, slightly insecure, naïve and brilliant young college student to becoming this horrible Mafia killer. In *Godfather II*, he's the same man from beginning to end—working on a much more subtle level, very rarely having a climactic scene where an actor can unload . . . The load on Al was terrific and it really ran him down physically."[15] Eventually Pacino had to take three weeks off, perhaps because he had pneumonia, perhaps because he suffered mental fatigue. Coppola was obliged to rework the schedule to accommodate his absence and focus on sequences where Pacino was not involved.

In an author's interview, director of photography Willis talks about lighting the Little Italy and Ellis Island turn-of-the century period in *Part II*. "I perceive period in a flatter light. Francis kept saying when it's in the sun it looks more period. Although there were some pieces that were in the sun, most of it was done in shade because the values were better. There was not as much light in the period interiors. People go through books and look at photographs of Ellis Island and that's their only real reference point. If you combine your reference point with what you feel, many times you come up with something that seems real. You've embellished it to make people perceive it as real—it's not real at all."[16] A particularly challenging shot was the reflection of the Statue of Liberty on young Vito in the boat's glass porthole. Gordon Willis told production designer Tavoularis how he could resolve the reflection. "Just do a big black-and-white photo blow-up of it. We'll put it outside the window."

Willis provides several examples that explain how locations are used as substitutions for what the audience perceives as an actual site. For the interior of Ellis Island a fish market in Trieste, Italy, was used. "The apartment house scenes were done in Rome. Part of it was done in Los Angeles, part of it was done in New York—it was shot all over the place. The scenes with De Niro on the rooftops were stretched over a long period of time because the weather wasn't good. The sun was out and we had to match the other shots."[17]

The structure of *Part II* was complex, with the stories of young Vito Corleone at the turn of the century and Michael's ascendance to power after the Don's death interweaving throughout the film. Editor Marks, in an author's interview, explains the editing challenges.

> The structure of interweaving the old and present story was written into the script. It was the contrast and juxtaposition that was the underpinning of the film. It always existed, but not necessarily in the exact way it appears on film. One of our most difficult problems was finding where to go back and forth, because the pace of the two stories was different. The old story was legato and lyrical and the new story was more frenetic. When you put those two together, it kept lurching you in and out of the film. We were constantly experimenting. Because of the constant cutting back and forth in time, the editing calls attention to itself. The editing structure is implicitly part of the story, so the editing took on a bigger role.

Marks goes on to discuss Coppola's reliance on the editing process. "He shoots long. He shoots beginnings, middles, and ends. He loves the editing process and relies very heavily on shaping the film in the editing process." As to whether Coppola spends a lot of time in the cutting room, Marks indicates that Coppola "reviews, talking, trying things, coming in and looking at it, talking again, trying other things. Occasionally, he would sit and work on sequences but he didn't live in the cutting room and I think that's a healthier way to work for everyone concerned. It is important for the director to maintain perspective."[18] Coppola invariably trusted his well-chosen crew. He respected their skills. He would spend some time in the editing room because he enjoyed the process and in this case was aware of the complexities in shaping the structure.

Much has been written about the uncommon acting abilities of De Niro. Best known for his dynamic relationship with director Martin Scorsese, De Niro came to Coppola's attention after his breakout performance as Johnny Boy in Scorsese's extraordinary early film *Mean Streets*. De Niro had auditioned for the part of Sonny in *The Godfather*. Coppola and Roos began mulling over the possibility of De Niro as young Vito Corleone. They decided to take De Niro to lunch without discussing their intentions. They spent the lunch checking out De Niro's features, demeanor, and mannerisms to determine if they could identify him with Brando, the older Vito, and whether they thought he could execute this difficult reverse transformation. After the social meeting, Coppola went with his gut, and, despite Paramount's reservations, he cast him without so much as a screen test. Coppola's instincts would be rewarded. Although De Niro could be inarticulate, shy, and insecure when he was not acting, he was capable of incredible hard work—whatever it took—to inhabit a role. De Niro researched every aspect of a character until he could totally transform himself. For a jazz musician in *New York, New York* he learned to play the saxophone; for the role of Jake LaMotta in *Raging Bull* he gained over 40 pounds and learned to box.

For the role of young Vito Corleone, De Niro studied the Brando performance again and again. He knew he had the responsibility to replicate the physical characteristics and qualities Brando had established. De Niro has stated, "I didn't want to do an imitation, but I wanted to make it believable that I could be him as a young man. I would see some little movements that he would do and try to link them to my performance. What I did was watch videotapes of Brando's scenes looking for gestures to pick up. Or maybe just a variation on something he did. The voice we tried first. I thought we might be going too far and that it was too raspy. I think it turned out pretty good though."[19]

While Coppola was shooting in Lake Tahoe, De Niro was honing his character. Because the majority of his speaking part was in a Sicilian dialect of Italian, Robert De Niro took a crash course in Italian and while in Sicily went to converse with relatives of the film's Sicilian dialect coach so he could hear the spoken word in its natural setting. There was no question that De Niro delivered an Oscar-winning performance, if that is the measure of achievement. De Niro was nominated in the Best Supporting Actor category along with one of his mentors, Lee Strasberg, who is a Myer Lansky–type family head in the movie. De Niro did not attend the Academy Award ceremonies in 1975, and when he was announced as the recipient Coppola accepted on his behalf: "I think this is a richly deserved award. Robert De Niro is an extraordinary actor and is going to enrich the films that are made for years to come."[20]

The reception for *The Godfather II* was terrific. To this day there is argument as to whether the sequel even exceeds the first film in scope, acting prowess, visualization, subtlety, classical drama, and tragedy. Critic David Thompson notes:

> The phenomenon . . . is that *Part II* is in many senses the bolder work—not just filling in the story gaps from Puzo's novel but building an explanation of how this America came about and of how desperate innovation grew into the most baleful and conservative measures. Notice how far this transition—the shift from hope and arrogance to fatal gloom—repeats the emotional journey of *Citizen Kane*, that earlier film full of warnings about being a success in America.[21]

De Niro's Oscar that night was the first of many for *The Godfather II*. Coppola reaped the fruits of his labors. With *Part II* he won the trifecta: Best Picture, Best Director, and Best Original Screenplay (with Puzo). Also honored was Tavalouris for his production design. Of particular joy to Coppola, his father Carmine won an Academy Award for the musical score shared with Nino Rota. So Coppola was a rich man emotionally and financially. His next artistic choices were entirely in his hands and heart. Having completed *The Godfather* and *The Godfather Part II*, Francis Ford Coppola undeniably had realized a masterpiece.

5

Coppola's Dark Heart: *Apocalypse Now*

After a grueling edit and re-edit of *The Godfather Part II*, an exhausted Coppola was ready for the Christmas release of the sequel. Never one to sit still, he was thinking about his next project and accelerated his involvement in artistic affairs in San Francisco. He bought a radio station, KMPX-FM, with funds against future profits from *The Godfather Part II*. He purchased the Little Box Theatre and the building that housed it and became immersed in *City* magazine, an underfunded journal focusing on all things San Francisco. Over time, Coppola had infused the struggling magazine with needed cash, a magnanimous no-strings-attached gesture, but now, in addition to dollars, he sought to redefine the magazine. He put his name out and used it in a major ad campaign, fired and hired staff, and fired again, changed editorial policy, and brought in experienced editors from outside venues. Coppola attempted to put his imprimatur on *City*. His decision making, in an effort to make a major San Francisco magazine, was poor. Coppola did not really understand San Franciscans; he was a New York boy, and the San Francisco natives resented his reimaging of their town.

Pulitzer Prize–winning San Francisco journalist Herb Caen, who wrote columns for the *Chronicle*, put it this way: "Why would Francis Ford Coppola hire a Los Angeles advertising agency to persuade us Bay Areans to buy his *City* magazine? I suppose it should also be recorded that Coppola's new toy is being designed by Mike Salisbury—also of L.A.—but leave us not to be provincial. I'm not sure yet, but I think I preferred the OLD *City* magazine."[1]

City had a short period of increased subscribership and revenue, but Coppola's money was seeping out the other end. Ultimately the magazine folded in 1976. Caen eulogized it in his column, placing Coppola at the center of its demise. More than the failure of a magazine, Coppola's involvement was indicative of his extreme behavior during this period in his life. There is no question that his successes led to excesses. On one level, it had been an artistic endeavor, part and parcel of Coppola's nature; in another way it was sheer arrogance. Coppola was imposing his newly found power indiscriminately. This ego-feeding conduct was evident in social activities as well. Coppola began hosting extravagant parties at his large home, inviting the great and near-great and wannabes for whom he would cook lavish meals. The house was truly a mansion, and in the days of 1970s overindulgence, all kinds of hanky-panky was rumored to have taken place under the Coppola roof. Eleanor Coppola, a shy, private individual, was unhappy with this unrestrained hoopla and would greet guests early in the evening and then retire to another part of the house.

Gradually, Coppola began to realize that no matter how many creative enterprises he was involved with in San Francisco, he was still an outsider and not necessarily beloved. He required a kind of attention and stroking, and he was not getting it, despite his influence. Perhaps, in part, this prompted Coppola to purchase a sprawling estate in Napa Valley. Intended as a retreat, the property was located in Rutherford, about 90 minutes from San Francisco, complete with a vineyard. Coppola could not then know how serendipitous the presence of the Rutherford vineyard would be.

April 8, 1975, when Francis Coppola won his coveted Academy Awards for *The Godfather Part II*, was a magical night for him. Carmine Coppola, in his acceptance speech, quipped, "If it wasn't for Francis Coppola, I wouldn't be here tonight. However, if it wasn't for me, *he* wouldn't be here."[2] It was endearing. Academy Award recipients can be forgiven for overlooking significant individuals during their thank-you speeches, and when Francis won the screenplay award and director's award he told his mother Italia that if he won again he would thank her. Then *The Godfather Part II* won for best picture, and, in addition to other remarks, he thanked the Academy for giving his father an Oscar and remarked there was something else he wanted to say but couldn't remember. Neither Carmine nor Francis thanked Italia. She was furious. In that sense, it was not Francis's finest moment as a devoted family man. Italia had been an actress in her youth, and her family had strong show-business ties in Italy. The Penninos had come to America from Naples, Italy. Italia's father composed Italian songs and was an early supporter of Italian films. As owner of the Empire Theater in Brooklyn, Francesco Pennino imported Italian films to air in his theater. From Italia's point of view, her influence on Francis's career was at least as major as Carmine's. Italia's father was a popular songwriter in Naples, and she referred to him as the "Irving Berlin of Italy."[3] Despite bickering about who deserved credit for Francis's artistic success, the reality was that like many first-generation American parents, Carmine and Italia would have preferred their children be doctors or lawyers, or in Francis's case an engineer; but since that was not the path they chose, Italia certainly felt she had earned recognition from her son on this occasion. There was also an unhappy Talia Shire, who had been passed over for best supporting actress in favor of the sentimental favorite, Ingrid Bergman in *Murder*

on the Orient Express. Talia was a   that her brother had not acknowledged her. As she observed caus   , "All of a sudden there are a lot of
relatives—aunts and uncles and c   s—all too willing to kiss Francis's ass
and trade on his status."[4]

Directly after *The Godfather Part II's* big win at the Academy Awards,
Francis and Ellie went to Rio for two weeks of alone time. On their return
from vacation, Coppola began formalizing *Apocalypse Now* so he could go into
preproduction. As a gift to himself he had also bought a rare Tucker automobile; he admired Preston Tucker's life story. The car was a concrete tickler to
remind him that he wanted to develop his biography into a film someday. He
had been buying himself a lot of lavish gifts. He owned a helicopter, a
Wurlitzer jukebox loaded with rare Caruso records, a room filled with trains,
and many other purchases indicating Coppola was on a manic buying spree.

The *Godfathers* were so phenomenally popular that television rights were
purchased by the summer. In July, NBC bought the rights to the two
Godfathers, including all unused footage, in order to make a nine-hour miniseries that Coppola would reassemble in chronological order. The deal was
purportedly for $15 million.

Coppola was now seriously focused on his next project, the Vietnam War
story *Apocalypse Now.* The backstory of *Apocalypse Now* began when George
Lucas and USC classmate John Milius were discussing the war in Vietnam in
the late 1960s. The two were members of the original Zoetrope group.
Milius, a crackerjack screenwriter, had heard of and spoken to returning sol-
diers about their experiences in Vietnam. He began to develop a project he
originally called *The Psychedelic Soldier*, which eventually became *Apocalypse
Now.* The plan was that Milius would write the script and Lucas would direct.
The script became part of the bundle that American Zoetrope lost to Warner
Bros. after *THX-1138* flopped. When Coppola was in the black he repaid the
money originally owed to Warner, and the developing scripts for *The
Conversation* and *Apocalypse Now* reverted to his ownership. Originally, Lucas
had owned the rights to *Apocalypse*, and in 1973 he refreshed Coppola's
memory about the project. In the ensuing year Lucas and Coppola argued
about monies to be paid for directing and producing and who would do what.
These were old financial tensions resurfacing on yet another project. The two
men were opposites when it came to money and how to use it. Ultimately,
Lucas turned away from *Apocalypse*, but not without resentment. John Milius,
who was a card-carrying member of the National Rifle Association (NRA), was
brought on board to reshape the script, with Francis instructing him not to hold
back. In the end, Lucas and Coppola came to a more amicable financial agreement for Lucas's lost rights and for his inability to direct *Apocalypse* in the future.

At the start of production, the only completed mainstream film about
Vietnam was the jingoistic *The Green Berets* (1968), starring an aging, prowar
John Wayne. The studios were skittish about Vietnam War vehicles so close in
proximity to the contentious environment that had divided the nation for

years. On May 7, 1975, President Gerald Ford declared the official end to the Vietnam Era, but the nation was yet to heal. Coppola was hard at work reshaping the voluminous Milius rewrites. Coppola was bringing the screenplay closer to its original conception—a river journey loosely based on Joseph Conrad's story *Heart of Darkness*.

Francis Coppola began to assemble his production team, believing at the time that the film would turn over in about a year. Initially planning to self-finance, he decided instead to strike a part-ownership deal with United Artists. He had already personally invested several millions in preproduction. Dean Tavalouris was again on board as production designer. Coppola was anxious to use Vittorio Storaro as the director of photography because he admired his photography on Bernardo Bertolucci's *The Conformist, Last Tango in Paris*, and *1900*. Storaro hesitated, not wanting to trump Gordon Willis and knowing how difficult it was to shoot a war film. Coppola convinced Storaro to accompany him to Sydney to look at potential locations. On the 27-hour plane trip Storaro read the screenplay. In Peter Cowie's *The Apocalypse Now Book* he is quoted as saying,

> I never went to sleep, I just sat down, and I started to write down my visual concept of *Apocalypse Now*, inspired by Conrad's book, which I'd just finished. I landed in Sydney . . . and met with Francis. . . . We were able to discuss the main concept . . . and later he called Gray Frederickson (producer) to translate my outline. . . . That was my first creative meeting with Francis and it was wonderful. It was one of the most remarkable encounters I've ever had in my life.[5]

Meanwhile, Fred Roos and Tavalouris were scouting locations. They determined that Queensland had tropical tracts that would be suitable. But the idea did not prove acceptable to Australia's burgeoning film community, which did not want Coppola's presence to dominate Australia's film industry. Coppola made the snap decision to shoot in the Philippines under the regime of Ferdinand Marcos, who for a hefty price would provide him with men and helicopters. Coppola chose Richard Marks as supervising editor. Walter Murch was in charge of sound design. Carmine and Francis Coppola would create the music.

For the lead role of Captain Willard, Coppola approached Steve McQueen, who wanted $3 million.[6] Coppola was forced to alter his strategy and set his sights on a less expensive selection. Marlon Brando said he would accept the role of Colonel Kurtz. For the part of Willard, Coppola wanted Martin Sheen, but he was not then available. He selected Harvey Keitel, who was dismissed very early on and replaced with a now available Sheen, considered by some as the next James Dean after his performance in Terrence Malick's *Badlands*. Robert Duvall was cast as the irrepressible Lt. Colonel Kilgore, and Frederic Forrest, who had been in *The Conversation*, was cast as Chef. Sam Bottoms, who had appeared in *The Last Picture Show*, was part of the boat crew, and a 14-year-old Larry (Laurence) Fishburne was cast as Clean. Harrison Ford and Scott Glenn, a Vietnam vet (who would take a role in Sofia Coppola's *The Virgin Suicides*) were also part of the cast. Albert Hall was cast as Chief Phillips, and easy rider Dennis Hopper does a star turn as a whacked-out photojournalist.

Apocalypse Now takes place in-country at the apex of U.S. involvement in the Vietnam War. Captain Willard, a man conflicted by duty and virtue, is assigned a confidential mission to hunt down and terminate with extreme prejudice Colonel Walter Kurtz, a former rising military star operating outside the purview of the industrial military complex.

The central metaphor of *Apocalypse Now* resonates in its title: the confrontation of good and evil, the quest for a spiritual path, and an inquiry into eternal truths. These themes address war, morality, and for director Coppola the very foundations of moviemaking as they then existed. He set out to create a film about America's military participation in Vietnam that would travel through what Conrad called the *Heart of Darkness* to examine and question the ethical code of the United States by employing an emerging cinematic language that rebelled against the notion of the "well-made" studio film.

From the outset the project infected everyone in its path with megalomaniacal fervor. Milius raved about actually shooting the film in Vietnam as the war continued to rage in Southeast Asia. On location in the Philippines, Coppola lost touch with reality and began to fantasize that he was Willard and that the out-of-control production was his own private trip into the belly of the beast. In reality the director was actually behaving more like Kurtz, operating out on his own, risking his sanity, career, possessions, and even his family.

Eleanor Coppola, Gio (age 12 at start of production), Roman (age 10), and Sofia (age 4) spent the better part of the production on location in the Philippines with Francis. The boys spent some of the time back in the states at school, but for the most part they were in the jungle. Francis had asked Eleanor to photograph the entire experience to create a documentary record of the making of *Apocalypse Now*. Ellie had a small crew and took on the assignment with great dedication. She shot copious footage and also amassed many stills. To maintain a record of times and places while she was working, she began writing what became *Notes*. It is a volume of enormous value in detailing the events of the filming, and, unplanned at the start, it is also the personal diary of Eleanor Coppola at a time of great strain and chaos in her marriage.

Notes is insightful in its descriptions, observations, and shared experiences with Francis Ford Coppola as he spirals downward psychologically during production and postproduction. It is courageous in its self-reflection as Eleanor Coppola struggles to cope with the belief that her husband is having an extramarital affair and that she has a great need to reevaluate her life as a person and wife.

Apocalypse Now was a culmination of directorial expression and excess during the American New Wave of the 1970s, when a new generation of filmmakers took over Hollywood and transformed what had largely been entertainment into personal statements with lofty narratives and aesthetic goals. After taking on organized crime to meditate on the corruption of American political and corporate values in *The Godfather* and *The Godfather Part II*, and the invasion of privacy resulting in the destruction of self in *The Conversation*, Coppola amassed the power and artistic hubris to tackle the nature of evil as personified by the country's aggressive engagement in the affairs of Vietnam.

Apocalypse Now is a series of narrative tableaus positioned in sequential order. We are introduced to Willard as he begins to unravel mentally in a hotel room; the officer is given his orders; a boat and crew are at his disposal; and he is escorted to his point of departure. Willard then embarks on a journey upriver to the Kurtz compound deep in the jungles of Cambodia. Each scene block of the odyssey is a saga unto itself. The crew progresses into an increasingly surreal set of circumstances until Willard reaches what Jim Morrison of The Doors quantified as "The End." The structure is linear, without parallel storytelling, flashbacks, or flashforwards. Like Dante's *The Inferno* it is a descent into Hell. Coppola does not drive the story downward but horizontally—it is a cinematic trip up-river to Hades.

Cinematographer Storaro utilizes light, color, composition, and movement to illustrate the story, visualize motifs, and convey the emotional actuality of the characters—their time and place. Storaro's cinematography reproduces the reality of the moment and space through diaphanous layers of light. The images of Vietnam are illuminated with a sense of empirical truth. Storaro photographed *Apocalypse Now* in the anamorphic widescreen format to capture the horizontal axis of the sky, the jungle, and the river that is the conduit of this road movie traveling by boat. TechnoVision in Italy had just developed lenses with the optical properties to duplicate the high level of definition seen by the human eye. This registers in the brain's storage bank and is filed along with selective memories of a given period. The light in *Apocalypse Now* produces glare, contrast, and saturated colors, which embody the immediacy of the tumultuous 1960s.

Lateral tracking shots evoke the film's central metaphor. Throughout *Apocalypse Now* the camera often follows a character—most notably Colonel Bill Kilgore—as he briskly leads his men to his helicopter in a prelude to the air attack. Framed in a full shot in a straight-on profile, the camera tracks right to left, locked into the speed of Kilgore's confident stride. The trajectory of the camera movement not only defines the powerful charisma of the character, but the tabular direction is a gesture that continues to evoke a visual representation of the theme defining Willard's pilgrimage toward a confrontation with the other half of his psyche mirrored in Kurtz—his destiny is cinematically constant and inevitable.

Psychedelic drugs such as LSD transformed the consciousness of many young Americans during the late 1960s. *Apocalypse Now* takes place in 1969. Experiments with mind-altering substances that produce hallucinatory psychoactive states in the brain were spreading at home and at war. For the men fighting in Vietnam the experience of leaving boyhood for the terrors of the jungle and facing an enemy they didn't fully comprehend was a surreal and horrifying transition into manhood. For them, psychedelic drugs were both a rite of passage and a way to transcend the unimaginable existence they confronted.

In *Apocalypse Now* some of the members of the crew are under the influence of hallucinogens. Storaro's use of color sparks these psychic visions in the viewer's retina. Orange and green smoke fills the air with bright, gauzy fog. Lance (Sam Bottoms), the zonked-out California surfer, fires a canister of purple smoke he calls "Purple Haze," a reference to the seminal Jimi Hendrix song. Hendrix, who provided the sonic soundtrack for drugheads during the era, had named the tune after a variety of acids chemically concocted for the experimental electric musician by Augustus Owsley Stanley III, engineer of countless sensory excursions taken by Baby Boomers.

Cinematography is an art of chiaroscuro, the attention to light and dark in a pictorial work. As Willard and the crew float into Kurtz's heart of darkness through the atrocities of war, Storaro's photography emphasizes conflict with tonal contrast. The environmental serenity of green foliage, blue sky, and water is counterposed to the presence of warriors with dark camouflaged faces, black metal weapons, and the burning yellow and orange of explosions that ravage the land expressed in a surreal display of deadly fireworks. The Kurtz compound is heavy with brush. The Colonel dwells in a cave where light isn't absent but represents the other side of brightness. The stark pools of light and the gloom of its reflected rays unify to expose that light and dark—good and evil—are configurations of each other. In an interview in *Projections 6: Filmmakers on Film-Making*, Storaro told Ric Gentry,

> *Apocalypse Now* was the sum of my work up to that time. It was everything I did in the moment of my past, and everything I could do in the moment of my present. It was through Conrad, in part, and the title of his novella *Heart of Darkness* on which Coppola's film is based, that I began to re-evaluate everything that went before. The concept of "darkness" itself was revealing. It is where light ends. But I also realized that darkness is not the absence of light but the antithesis of light.... Light and dark are not only metaphors but the means by which we perceive and understand.[7]

The sound design by Walter Murch creates an aural environment that supports and enhances the thematic achievements of the visual narrative. *Apocalypse Now* is a sonic landmark which heralded a new era in the application of film sound analogous to the accomplishments in production design attained by William Cameron Menzies on *Gone with the Wind*.

Despite the incredibly stressful conditions that existed during the making of *Apocalypse Now*, both cinematographer Storaro and sound designer Murch elevated their crafts to a new level of competency, skill, and intricacy.

Sound effects and music interpenetrate to produce overlays of realistic, expressive, associative, and symbolic pertinence. The whirl of helicopter blades is a signature sound in *Apocalypse Now* that defines the authentic and sensory nature of the Vietnam War experience. In the opening of the film, Willard imagines the sound of a turning hotel ceiling fan into a synthesized blade thwarp that distinguishes his dream state. This is then blown out of his consciousness by the audio of an actual helicopter that flies over the building, thereby returning the psychically burned-out officer to the material world of Saigon.

Throughout the film, Michael Herr's narration[8] puts us inside Willard's thoughts as he tries to reason the purpose of his journey. This inner voice is up close and resonates as if it were emanating from inside his head. It allows the viewer to experience Willard's twisted cognitive condition.

During the helicopter battle Kilgore plays a tape of Wagner's "Ride of the Valkyries," which blares out of speakers mounted on the helicopter. The triumphant horn melody and the heavenly choral voices signify power and victory and bring associations of Nazi invasions and the superiority of a master race. The perspective of source and score interchange and interact with sounds of gunfire, helicopters, explosions, radio transmissions, and shouting voices of the combatants, which constantly shift to produce a hyperdramatic, cine-operatic encounter between sound and image.

To create the exterior ambiance of Kurtz's compound, Murch blended realistic Southeast Asian jungle sounds that had been recorded for the motion picture *Lord Jim*, music and singing of the Mung people of Cambodia taken from ethnomusicality records, Vietnamese dialogue spoken from various depths in a hidden valley, and a bird-presence track recorded at the San Francisco Zoo bird room.

The interior of Kurtz's lair is depicted as a dank, wet ruin. There are the sounds of seeping water and echoed drips from various parts of the dark location that acoustically outline the space. Jungle inhabitants are represented by cricket sounds and the suction-cupped fingers of a Philippine lizard known as a gecko.

Coppola and his team of film editors—supervising editor Marks, Jerry Greenberg, Murch, and Lisa Fruchtman—struggled incessantly to find a fitting conclusion for *Apocalypse Now*. After trying every available possibility inherent in the raw footage they arrived at the concept that after Willard's ritualistic killing of Kurtz, he reads the man's typewritten diary and finds the message "Drop the bomb—exterminate them all!" written in scrawl. The Doors song "The End" is heard at the beginning and end of the film. As sung by the Dionysian rocker Jim Morrison, who had attended UCLA with Coppola, the modal, tribal ode is an Oedipal drama that deliberates patricide. Its presence establishes a preordained affinity between Willard and Kurtz. Willard then emerges from the cave carrying the diary, throws down the murderous knife, and is acknowledged by the tribe as their new leader. Willard rejects this and leads Lance, the only survivor of his crew, back to the boat. They turn the vessel around to travel the river once again. They receive radio contact asking for conformation but Willard shuts it off. We hear Kurtz repeat Conrad's prophetic words, "The horror, the horror." In an author's interview, supervising editor Marks talks about the struggle of cutting the ending. "*Apocalypse* was the quintessential difficult ending, mostly because Brando was shot in such a strange way. It was just endless improvisation, with Brando covered with overlapping cameras. . . . I don't think there was ever a clear cut answer. Not that Francis didn't write an ending; he wrote them, but they weren't necessarily the ones that were filmed, and the ones that were filmed were changed a thousand times in the cutting room."[9] The fruitless search for a logical ending to a film about the Vietnam War is the consummate metaphor of *Apocalypse Now*. The war and the film can never truly be resolved and must lie within a conflicted American heart.

Time and cost overages on *Apocalypse Now* were stupendous. The quoted budget at the end of production was about of $31.5 million.[10] The film took three years to come to fruition. It had survived a massive typhoon and Martin Sheen's heart attack. Coppola was being vilified by the biting American press. In an attempt to mollify the naysayers, Coppola decided to screen an unfinished version at Cannes in competition where it received a warm reception and shared the Palme d'Or with Volker Schlöndorff's *The Tin Drum*. On August 15, 1979, *Apocalypse Now* opened in limited release. A playbill was created by famed graphics designer Milton Glaser.[11] The 16-page handout included a statement from Coppola to his audience. He says, "The most important thing I wanted to do in the making of *Apocalypse Now* was to create a film experience that would give its audience a sense of the horror, the madness, the sensuousness, and the moral dilemma of the Vietnam War." He continued, "It was my thought that if the American audience could look at the heart of what Vietnam was really like—what it looked like and felt like—then they would be only one small step away from putting it behind them."[12]

The Vietnam War was a seminal experience for the American public. The political divisiveness and the harrowing experience of visually seeing the war unfold on nightly newscasts left American society in pain and damaged. For those soldiers who had experienced Vietnam and for the families of those who died in the conflict, the trauma continued. Returning soldiers often received a hostile reception from the citizenry and had psychic wounds that took years to repair. Ultimately, Coppola hoped that his artistry could contribute to an arduous and lengthy healing process.

It took many years for *Apocalypse Now* to yield a profit. The overruns were enormous. In the end, the tally was positive, and the film received eight Academy Award nominations with Oscars for Storaro and Murch. With the tincture of time *Apocalypse* has been deemed by most to be a masterpiece. It was responsible for spawning a series of filmic endeavors addressing the war in Vietnam.

The *Apocalypse Now* chapter in Coppola's life had left him traumatized and hurt. For the major portion of the experience he had behaved badly toward many of his most trusted colleagues and most assuredly to his wife Eleanor. She had been denigrated in public and private while Coppola found reasons for pleasuring himself and justifying his uncivilized behavior. He still had hearth and home, but just barely. Francis Coppola, the gambler, had rolled the dice, but even with an ultimately financially successful film, it was questionable if he had won the toss.

Reinventing the Wheel of Life: Zoetrope Studios and *One from the Heart*

To understand Francis Coppola's passionate desire to own a Hollywood studio in 1980, it is necessary to place his fervor into the historical context of the Golden Age of Hollywood and the classic Hollywood studio system.

Hollywood as the mecca of moviemaking developed during the silent film era when the nascent American film industry relocated from New York to find better weather and light. In Los Angeles and environs, studios were founded under the strong control of the moguls by the 1920s. The moguls were a group of businessmen largely comprised of Eastern European Jewish emigrants who had left their home countries under the strain of prejudice, poverty, and pogroms. These men fled their homeland to partake of the American dream and, in establishing studios in Hollywood, often ended up defining the American dream through the motion pictures their studios produced.

The moguls varied in their aesthetic and artistic sensibilities. They were not driven to make art; instead they wanted to create thriving businesses. Most had come out of retail businesses where they understood what the public wanted. Being immigrants in a country of immigrants the moguls could identify the tastes of the people who would become the prime audience for motion pictures. They strongly identified with the immigrants' desire to assimilate and become part of the fabric of America. It was their desire, too. In a landmark book on the subject of the Jewish moguls of the Golden Age of Hollywood, author Neal Gabler traces how this group of men created the Golden Age and literally invented Hollywood. The book, titled *An Empire of Their Own: How the Jews Invented Hollywood*,[1] painstakingly examines the process by which these men gained power and placed their stamp on an entire industry for decades.

As recently as September 2011, Coppola told Cameron Bailey at the Toronto International Film Festival that he was "in awe of the Hollywood Studio System."[2] Probably more than most of his filmmaking peers who came out of the California film schools in the 1960s, Coppola was a student of film history. He didn't find it necessary to totally reject the accomplishments of the classic Hollywood studio system in order to function as an independent film artist in a new time. Coppola could embrace the enormity of the moguls' contribution and, at the same time, respond with enthusiasm to Italian neo-realism,[3] the nouvelle vague of the late 1950s and 1960s, and filmmakers in Japan and worldwide. His response to any film movement or any filmmaker was based on artistry. Coppola embraced any circumstances that fostered innovation and the artists' ability to create without hindrance. Coppola appreciated most of the Golden Age studio structure. As explained in extraordinary detail in *The Genius of the System: Hollywood Filmmaking in the Studio Era* by Thomas Schatz,[4] the major studios (Universal, MGM, Warner Bros., Paramount, RKO) and the moguls and executives identified with them—such as Irving Thalberg, Jack Warner, David O. Selznick, and Darryl Zanuck—organized the film studio utilizing solid business concepts. Each discipline necessary to ensure the success of a final product was categorized as an organizational unit and had lines of progression that were clear-cut and definable. Departments had supervisors and staff, the majority of whom were under contract to the studio. The studio methodology was instituted with one concept in mind—a successful and profitable end product. Among the departments were Art Direction, Editorial, Screenwriting, Casting, Producers, Directors, Directors of Photography, Sound, Make-Up, Wardrobe, Music, and Publicity. The studio also had a stable of actors under contract. There were talent scouts searching for the next great star, elocution and dialect coaches, and dancing and singing instructors. Most critical was bottom-line profitability. The studios maintained careful accounting systems. Productions were budgeted and schedules adhered to. All this assembly-line production created a commanding corporate business model that flourished for over two decades from the 1930s to the mid-1950s. Those studios that were tightly controlled by the moguls and their executives and central producers turned profits and became known for their special strengths and genres. Movie stars were attached to specific studios. Prestige directors were hired by the studios to direct in their genres. Prominent novelists of the day were attracted to studios, lured by steady salaries. Scouts combed Broadway searching for new stars. Those with favorable screen tests were offered lucrative studio contracts. Within the rigors of the studio system and the imposition of demands on its employees top to bottom, the opportunity for motion pictures to advance as an art form coexisted in equal measure with artifice and forgettable fare. There are countless examples of directorial greatness, acting genius, wonderful storytelling, photographic beauty, breathtaking costumes, ingenious make-up, and advancement in sound, skillful editing, and art direction that merged with production design. Likewise, some studios didn't get it right, had unsteady balance sheets and poor results, and were either reengineered or folded. Coppola recognized that moviemaking was a business and there was a profit motive, but he also believed the studio heads of the Golden Age had taste and cared about a good show. So if both could be accomplished, it mattered to the moguls.

The myriad elements of the extraordinary motion picture industry during the Golden Age were well understood by Coppola. He wanted to extract the best of that unique era and transform it into an updated version of a self-contained, technologically cutting-edge studio entity. Without a concrete studio property, Coppola had been using the American Zoetrope brand and the substantial influence of the Francis Coppola moniker in the 1970s to support, influence, and engage in a wide and varied amalgam of artistic endeavors. Coppola, as the oldest of the New Generation, aka American New Wave, and the first to achieve commercial success, was viewed by his colleagues as a mentor.

It was in Coppola's nature to assume this guiding role and expand it further to include backing and underwriting ventures he believed sustained the world of film as an art form. If he had money or could negotiate it using his influence, he took that route. If he couldn't provide financial support, he found other ways to make contributions. Coppola was an impresario in the broader sense of its meaning.

The definition of *impresario* was a remarkably good description of Coppola. The origin of the term is in Italian opera of the eighteenth century. The impresario was a pivotal figure in the success of a season of opera. It was the responsibility of the impresario to organize new material from composers and assure it was prepared for presentation. All the requirements to bring the operas to the stage rested with the impresario—singers, sets, costumes, and orchestra. The impresario was expected to finance the entire enterprise. If the season was a success, the impresario reaped the benefits. If it failed, the losses were his losses. To be a gainful impresario, it was useful to be a risk taker comfortable hazarding a gamble. The impresarial concept evolved over time and exists to this day in broader conception in the entertainment industry. An example of a modern-day impresario was the renowned Sol Hurok, who was responsible for facilitating American presentations by performing artists from around the world. These artists might not have been showcased without his sponsorship. Under the banner "S. Hurok Presents . . . " Hurok was responsible for bringing the Bolshoi Ballet to the United States in 1959 when the Cold War had prevented their appearance there. He presented dancer Isadora Duncan, considered the creator of modern dance, to the United States when she had previously appeared only in Europe and the Soviet Union. He showcased famed pianists Vladimir Ashkenazy and Van Cliburn and presented violinist Isaac Stern, classical guitarist Andres Segovia, and many other musical luminaries who might not have received such heightened exposure in the United States without his efforts. Arthur Rubenstein introduced Hurok to singer Marian

Anderson, and he became her manager. In 1939 Hurok used the clout of First Lady Eleanor Roosevelt to negotiate the magnificent Ms. Anderson's iconic Easter Sunday performance on the steps of the Lincoln Memorial.

Coppola had seen a version of German film director Hans-Jürgen Syberberg's *Our Hitler*, aka *Hitler: A Film for Germany*. This seven-hour film was highly controversial in theme and idiosyncratic in presentation. With the spirit and artistic commitment of an impresario, Coppola was enthralled with the film's ingenuity and wanted it to have an airing. He sponsored the film at special screenings for $10 a ticket and sold out a 2,000-seat theater in San Francisco. The film travelled to other venues with the same enthusiastic reception. Coppola took a similar approach with Abel Gance's 1927 masterwork *Napoleon*, which was being restored by famed film historian Kevin Brownlow. Brownlow's reconstructed version was re-edited and American Zoetrope released it through Universal Pictures. Planned as an event, *Napoleon* was screened in New York City's Radio City Music Hall, where it appeared from January 23 through 25, 1981, to standing-room-only crowds. Coppola engaged his father, Carmine, to write a score for the silent film, which was performed live as accompaniment to the viewing. Playbills were given to the audience members. There is an essay written by Carmine Coppola titled *Writing the Score for Napoleon*, in which he says, "The style of the music had to be of the time. I researched the songs of the French revolution . . . C'ira, the song they sang following ox-carts bearing nobility on the way to the guillotine . . . and of course the daddy of them all 'La Marseillaise'—the film has a thrilling scene showing the birth and acceptance of this wonderful anthem."[5]

Francis was awestruck by the early invention and scope of *Napoleon*. Well before its time, Gance employed a three-screen visualization, which required three synchronized projectors. This triptych approach allowed for panoramas long before the existence of widescreen formats or 70mm projection. The triptych was also used to show simultaneously different actions projected onto each third of a screen.[6] Rightly, Francis Coppola believed film audiences would respond enthusiastically to film artistry of this caliber if given the opportunity. Coppola continues to expose the film-going public to these spectacles. On occasion he has used the phrase, "Francis Ford Coppola Presents . . . " in the same manner as the impresario Hurok.

In his mentoring role, Coppola lent support to films and filmmakers who were having difficulty at some stage of their projects. Most notably, he and George Lucas were responsible for bringing esteemed Japanese director Akira Kurosawa's *Kagemusha* to the international community. Lucas had discovered Kurosawa was having funding difficulties in Japan. He brought the issue to Coppola, who immediately agreed to lend his support. Coppola and Lucas executive produced the film internationally, and Lucas convinced Alan Ladd Jr. at Fox to bolster the financing.

By the end of the 1970s the legendary master of the French New Wave, Jean-Luc Godard, had fallen out of favor largely due to the extreme political tone of his films during the decade. He had plans for a film about Bugsy Siegel, but not the capital. When Coppola colleague Tom Luddy,[7] who knew Godard, told him Godard was out of funds, Coppola felt compelled to support the filmmaking icon of the film-school generation and advanced him $250,000. Although the project fell through, he made a feature entitled *Sauve qui Peut (La Vie)* and to meet his financial commitment offered the U.S. rights to Coppola and Luddy. The film was released by New Yorker Films.

In 1977 Coppola's UCLA classmate and member of the original American Zoetrope team Carroll Ballard began directing *The Black Stallion*, the first of a children's book series by Walter Farley. This was at Coppola's request. Coppola was so high on the idea of *The Black Stallion* he bought the rights to the entire *Stallion* series. He envisioned sequels and perhaps a TV series. He asked Walter Murch to couple with Ballard on the film's development. Ballard, son of late famed cinematographer Lucien Ballard (*The Killing*, *The Wild Bunch*, *True Grit* [1969]) had been raised in Los Angeles. After graduating from UCLA he spent most of the 1960s working for the United States Information Agency shooting documentaries.

Both Ballard and Murch thought the *Stallion* material was not particularly original and perhaps a bit sappy. They talked about their feelings and then met with Coppola. Ballard told Michael Schumacher in an interview in *Francis Ford Coppola: A Filmmaker's Life,* "I really didn't like the book that much. I thought it was kind of a *Leave it to Beaver* story."[8] Coppola was furious and told Ballard and Murch they could get out if they didn't like the project. Coppola was very committed to the story and felt hurt, angry, and betrayed. Not only did Coppola think the film would be a success, he also believed he was providing a solid work assignment. In the end, cooler heads prevailed and Ballard completed the film. When Coppola executive produced *The Black Stallion Returns* (1983) he chose to assign Robert Dalva as director. He had been the editor on the original.

The Black Stallion opened in 1979. Coppola was the executive producer. Murch worked uncredited. In the cast was Teri Garr, who had appeared in *The Conversation* and would join Coppola as part of his repertory at Zoetrope Studios. Carmine Coppola was responsible for the original score. Preproduction was not without friction. Coppola and Ballard disagreed on the script. In the end the film was a success and was nominated for two Academy Awards. Although Ballard felt that Coppola had interfered during filming, he did come to recognize that without Coppola he would never have made a film in Hollywood. Further, it positioned Ballard to go on to other projects in the next phase of his career.

During the timeframe before *Apocalypse Now* was finally released, Coppola was in a fragile mental state. The protracted production and postproduction period had worn Coppola down. His extramarital affairs had frayed his marriage and left him in conflict and despair. The press was nipping at his heels.

Coppola, who was typically skillful and an excellent self-promoter, had always made himself accessible to the press. He had been the press's darling after the triumphant *Godfathers*; now he fell victim to a voracious rumor mill that produced story after story anticipating the failure of *Apocalypse Now* and alluding to Coppola's loss of control. Coppola was hurt and angry, frustrated by the manipulation of information bombarding the media about *Apocalypse Now* and its ultimate fate.

At the end of April, 1977 Coppola transmitted an internal memo to his fellow employees at American Zoetrope in San Francisco. In the memo, Coppola communicated several edicts that seem to reflect his unstable state: paranoid, dictatorial, and defensive. It began: "This company will be known as American Zoetrope and, purely and simply, it is me and my work. We will not be in the service business ... but rather will maintain these facilities in order to realize my own projects. Therefore, you really are not employees of a company—instead the staff of an artist, very much like the crew of a motion picture. Wherever I am will be considered the headquarters of the company." Coppola, who throughout his career juggled finances and gambled with his own funds, went on to say, "I am cavalier about money because I have to be in order not to be terrified every time I make an artistic decision. Remember, the major studios have only one thing a filmmaker needs: capital. My flamboyant disregard for the rules of capital and business is one of my major strengths when dealing with the studios. It evens the score, so to speak." Coppola continues by noting: "Please remember, my name is Francis Coppola. I am dropping the Ford. This comes from a statement I once heard: Never trust a man with three names." In conclusion he declares, "I've heard that success is as difficult to deal with as failure—perhaps more so." And finally, in an intentionally warped paraphrase of a proverb sometimes attributed to Euripides, Coppola concludes, "Euripides, the Greek playwright said thousands of years ago: 'Whom God wishes to destroy, he first makes successful in show business.' "[9]

If the staff who received the memorandum were nonplussed, that was not the worst of it. The memo was leaked to the press and appeared in *Esquire* in the November 1977 issue. The public issuance of the memo deeply humiliated Coppola and added grist to the rumor mill. He surely sounded off-kilter in the memo; his usual swagger and confidence were gone, replaced by defensive, inarticulate pronouncements. Coppola's image suffered a major blow and perhaps irreparable damage.

The delay in the release of *Apocalypse* caused another agony for Coppola. Whereas he expected it to be the first major film release to tell the story of the war in Vietnam, the market caught up with him, and several motion pictures on the subject were in circulation first. Most significant was the late 1978 release of Michael Cimino's *The Deer Hunter*. Coppola tried to keep his feelings *sub rosa* as he attended the New York premiere. He may often have worn his heart on his sleeve, but when Coppola was asked in 1979 to present the Academy Award for Best Director, he accepted graciously. As fate (and the odds makers) would have it, the award was granted to Italian American filmmaker Cimino for his direction of *The Deer Hunter*. For the world to see, moviegoers and colleagues of all stripes, Coppola bear-hugged Cimino and called him *paisan*. It was a vintage Coppola moment, reminding the international viewership why they believed throughout the 1970s that Francis Ford Coppola was the father of New Hollywood. A few days later, back in Napa Valley, the Coppolas, friends, and relatives celebrated Francis's 40th birthday in style.

The epic story of the rise and fall of Zoetrope Studios began on March 25, 1980, when Coppola purchased Hollywood General Studios for $6.7 million.[10] The studio site had been built in 1919 by John Jasper and had been called Jasper Hollywood Studios. It then became General Services Studios and through resale was Hollywood General when Coppola took title. Coppola had started looking for a Hollywood property in the summer of 1979. He had lost his taste for location shooting after the torturous experience of two years in the jungle on *Apocalypse Now*. Then too, after being skewered in the press during production and postproduction with *Variety* issuing alarming stories practically on a daily basis, Coppola was desperately in need of the control and status he had enjoyed throughout most of the decade. He was emotionally bruised by the fallout of his "private" memo and the embarrassment it caused him, and also needed to absorb the impact of Eleanor Coppola's diary published in August 1979, which chronicled the *Apocalypse Now* experience from her perspective. *Notes*, as the journal was titled, had not been intended for publication when Ellie started writing it in March 1976. By the journal's final entry in November 1978, she had been encouraged by friends and colleagues to publish her notes. Eleanor Coppola had been through a life-altering experience during this period. She had held to her agreement with Francis to document the making of *Apocalypse* while enduring extreme physical and emotional hardship (at one point she weighed 90 pounds.) She cared for Sofia, who was age four when the move to the Philippines occurred, and her two boys Gio and Roman, who shuttled back and forth between school in the United States and the rest of the family on location. On occasion Eleanor returned to San Francisco, but for the vast majority of location time, she was there, functioning as a wife, mother, and film documentarian. Francis Coppola suffered massive mood swings and erratic behavior as he directed *Apocalypse*. Unbeknownst to Eleanor, Francis was having an affair during most of production and postproduction, and many members of the cast and crew were aware of the situation. As is often the case, Eleanor was among the last to know. Suffice it to say, with tincture of time Francis and Eleanor moved through this stage of their marriage, but while it unfolded, Francis, who loved his wife and was a devoted family man, was deeply pained. On the other hand, he could not bring himself to end his clandestine relationship. Eleanor Coppola was and is an extremely private person. Ultimately *Notes* was therapeutic. As she began to examine her life with Francis, she realized she had always acceded to his needs. She had lived a life of "waiting." She likened herself to Kay Corleone in the *Godfather*. Occurring at the height of the women's movement, Eleanor did not need to look too far for support from her community of friends. Before its publication she read passages to Francis, and he acknowledged it should be published—although, in truth, he may not have been the decider. On one level the diary was an informative companion piece to the film, but on the flip side it would reveal his infidelity and be yet another source of embarrassment to him.

At the beginning of 1980 Francis Coppola planted a small palm tree on the Hollywood General property. It was a symbol of the Zoetrope Studio dream he believed would serve as the utopia of his professional life. Coppola had chosen *zoetrope* as the name for his studio back in 1969 with Lucas when he founded American Zoetrope. He had been given a zoetrope, which was a pre-film wheel-like device for producing moving images, by Mogens Scot-Hansen, a European filmmaker who ran a welcoming film company called Lanterna Films.

Coppola thought he had the deal locked up, but there were complications involving transfer of property rights and lawsuits about ownership. To resolve them, Coppola had to lay out more than originally contemplated for the purchase and at higher rates of interest; thus, as was so often the case with Coppola transactions, the monetary ante was already upped. Lucas counseled against the whole transaction. He told Coppola, "being down there (Hollywood), you're just asking for trouble, because you're trying to change a system that will never change. Here (in San Francisco and environs), we don't change a system because there is no system." Lucas, in talking about his newly founded Lucasfilm, remarked, "I'll have mine, and it will take a lot longer to get built, but I don't think it's ever going to collapse out from under me."[11] Lucas's statements were prescient. He had released the first *Star Wars*, which ranked as one of the biggest blockbusters of the decade, and it evolved into a franchise worth billions of dollars. But Lucas and Coppola were not cut from the same cloth. Coppola had chosen a simple love story, *One from the Heart*, as his first project and believed its returns would pay for the start-up of the studio. Coppola did not consider, or perhaps could not comprehend, the business or financial environment in which he was functioning, nor did he address the trends unfolding in the film market, although Lucas's *Star Wars* was a prime example. Some of the Hollywood studios still retained the same or similar names as during the Golden Age, but in all respects they were a far cry from that era. Generally, Hollywood was run by conglomerates and spilled over into hybrids encompassing films, television, and music divisions. The sole purpose of these entities, which grew more and more complex, was to sell tickets, and the best way to insure a project was to replicate what had succeeded already. The concept of a sequel, which had been at its zenith with *The Godfather II*, became an ordinary vehicle for recycling familiar fare. Franchises became part of the film vernacular, and branding of commercial products attached to the franchise was another way to exploit a film product. Inflation was sky high, and bank interest rates were approaching double digits. But Coppola was confident that Zoetrope, which would be a state-of-the-art facility encapsulating both theatrical cinema and never-before-used electronic wizardry, would be a perfect antidote.

Zoetrope Studio (briefly called Omni Zoetrope), on $10\frac{1}{2}$ acres with nine sound stages, was organized with 1,500 employees on its roster. Coppola as mogul hired his classmate from Hofstra, Robert Spiotta, as the president and CEO of the studio. Spiotta, an oil executive, had been cast as Stanley Kowalski in Coppola's Hofstra production of *A Streetcar Named Desire*. Lucy Fisher, who had been a vice president at Twentieth Century Fox, was vice president–head of production. Department heads included Dean Tavoularis for art and design, and Jennifer Shull for casting (she had cast *The Conversation*); Dennis O'Flaherty and Dennis Klein, both young TV series writers, and William Bowers, a veteran screenwriter, were hired as resident writing staff. Fred Roos, whose skills in identifying talent were legendary, was the commissar of talent. Coppola brought on members of the old guard. Rudi Fehr, a venerable film editor who had also been a key executive at Warner Bros. under Jack Warner, was editorial consultant. Friend, confidante, and colleague Walter Murch was the head of the sound department. Coppola also had on staff the legendary Gene Kelly as dance consultant. British director Michael Powell, who had worked at the very same studio directing *The Thief of Baghdad* during World War II (supposedly one of Coppola's favorite films) acted as an advisor on occasion. Finally, Tom Luddy, who screened films from an enormous archive for public enjoyment and became a producer, was placed in charge of special projects.

Coppola indicated that San Francisco would still be the base for research and development and the think tank for the studio. Francis Coppola would remain in Napa Valley, but physical production was in Hollywood. Replicating the actors' contract system of classic Hollywood, Coppola enlisted talent who would form a repertory company prepared to appear in projects as they unfolded. Members included Teri Garr, who had been in *The Conversation*; Laurence Fishburne and Albert Hall from *Apocalypse Now*; Frederic Forrest from both *The Conversation* and *Apocalypse*; and Raul Julia. A young Rebecca De Mornay was part of the troupe.

One from the Heart was conceived as a simple love story: a young couple has lost their sense of contentment. The setting is Las Vegas on July 4 the fifth anniversary of Frannie (Teri Garr) and Hank (Frederic Forrest). Each has a one-night affair with an exciting partner—Frannie with a handsome dancer (Raul Julia) and Hank with a beautiful and sensual circus high-wire performer (Nastassia Kinski.) Coppola envisioned the story as a musical with the songs sung off-screen by Tom Waits, who wrote the score, and Crystal Gayle. After one night apart, the couple reunites, perhaps wiser. *One from the Heart* was to be the first film to use electronic cinema, a technique that would allow Coppola and his crew to visually conceptualize and edit the film as they shot. The cutting-edge equipment was provided by the Sony Corporation.

Coppola resided in a trailer called the Silverfish and addressed the actors as they performed. Coppola contended that this revolutionary method would be economically cost-effective and would revolutionize moviemaking. To photograph the film, Coppola called on Vittorio Storaro. The American unions immediately balked at the use of a foreign cameraman, but Coppola won out. The entire production was planned and designed to be shot on the studio lots. Its look was to be fantastical.

The challenges of studio production for the sets, lighting, and composition were enormous. Tavoularis designed a street in Las Vegas on the studio lot and Las Vegas's McCarran Airport. A real plane was brought in as one of the props. Storaro, at Coppola's insistence, shot in an aspect ratio to give the show an older 1940s look. They then had to change course and reconfigure the format to accommodate the sets top to bottom. Cost overruns made the notion of cost effectiveness with new technology moot. What might have been a sweet, stylized confection of a movie that came in on-budget to support Coppola's technological assertions became a bloated hodge-podge at an estimated cost of $27 million.[12] Coppola was not in control at the helm. The story seemed secondary when lacquered over by the artistic excess Coppola demanded.

When asked by writer Gay Talese in a July 1981 *Esquire* interview ("The Conversation"), "How do you feel about the picture you've just finished?" Coppola replied, "*One from the Heart* is interesting to me because I think it represents a new direction in my work that I'd like to pursue in the next ten years. Stylistically, and in its use of film language, it's different from anything I've done before—anything *anyone's* done before. On one level it's a thrust into a new technology and way of working; on another, it's an examination of love and jealousy themes. I see myself becoming more of a film composer. All my future films will be musical—with songs and dances and more fluid imagery."[13]

It's fair to say that most of the Hollywood establishment was gunning for Coppola, the maverick mogul of Zoetrope Studio. Advance press about *One from the Heart* had been negative. The industry was cynical about the concept of electronic cinema. Critics were mostly brutal, but even minority praise fell on deaf ears. Such was the predestined providence of *One from the Heart*. Box office receipts were abysmal, and the studio was bankrupt. In these more pitiless financial times, Chase Manhattan Bank demanded Zoetrope Studio in Hollywood be put up for sale. About one issue, Coppola had been on target. In the ensuing years Coppola's technological predictions came to pass.

One from the Heart has not been revisited as a masterpiece before its time. Its execution was simply misguided. Francis Coppola would not spend the next 10 years making musicals; instead the majority of his films would be made as a director for hire, in need of work to pay off his debts and protect his house and home.

7

Back-to-Back Personal: *The Outsiders* and *Rumble Fish*

With the loss of Zoetrope Studio in Hollywood, Francis Coppola needed to pull his professional life back together and regroup. The failure of his quixotic dream left him at bay, but he knew he had to keep going. There were so many issues Coppola had failed to grasp during the *One from the Heart* fiasco. Many realities eluded him. He did not recognize the enormity of the blockbuster concept and how it was pervading industry decision making. United Artists was staggering under the weight of the enormous failure of Michael Cimino's epic western *Heaven's Gate*. Cimino, just two years after his Academy Award–winning director's turn for *The Deer Hunter*, was thought to be a bankable commodity. The anticipation was that *Heaven's Gate* would emerge as a blockbuster western. Its original budget had been modest at $7.5 million. United Artists was in the catbird seat, and then the project began spiraling out of control, with a budget that eventually ballooned to $36 million. No one seemed to be in charge of the director-run-amok. It is unfathomable that Cimino was able to extract millions and millions of additional working capital with no red lights or stop signs. In Steven Bach's enthralling book *Final Cut: Dreams and Disaster in the Making of Heaven's Gate*, Bach explains how the studio buckled and allowed Cimino *to* bring the studio to its knees. With this backdrop and the industry's knowledge of Coppola's excesses on *Apocalypse Now*, the film industry had ample reason to steer clear of Coppola and Zoetrope Studio. Despite Coppola's feeling of autonomy, that fact was he needed ample amounts of money from investors in the short run; he was expecting *One from the Heart* to provide financial stability—Coppola invariably borrowed from Peter to pay Paul, using his own assets as collateral. For the first time in his career, Coppola likely had more detractors than acolytes. His perennial swagger and air of self-confidence were lacking, replaced by bluster and tantrums. Coppola was no longer the respected renegade of the 1970s. Editor Rudi Fehr had come to

Zoetrope at Coppola's request after many years working for Jack Warner. In an author's interview, Mr. Fehr described Coppola on *One from the Heart*:

> He's very talented, very insecure, very self-indulgent. I felt so badly that he lost everything he ever made. *One from the Heart* wiped him out. He got so burned when he took *One from the Heart* to a sneak preview in Seattle without titles, dissolves, the final music, or an ending. I said, "Francis, you're making a big mistake. You always want to know what Mr. Warner did. Mr. Warner said not to show the picture to anyone until you can put your best foot forward, when you have everything ready. If you and I don't know what's wrong with the picture, we shouldn't be in this business." There was a reviewer in the audience and it was a devastating review. Theatre owners wouldn't book the picture.[1]

Coppola and American Zoetrope, no longer a concrete Hollywood studio, began to assess the film projects they had in the works and those upon which they could build. The idea was to bring these films to completion and come out in the black.

Coppola and his team had been developing *Hammett* during preproduction of *Apocalypse Now*. Fred Roos was the lead person managing the project. The film's story was to be based on a novel by the late Joe Gores about a detective in a life transition—it was a thinly guised portrait of writer Dashiell Hammett in his early years.

As happens frequently as projects develop, the cast and crew evolve and change. The budget had been set for $8 million with Nicolas Roeg (*The Man Who Fell to Earth*, *Performance*) to direct. Zoetrope wanted Frederic Forrest, who was now one of Coppola's regular actors, to play *Hammett*, but United Artists, then Zoetrope's distributor, did not think he was substantial enough to carry the picture. While they searched for another lead, Roeg left the project. Roos had seen *The American Friend* directed by German filmmaker Wim Wenders and thought he would be perfect for Hammett. Tom Luddy screened several Wenders films for Coppola, and Wenders was brought onto the project. Wenders wanted *Hammett* to be like a film noir and favored shooting it in black and white. He saw the film as relying on flashback and narration. Working with Joe Gores, they labored to achieve a script upon which they agreed. In *On the Edge: The Life & Times of Francis Coppola*, Roos told its authors, "Joe was working in odd territory, trying to please Wim, but he was off his own basic story, it was a hybrid."[2] Gores left the project because of other commitments, and the screenplay went through other hands. The preproduction dragged on without a usable script. Obviously, money was expended with no tangible result and film-industry publicity racking up more negatives for Coppola. Sam Shepard, who had agreed to the lead, bowed out because of all the delay. There were many, many script rewrites. By this time, Forrest's reputation had grown due to his acting chops in *The Rose* as Bette Midler's boyfriend and his performance as Chef in *Apocalypse Now*, which was now in release. The problems on *Hammett* seemed almost insurmountable, and, to be sure, time was money. Coppola screened the work in progress in July 1980 and thought it came up short. Completion was again postponed to March 1981.

On forced hiatus, Wenders returned to Europe with his then wife Ronee Blakely (the marriage would last barely a year) and made a documentary homage to dying film director Nicholas Ray—*Lightning on the Water*. He also completed *The State of Things to Come*, perhaps to get his frustrations with *Hammett* and Coppola out of his system. Wenders had come to the United States in 1978 at age 33 at Coppola's invitation and was thrilled at the chance to work with Coppola. In an October 22, 2011, interview with *The Playlist*, Wenders told Edward Davis: "It was a long, amazing experience (but) too good to be true." Wenders said he shot the first version "under the radar" because Francis had his mind on *Apocalypse Now*.[3]

When *Hammett* was finally afforded a token release in 1983, it was axiomatic that it failed. Commercially and critically the manipulated picture tanked. The only absolute result was that it added to Coppola's debt structure. Also on Coppola's roster was *The Escape Artist*, directed by cinematographer Caleb Deschanel and starring *One from the Heart* actor Raul Julia. *The Black Stallion Returns* was also on Coppola's production in the planning phase. Roos and Tom Sternberg would produce.

Coppola now turned his attention to the first project that attracted him artistically since *One from the Heart*. It would come from the youth market. In late 1980 Francis Coppola had received a letter from the librarian of Lone Star Junior High School in Fresno, California. It had been signed by librarian Ellen Misakian and cosigned by many of her students. The teenagers had responded positively to *The Black Stallion*, which Coppola had executive produced, and turned to him with the idea of making the best-selling *The Outsiders* into a film. The letter came into Roos's hands, and he passed it along to Francis. Roos read the novel and immediately saw the possibilities despite the simple teenager theme. What Roos perceived with his astute casting eye was a young male cast that would capture the youth audience, especially nubile teenage girls. It would be another opportunity for Coppola to spawn a young generation of superstars.

To make this project a reality, Coppola had to go cautiously, hat in hand, shopping the project to the studios so he could option the book and begin production with a distribution deal. He simply had no funds, and Zoetrope would have a minor role, but the studio name would be in the credits.

The final deal involved multiple players, which was the norm. Warner Bros., despite its past history with Coppola's instability, was the lead studio. Coppola then obtained completion guarantee and production financing from Chemical Bank. There was no Coppola mortgage or collateral in the deal. Coppola would have to adhere to a strict budget and schedule—clearly not Coppola's modus operandi.

To keep the budget down, Coppola decided to forgo Vittorio Storaro, who was out of his price range, and hired director of photography Steven Burum, who had been the second unit director of photography on *Apocalypse* and a classmate at UCLA. Coppola used electronic cinema moviemaking techniques and brought his Silverfish trailer on set. When the picture was cast all the young actors agreed to work at lower than their usual salaries for the opportunity to be directed by the film artist Coppola. The location would be in Tulsa, Oklahoma, since that is where the story is set. It also provided an out-of-Hollywood haven for the financially embattled director. Coppola told Aljean Harmetz of the *New York Times*, "It was chaos incorporated at Zoetrope, like fighting a war. I used to be a camp counselor, and the idea of being with half a dozen kids in the country making a movie seemed like being a camp counselor again. It would be like a breath of fresh air. I'd forget my troubles and have some laughs again."[4] Gian-Carlo Coppola, Coppola's young heir apparent, was the associate producer. Carmine Coppola would write the original music, and Domino (aka Sofia) Coppola had a small part as the "little girl."

S. E. (Susan Eloise) Hinton, the author of *The Outsiders*, began the book when she was 16. Because she was a young girl, she used only her initials as she was concerned about readers questioning her authenticity. By the time Misakian contacted Coppola, the book had sold over four million copies and was required reading in many schools. A market for the film seemed assured. Although there was virtually no promotion budget, Coppola himself began referring to the film as a "*Gone with the Wind* for fourteen year old girls."[5] Coppola had great respect for Hinton and included her on the set.

Once again Coppola was responsible for jumpstarting or cementing the careers of a group of young actors. C. Thomas Howell, Matt Dillon, Ralph Macchio, Patrick Swayze, Rob Lowe, Emilio Estevez (Martin Sheen's son), Tom Cruise, and Diane Lane all went on to have enduring major careers after *The Outsiders*. *The Outsiders* is the story of the Greasers, small-town Oklahoma outcasts with not much going for them. They are the have-nots opposing another gang, the socs, who have means. Through a series of tragic confrontations and losses, *The Outsiders* dramatically conveys the love of three brothers and the rite of passage of Ponyboy, the protagonist who narrates the film. In a scene where Ponyboy and his best friend Johnny spend several days hiding in a church, Ponyboy reads *Gone with the Wind* aloud and recites the Robert Frost poem "Nothing Gold Can Stay." This was echoed by Stevie Wonder on the soundtrack singing "Stay Gold." Coppola is able to heighten the drama of story by the use of Carmine Coppola's sumptuous score. The film was shot in widescreen and vivid color, with Coppola likely attempting to suggest the ultimate teenage angst film, *Rebel without a Cause*.

The Outsiders was released in March 1983. It had no advance publicity but earned $5 million in the first weekend. It was not the critics' darling, but the target audience came in droves. *The Outsiders* held the number one box office spot for one month until the release of the high-concept film *Flashdance*.

Still, although the film was financially successful, Coppola was personally injured by the negative critical comments. David Denby in *New York* magazine had called it "a frightening failure."[6] Coppola ruminated about the negative reviews proffered by New York critics since *The Godfather* and wryly pondered whether his films were really so bad or if they just liked exaggerating about his work.

By the middle of production on *The Outsiders*, Coppola had already decided that he wanted to film Hinton's *Rumble Fish* with Hinton's blessing. They wrote the screenplay on Sundays, and Coppola prepared to remain in Tulsa to use many of the same crew and the existing equipment. This was the cost-saving approach Roger Corman had taught him when Coppola made his first legitimate film, *Dementia 13*, back in Ireland. The approach to *Rumble Fish* was entirely different artistically. Coppola saw it as a fitting opportunity to apply German Expressionism to a dysfunctional father and two brothers, the elder hero-worshipped by the other, and the younger brother's group of friends. They are all at bay in small-town Oklahoma. Once again Coppola called on Burum to shoot the film. This time Burum studied older films shot in this cinematic style. Longtime colleague Dean Tavoularis concentrated on creating a claustrophobic, exaggerated physical environment. The film was to be shot in black and white. The streets the boys walked would be filled with shadow and outsized symbolic dressings. Clocks figure prominently in the atmosphere, perhaps reminiscent of one of Coppola's cinematic heroes, Ingmar Bergman in *Cries and Whispers*— the ticking of the clocks and the passage of time. Instead of a lush score created by his father, Coppola decided on a percussion score in the film's background and chose Stewart Copeland of the rock group The Police. Copeland proved to be very creative and mixed the sounds of the local Tulsa milieu with the percussive score. This soundtrack, for which he received a Golden Globe nomination, began a second career for Copeland, who since then has scored many successful films. Both Coppola boys, Roman and Gio, were associate producers.

Coppola chose some cast members from *The Outsiders*. Dillon plays Rusty James, the younger brother. Diane Lane is cast as his girlfriend. Domino Coppola is Lane's younger sister. From *Apocalypse Now* Coppola cast Larry Fishburne and Dennis Hopper. Tom Waits from *One from the Heart* appears. Mickey Rourke, Vincent Spano, the late Christopher Penn, and Diane Scarwid were part of the *Rumble Fish* ensemble, and Francis Coppola's nephew (son of August) joined the group using his stage name Nicolas Cage.

As he tried to do consistently, Coppola had a two-week rehearsal time and then videotaped a final run-through as a previsualization as he had on *One from the Heart* and *The Outsiders*. Longtime collaborator Barry Malkin worked closely with Francis on the final cut. Malkin was especially meticulous in editing the rumble scene, which had been choreographed by San Francisco Ballet director Michael Smuin.

One of the plot points in this film is getting out from under and getting away before time runs out. It is Motorcycle Boy who has tried to get away but knows he must help his inarticulate younger brother, Rusty James, find a way out. Motorcycle Boy has color blindness. The Rumble Fish in the pet store are symbolic of freedom, and when the boys go to look at them, they are the only color that is seen in the film (similar to the girl in the red coat in Spielberg's *Schindler's List*). Motorcycle Boy wants to set them free and in so doing is shot by the police, who believe he is robbing the store. Coppola cast Hopper as the boys' alcoholic father. It didn't seem a far stretch for Hopper. In commenting on Coppola's choice of Hopper in *Hollywood Hellraisers* by Robert Sellers, Coppola notes, "I hire Hopper for the two percent of ultimate brilliance, not the ninety-eight percent horseshit."[7]

When the movie was completed, the decision was made to feature the film at the New York Film Festival. *Rumble Fish* would be the first Coppola film to appear in that venue. Unfortunately, it did not go well. The critics totally panned the film, and the audience booed it. Not only was Coppola devastated by the reception, Universal, the distributor, was at a loss in terms of marketing. With negative reviews, failure at a major film festival, the choice of black-and-white cinematography, and a strange visual style, *Rumble Fish* quite rapidly sunk into oblivion. What was meant as an "art film" for kids was crucified by adults. At least, the film was dedicated with a sincerity that could not be challenged: "This film is dedicated to my older brother, August Coppola, my first and best teacher."

8

Coppola for Hire: *The Cotton Club, Peggy Sue Got Married, Gardens of Stone*

By the time the press had delivered their body blows to Francis Coppola in response to his deeply personal, experimental film *Rumble Fish*, he already knew his next project was *The Cotton Club*. The assignment started off slowly. Producer Robert Evans was now working independently after several down years. He had been at the top of his game with the extraordinary success of Roman Polanski's *Rosemary's Baby* and *Chinatown*, but his career suffered when he was convicted of cocaine possession. In 1982 Evans optioned James Haskins's *The Cotton Club*, which was a photographic history of Harlem's famed Cotton Club. The club had flourished during Prohibition with an array of black entertainers and white customers. It was Evans's idea to make the film as a lavish musical and a gangster story. He thought the melding of two popular genres would have audience appeal. Evans was able to obtain backing for a $20 million project from the Doumani brothers, who owned casinos in Las Vegas. Initially Evans had Robert Altman as director and floated star names like Al Pacino and Sylvester Stallone. When Evans's drug issues stalled the planning, Altman exited. Evans got a commitment from Richard Gere to appear in *The Cotton Club*. Gere was considered a guaranteed draw after the megahit *An Officer and a Gentleman*. Because the film was to be part gangster plot, Evans hired Mario Puzo to prepare a first draft script. The script Puzo presented to Robert Evans in mid-1982 was not acceptable to him, and Evans decided to contact Coppola for help. Coppola and Evans were not pals, but Evans knew that Coppola was in dire straits, and he took advantage. Evans phoned Coppola and said, "I have a sick child. I need a doctor."[1] Coppola said he would be happy to help with the script for a week or so *gratis*.

What began as a week's obligation ended in over a year's worth of Coppola's professional life.

When Coppola read Puzo's draft he found a jumbled and unusable blueprint. After a discussion with Evans, Coppola agreed to totally rework the script for $500 thousand. Coppola had delivered before when scripts were in trouble, and his writing talents could be put to good use on this project. Francis mapped out an approach that involved key players in a reconstruction of the script. Evans, Gere, and Gregory Hines were invited to Coppola's Napa estate for a week-long brainstorming conference. As Coppola began to familiarize himself with the backdrop of the Cotton Club he became intrigued by the Harlem Renaissance starting in the early 1920s and ending as the Great Depression began. Coppola became enamored of the period and excited about participating on a Jazz Age epic.

With the Doumani brothers getting anxious and threatening to pull their investment, Evans approached Coppola and asked him to direct the picture as well. In June 1983, Coppola agreed to direct the film.

In an interview with David Thomson and Lucy Gray for *Film Comment* magazine in the fall of 1983, Coppola reflects on the need to be in control of the film. "I made it very clear that if I were to do the film, I would need to really control it on every possible level. And then of course I come here and although I have those rights, the same thing goes on. So finally I've just put them all in their place, for the sake of the picture."[2]

When Coppola came on board he immediately encountered preproduction overruns. The club was being rebuilt in the Astoria Studios in Queens, New York. Robert Evans had hired the famed production designer Richard Sylbert. The replica was magnificent but costs were already at $1 million (they would ultimately swell to $6 million). In common, Coppola and Sylbert had both worked with Vittorio Storaro; Sylbert designed *Reds* for Warren Beatty and Storaro shot it. Sylbert laid out the club with meticulous care. In an author's interview, Sylbert explains the research he did to design the legendary club. "I laid out the club by talking to the men and women who used to dance there and from some pictures that I found." He had a team of researchers in Los Angeles that gathered an enormous amount of detail. Sylbert explained that he built the whole street: the front of the club, the marquee, and all the shops around the corner and across the other corner on an empty lot he found in Harlem. He describes, "One crew worked to get that done, and then this huge crew was in the studio to build the club. The costumes cost three and a half million dollars, and the sets cost nine million dollars."[3]

Once Coppola assessed what he had inherited he knew he had to take the reins. He told Evans the script needed more attention and hired Pulitzer Prize–winning William Kennedy, who had written a trilogy about the Roaring Twenties (*Ironweed* was based on Kennedy's work). Kennedy was able to bring specificity and authenticity to the script, although, working with Coppola, rewrites continued throughout the shoot. The cast and crew were enormous with some members pre-Coppola and others hired after he was at the helm. Coppola made changes. He hired Michael Smuin as choreographer;

he had laid out the rumble scene in *Rumble Fish*. Coppola brought on many of his regulars, including family members. Nicolas Cage was to act for his uncle. Because Coppola was continuing to utilize the electronic cinema there was a lot of waiting involved on the actors' parts. Diane Lane, who had worked with Coppola a number of times, speaks of the frustration. "This went on for months. We never knew when we were going to shoot."[4] Nephew Nicolas Cage had a tantrum and trashed his dressing room. Coppola was protective of Nicolas and said he was preparing for one of his scenes as "Mad Dog" Dwyer.

Regulars Laurence Fishburne and Tom Waits were in the cast. Sofia had a small part using the Domino moniker. Gio was a second-unit director and also credited with editorial montage. Marc Coppola (now a venerated disc jockey) had a small role.

The Cotton Club was a showcase for numerous black actors, singers, and dancers of the day—Gregory Hines, Lonette McKee, and Maurice Hines. The story involves the rise, fall, and romances of several of the denizens of the club.

The less-than-savory backers were not pleased with the escalating costs of the production. The scope and ambition of the entire production was simply not manageable. Because Francis had not developed the project initially his displeasure was exacerbated by personnel he had not chosen and with whom he could not work. He fired a lot of individuals and hired replacements. This made for additional turmoil and anxiety on the set. The overall atmosphere was chaotic. By August the production was two months behind schedule. Evans receded to the background while Coppola ran the show, unperturbed by the tumult. Finally, by the end of December 1983, production was complete at a cost of $47 million.

The Cotton Club finally opened at the end of 1984 to mixed reviews. For reasons that are not entirely clear, Orion, the distributor, rather than see how it might fare over time, decided to pull the picture after a scant two weeks. Perhaps they wanted to put all their eggs in the *Amadeus* basket. At that point the picture was a distinct financial failure. Its gross was a bit shy of $26 million, about half of its budget. It was another failure for Coppola, but not in the same manner as *One from the Heart*. Robert Evans hired Coppola because he needed him. For this gangster musical with tough-guy backers, Coppola was truly a hired gun. At least he had drawn a salary and didn't lose any of his own money.

When *The Cotton Club* was completed and released there was considerable bad blood. Producer Evans lost his shirt and put the responsibility squarely on Coppola. In postproduction it was alleged that 11 musical numbers were cut out. It may be true, and it also may have been necessary. There was disagreement about retaining numbers and the length of the finished film, but those decisions lie on the editing-room floor with Coppola and Malkin, his trusted colleague. Evans, let us remember, came crawling to Coppola pleading for a script doctor and then went one step further and asked him to direct the whole project, picking up a work in progress. Still, Evans felt sabotaged. In the *Hollywood Interview* with Alex Simon, Evans talked of his relationship with Coppola:

> Francis is the most charming, seductive man I've ever met. I think he's a direct descendant of Prince Machiavelli. Once you leave his kitchen, you're enamored of him. He's so talented, so brilliant, and a dreamer. And I think self-destructive. We've only spoken once since that time, at the 25th anniversary screening of *The Godfather*. We all went down to the front of the theater afterwards, to tremendous applause. Francis started to pass me. Then he stopped, put his arms around me and whispered in my ear, "We did something right." That about sums it up.[5]

Now midway through the 1980s, Coppola was strictly a director for hire; not only was it difficult for Coppola, it could be truly messy. *The Cotton Club* was an expensive failure, and Coppola was the director of record, even though he spent much of his tenure undoing and reorganizing the production he inherited when he came onto the project.

Coppola had vowed he would work as a director for hire for as long as it took to be debt free. Although he had been advised to declare bankruptcy, he refused. It wasn't his way. He believed it was his responsibility to work his way out of his financially precarious situation. So when he was offered the job as replacement director on *Peggy Sue Got Married* he accepted. The film was a Rastar/TriStar production, and Rastar was famed Hollywood stalwart Ray Stark, who was responsible for *Funny Girl* and many other film hits. Jonathan Demme was the original director but left citing creative differences. Debra Winger had been cast as Peggy Sue, and she wanted Penny Marshall to direct. Marshall had conflicts with the screenwriters. That left Stark and producer Paul R. Gurian looking for another director. Stark remembered Coppola from the late 1960s when they were both involved with Seven Arts; Coppola had been a screenwriter there. Stark asked Francis to direct *Peggy Sue*. No sooner had Coppola accepted the assignment than Winger developed a back injury and had to withdraw from the picture. Kathleen Turner, who was building a star-studded résumé with *Body Heat* and *Romancing the Stone*, was approached and accepted the role specifically for the opportunity to work with Coppola. Turner states, "I really wanted to work with Francis. I was intrigued by the thought that this was a great filmmaker who had never really had a leading lady. His films had basically dealt with men. In fact he said to me, 'I really don't know how to treat a leading actress. You'll have to tell me.' I said, well you have a glass of wine ready for her at the end of every day."[6]

Turner was completing *The Jewel of the Nile*, so production was delayed until she was available. Coppola used the time to consider a long-dreamed-of project of his own—a biopic of Preston Tucker, the auto maker, which he still hoped to realize at some time in his professional future. He directed a 3D short intended as a kick-off for a Disneyland/Disneyworld attraction. The short was titled *Captain EO* and starred Michael Jackson. It was a Michael Eisner conception that George Lucas produced. Lucas asked Coppola to direct, and Coppola was interested in the technical aspects of the project and how the use of electronic cinema might mesh with 3D. The production cost an extraordinary $20 million for a short high-tech specialty product. Also squeezed into Coppola's schedule was a segment for Shelley Duvall's successful Showtime series *Fairie Tale Theatre*, which retold classic fairy tales. Coppola directed "Rip Van Winkle," starring Harry Dean Stanton as Rip and Talia Shire as his unforgiving wife. The segment was well received, and Coppola enjoyed working in the medium.

It was not as if Coppola would have been drawn to *Peggy Sue* if money weren't an issue. The film was an accessible story of a woman, unhappy with her philandering husband and on the verge of divorce, who attends her 25th high school reunion and after fainting has a fantastical time-travel experience that allows her to return to her senior year with the ability to reflect on her life and the decisions she made. It is reminiscent of George Bailey's angel-facilitated flashback in Frank Capra's *It's a Wonderful Life*. More current was Steven Spielberg's vehicle *Back to the Future* (directed by Robert Zemeckis), which was a fun-loving exploration of time travel. The *Peggy Sue* production actually wanted to put some distance between these two films, worrying they might be perceived as too similar. But the association that resonated most for Coppola was the iconoclastic play *Our Town*—specifically the scene when the departed Emily reflects on her young life with her mother and George, her husband. It was as if that frame of reference gave the story some gravitas for Coppola. Paul Gurian notes that Coppola did not desire "A Francis Coppola Film" credit for this film. Gurian notes, "I felt this film was a chance for Francis to make a small, intimate film with a simple story and the critics would say, 'Hey. Francis, it's good, you made a nice simple story. It's not a brilliant Francis Coppola film,' and frankly it isn't, and anyone who says it is, is crazy."[7]

Coppola had his reservations about *Peggy Sue*, but he needed to push forward whittling away at his enormous fiscal problems. Fred Roos, his trusted colleague and arbiter of good taste, reassured Francis, predicting it would be an audience pleaser.

The most challenging cast member was Nicolas Cage, Coppola's nephew, who would play the male lead opposite Kathleen Turner. Cage was not actually Coppola's choice. Producer Gurian was very anxious that he play the role. Cage refused it several times but ultimately agreed to play Kathleen Turner's husband. Cage was August Coppola's son. His father, Coppola's revered older brother, was dean of creative arts at San Francisco State University. Clearly, Cage had the artistic genes but not the academic. While still in high school, he approached his father and told him that he wanted to act and didn't want to stay in school. August, to his credit, told Cage to get his General Educational Development (GED) certificate and gave him his blessing.

Coppola had directed Cage in a small role in *Rumble Fish* and a more substantial one in *The Cotton Club*. Cage liked working with his uncle although *The Cotton Club* had been a difficult experience. In the *Hollywood Interview* with Alex Simon, Cage remarks,

> I liked working with him. I found him to be very open to some far-out ideas. *Peggy Sue* I didn't want to do. I actually turned it down originally. He really went through the paces with me on that. TriStar wanted to fire me and he talked them out of it. I was going for something different with that character.... During rehearsal, I came up with this idea to be Pokey from the Gumby show, and create this cartoon character. There were some very tense days on the set.... Kathleen Turner was not happy with the performance. She thought she was going to get the boy from *Birdy* and instead she got Jerry Lewis on acid![8]

Opinions vary as to whether Cage's experiment (especially an inconsistent high-pitched vocal pattern) was a wise choice. He did, however, have some endearing moments, particularly his singing audition *He Don't Love You (Like I Love You)* in a black nightclub where Peggy Sue is able to see him in a more serious and intense perspective. In a 1996 interview for *Playboy* Cage thought back to the experience, remembering he was worried about the perception of nepotism if he took the part. "I started acting when I was seventeen, my fellow actors didn't accept me. They said I was there because of Francis Coppola. I felt I had to work twice as hard as the next guy to prove myself..."[9] In 1995 Cage won an Academy Award for his heartbreaking performance in *Leaving Las Vegas*. He has countless films to his credit and continues to push the envelope in many of his performances. His Elvis obsession is transformative in David Lynch's *Wild at Heart*. In Ridley Scott's *The Matchstick Men* he delivers an endearing characterization of an obsessive-compulsive con man with a sensitive, vulnerable interior. *Peggy Sue* marks the last time Cage and Coppola collaborated, but as is invariably the case, Cage remains a beloved nephew.

Also appearing in the film was Sofia Coppola as Peggy Sue's younger pesky sister. Sofia, with braces, performs adequately under her father's direction but has a weak vocal quality that may be a reflection of her personal reserve. She has many of her father's talents, but she is not flamboyant or extroverted.

The film benefits greatly from the participation of director of photography Jordan Cronenweth, who said working with Coppola was the "highlight of his career." He observed, "He delegates more than any other director I've worked with. He's a hands-off director."[10] Coppola's faith in Cronenweth's ability was well placed. The look of the film reflects the dream-like experience of the protagonist reverted to her teen years. The colors are saturated and create a heightened reality so appropriate for the time-travel sequences. Coppola delivered the picture on time and under budget. It was a very tight schedule with 18-hour days. Whether he was for hire or on his own, Coppola had standards he would not betray. When he screened the ending he asked for the opportunity to reshoot it, believing it wasn't quite sharp enough and that the actors looked tired. There was consensus that the reshoot improved the picture.

Peggy Sue Got Married was released in the fall of 1986. It closed the New York Film Festival, where it was received positively. It went on to be a box office hit, grossing about $22 million. Of all the films in the 1980s that Coppola directed for hire, it was the only one that ended up in the black.

Francis Coppola's success with *Peggy Sue Got Married* positioned him to receive an offer to direct an upcoming project for TriStar. They had a property called *Gardens of Stone* from a 1983 novel by Nicholas Proffitt.

Proffitt's novel focused on the Army's Old Guard unit, which is responsible for soldier burials at Arlington National Cemetery. The novel was largely autobiographical as Proffitt had spent most of his Army tenure with the Old Guard unit. After discharge, Proffitt obtained a journalism degree, was hired by *Newsweek* magazine, and became the Saigon bureau chief.

Coppola responded well to the idea of a film that dealt with army ritual and the "family" of the Old Guard. It told a personal story of a career army sergeant who had tours of duty in Vietnam as a young soldier and suffers emotionally burying young soldiers who are casualties of that difficult war. When Coppola was offered the film, the screenplay had already been written by a young screenwriter, Ronald (Ron) Bass. The following year Bass would write the screenplay for *Rain Man* and receive an Academy Award.

Coppola knew that he would need Army cooperation for the film to succeed. It would require the authenticity of the actual location at Arlington National Cemetery and access to Old Guard personnel. Coppola, who had angered the Pentagon during *Apocalypse Now*, negotiated skillfully and, with some minor alterations to the script which he reworked with Bass, the Army provided a military adviser and access to the cemetery, Fort Myer, the U.S. Army Marching Band, and Old Guard troops.

As was his wont, Coppola employed many crew members and actors who had regularly been part of his filmmaking team. Fred Roos was one of the producers. Roos's contribution to any Francis Coppola venture cannot be overestimated. Roos met Coppola when his sister Talia Shire was being considered for *The Godfather*. He was a casting director and managed Shire's early career. Roos was a graduate of UCLA in 1956. He acknowledges that seeing the Academy Award–winning 1946 film *The Best Years of Our Lives* as a young person inspired him to pursue a career in film. In the industry he is known for his uncanny ability at spot-on casting choices. Roos, with a gentle and reassuring demeanor, has been an integral and critical part of the Coppola creative family for decades. He provides the perfect counterpoint to Coppola's extroverted firebrand personality. His presence on the set of *Gardens of Stone* would be more essential than either of them could possibly know. Another constant in Coppola's professional life was Dean Tavoularis, who was responsible for the production design, as he had been since *The Rain People*. Coppola asked Cronenweth, who shot *Peggy Sue*, to be the director of photography. Another key crew member was Richard Beggs, who had been working as sound designer on Coppola's films since *Apocalypse Now* (for which he won an Academy Award as a member of the illustrious sound team including Walter Murch) and would continue to work with Coppola and Roman and Sofia on their projects. Barry Malkin again served as film editor on the production. Coppola had asked his father Carmine to prepare the score for *Gardens of Stone*, and he wrote the music for the Old Guard marching band. On the acting side, Coppola cast James Caan in the leading role of Sgt. Clell Hazard. Caan and Coppola had worked together professionally since *The Rain People* and were classmates at Hofstra, where Caan played football and Coppola directed plays. Also in the cast was Angelica Huston, with whom Coppola had just worked on *Captain EO*, and Lonette McKee, who appeared in *The Cotton Club*.

Coppola's eldest son, Gian-Carlo, was slated to be Coppola's right hand. Since he had left high school to pursue a filmmaking career at age 16 (with permission from his parents), Gio had been on the set with Francis at every opportunity. With each production he assumed a little more responsibility. On *The Outsiders* and *Rumble Fish* he was credited as associate producer. For *The Cotton Club* he is credited as second unit director and developed an editorial montage for one of the scenes in the film. He also was second unit director on the *Captain EO* short. Gio was a serious student with the extraordinary fortune of learning from a master. In the preproduction phase of *Gardens of Stone* Gio was responsible for videotaping all the rehearsal sessions that Francis invariably conducted to prepare his actors for scene direction. He supervised the electronic cinema staff. Plans were in the offing for Gio to branch out and work with other film-industry professionals. He was set to begin an internship with Spielberg on the television series *Amazing Stories*, which would feature episodes executed by different directors. This would be a great exposure for Gio, who could observe different work methods of established directors. Gio had also been hired by Penny Marshall for second unit on her next feature, *Jumpin' Jack Flash*. Marshall's daughter Tracy Reiner was Gio's close friend, and they had at one point been a couple.

On May 26, Memorial Day, Gian-Carlo Coppola and his friend Griffin O'Neal, son of Ryan O'Neal, decided to go speed boating on the South River near Annapolis. With them was Gio's girlfriend, Jacqueline (Jacqui) de la Fontaine. Gio and Jacqui were in love and in a steady relationship. Gio had met O'Neal on the set of *The Escape Artist*, one of O'Neal's few substantial roles as an actor. By all accounts Gio was a sensitive, caring young man, and he knew that Griffin had an unstable life and had spent a year in drug rehabilitation. Only days before he had been stopped by Virginia police for speeding and was charged with reckless driving, driving without a license, and carrying a switchblade. O'Neal was scheduled to play a small part in *Gardens of Stone*, and the production company bailed him out.

Initially, Jacqui went on the boat with the two young men but asked to be taken ashore. Gio and Griffin were on the river with Griffin driving the boat at a speed that would later be described as excessive. He maneuvered between two boats on the water, not aware they were attached by a towline. Griffin realized the towline was connecting the two boats just seconds before the line struck their boat. Griffin was able to duck, but the line struck Gio Coppola with enormous force, knocking him over backwards. When his head hit the deck the contact killed him instantly.

What unfolded from the moment Gio's death became known is a nightmarish story that would be unbearable for any family. The facts of the accident became known. O'Neal lied initially to the investigators, telling them Gio was driving the boat, but there were many eyewitnesses, and he was forced to admit he was the driver. O'Neal was charged with manslaughter but pled to a lesser charge of negligence while driving a speedboat. Ultimately he received probation and was required to perform community service.

In the larger sense O'Neal's role in the boating accident is only factual. It didn't change reality. The Coppola family was painfully altered forever. In an interview with Schumacher, Eleanor Coppola reflects on the effect of Gio's death on Francis Coppola. "I think there is something unique about the relationship of a father to his first child . . . we used to say he was an 'old soul'. He could sit quietly on the set for hours. . . . Gio had a healing, observant 'old soul' personality—more like mine—that was a soothing complement to Francis's tumultuous Italian personality."[11]

In an article about the tragedy in *People* magazine, Reiner also refers to Gio Coppola as an old soul. "Gio was a very, very old soul. He had a magic about him. He taught me more about life than anyone I've ever met. There's no elaborate story to Gio. He loved art. He painted and wrote and wanted to make films and he could fix just about anything. He was a very formal, classic gentleman."[12]

In the expanded version of her personal diary, Eleanor Coppola's entry on May 29, 1986, recounts her feelings after Francis told her of the death of her son:

> My mind keeps jumping back to Memorial Day. . . . The telephone rang. Sofia answered it downstairs and I picked up the extension. We both heard the strange, strangled sound of Francis's voice, as if he were speaking without breathing: "Ellie, we've lost our beloved son. Gio is dead." . . . Sofia went to the other line and called Roman, then she came in my room in agony. I pulled her into my arms. She sobbed, "I never heard Roman cry before."[13]

Francis Coppola knew he would never be complete again. With the death of Gio he lost a part of his body and soul. He chose not to stay home and mourn.

He couldn't face being near Gio's room and his belongings. He returned to the set to begin the direction of *Gardens of Stone*. O'Neal requested a release from his role in the film. It was granted. Coppola wanted no retribution; he couldn't see the point. It wouldn't bring Gio back, and O'Neal was in need of help. Coppola had no need to cause him any harm.

Caan told Michael Kay in an interview on YES network that he was with Coppola at the worst moment of his life—the time after Gio's death. He describes Coppola on the set in deep despair, at times breaking down while moving through his obligations. In retrospect, Coppola says he remembers almost nothing about the making of *Gardens of Stone*. Caan absorbed the experience as an opportunity to reexamine his own life and choices. He had been battling substance abuse for years. The death prompted him to get his house in order. Roman came to the set every day to be at his father's side. The shoot was painful for all the participants; the atmosphere on the set was subdued. Those who had been members of Coppola's creative family carried the weight of the production. Their support and Coppola's intangible capacity to perform at all under unbearable conditions brought *Gardens of Stone* to completion. Coppola told Peter Keough in a 1987 interview, "I was in a dream. I just wanted to get through it. Some nice people got me through that, people I worked with before. That's one of the really beautiful things about having a close crew."[14]

The film was not received well. Amazingly, critics only did their jobs and examined what they saw on the screen. They remarked that Coppola seemed detached; they couldn't feel his presence as director. Critic Dave Kehr, writing in the *Chicago Tribune*, was an exception. "It's impossible to watch *Gardens of Stone* without remembering the tragedy that intervened in Coppola's own life. . . . The film is so distant, perhaps, because it is so close."[15] None of the film analysis mattered to Coppola and his family. When the last scene was covered, the Coppolas left for Paris and some consolation.

The death of Eleanor and Francis Coppola's son defined much of the future for the Coppola family. In an interview for *Film Comment* in 2008, Coppola observes, "Few people, thank God, go through the experience of losing a child. . . . It's not an experience you get over. . . . You don't get over it, you can't get over it, you'll never get over it. I think of it as the loss that keeps on losing; there isn't a day that goes by that you don't say, 'Gee, what would he be contributing?' "[16]

In the months that followed Gio's death, his final year came into sharp focus. Gio had met de la Fontaine when she attended Beverly Hills High School. Jacqui, with her mother, had moved to Los Angeles from New York when her father, a restaurateur, abandoned them when Jacqui was 12. Jacqui and Gio became a couple at the beginning of 1986 and by Memorial Day were developing plans to marry. They were sharing an apartment, and Eleanor perceived that Jacqui was a wonderful influence on Gio. Jacqui had remained on shore when Gio and Griffin went out for the fateful late-afternoon boat ride.

After Gio's death it became known that at age 19 Jacqui was pregnant with Gio's child. Eleanor and Francis totally embraced Jacqui. Immediately she became a fully accepted member of the family. Jacqui, with artistic propensities, was especially interested in costume design. It was easy to nurture Jacqui's ambitions; remarkably they aligned exactly with Sofia's abilities and Eleanor's aptitudes.

On January 1, 1987, inaugurating a new year on a life-affirming note, Gian-Carla Coppola, daughter of Jacqui and Gio, was born. At the time of Gio's speed-boating accident Jacqui had been over two months pregnant. The little girl became known as Gia. She was Eleanor and Francis's first grandchild and was showered with love and affection. Eleanor and Francis helped care for Gia and Jacqui and purchased a home for them in the Hollywood Hills.

Coppola and His Dreams: *Tucker: The Man and His Dream, The Godfather III, Bram Stoker's Dracula*

After *Gardens of Stone* completed its brief and disheartening release, playing off quickly in the United States and Europe, Coppola again began to reflect on the American auto-making entrepreneur Preston Tucker and his story. Tucker had rolled around in Francis's psyche since he was a child. Carmine Coppola had been intrigued by Tucker's invention and respected Tucker's ingenuity and vision. Tucker was a patriotic American interested in designing an efficient, economical, and safe automobile for the American public. He was a dreamer and also a shameless self-promoter who produced commercial presentations featuring his entire family to enthuse the consumer about his visionary products. Tucker was far from a fool, but apparently he was unable to recognize the threat he posed to the all-powerful Big Three auto makers. Formidable forces were at play to squelch Tucker and his dream.

Francis Coppola retained his father's enthusiasm for Preston Tucker's gumption and responded to the aesthetic of the Tucker automobile he had seen on display with his father. Carmine had gone so far as to purchase stock in Tucker's company—all of which he lost when Tucker went belly-up. It was a David and Goliath saga, but Goliath prevailed. Tucker was hounded by lawsuits, accusations of fraud, and challenges to his key auto invention, the 1948 Tucker Sedan. He eventually lost the financial ability to produce the car although he had a huge factory in Chicago and planned to mass manufacture the Tucker on an assembly line. In the end, fewer than 50 sedans were manufactured, and the ones that are still in existence are cherished collectors' items. Both Coppola and George Lucas own 1948 Tucker Sedans. In 1975,

Francis had obtained the rights to Preston Tucker's story from the Tucker family and had their complete cooperation (absent the reality of Tucker's philandering.)

In the early days of Zoetrope Studios, when Coppola was mapping out plans for a series of productions to be accomplished under the Zoetrope banner, he conceptualized the idea of Tucker's story as a musical. Initially he imagined it as a dark piece because Tucker had been thwarted by corporate forces and did not actually achieve his dream of mass producing Tucker automobiles. Coppola contacted Leonard Bernstein, Betty Comden, and Adolf Green to gauge their interest in such a venture. (Perhaps if he wanted it dark, he should have contacted Stephen Sondheim.) The three visited Coppola's estate and for two weeks had lively conversations, drove around the Napa Valley in Coppola's Tucker, and discussed the conception of an *On the Town*–type musical. Although Bernstein wanted a clearer outline of the idea, they left with the door opened. The project was mentioned in the press and became part of Zoetrope's preproduction agenda. With the failure of *One from the Heart* and the collapse of the studio, this notion, along with many others was unrealized. Coppola claims to have been so embarrassed that he never contacted Bernstein to explain the plan would have to be shelved.

Yet Coppola held on to the desire to bring the project to fruition. Whereas once he could have found financing, now he wasn't bankable and the studio financiers stayed at a distance. The emotional draw of the project was intensified by the loss of Gio, who had loved cars and the Tucker story. After all, his grandfather had ordered, but of course had not received, a Tucker. In 1985 in a local July Fourth parade, Gio convinced Francis to ride in the caravan with the Tucker Sedan. The Coppola kids washed and polished the car, and Gio drove with Francis in a passenger seat. This was a vivid memory that kept the Tucker project alive for Coppola.

Because Coppola had just collaborated with Lucas on the *Captain EO* project, he contemplated approaching Lucas to executive produce *Tucker*. But Coppola was skittish. In their relationship, Coppola had been the mentor—he was the father figure. Coppola had been the kingmaker in launching *American Graffiti*. It was a big success. Yet over the years they had had their ups and downs, particularly over the *Apocalypse Now* property and the original intention that Lucas would direct it. When Coppola finally talked with Lucas about partnering on *Tucker*, George Lucas agreed to finance it. Coppola remembers, "It took a lot of courage on my part. I wanted to do something with George, but I didn't know if he wanted to do something with me."[1] Lucas, now a kingmaker himself after the enormous success of the *Star Wars* franchise, had his own opinions on the shape and direction of *Tucker: The Man and His Dream*. Lucas envisioned an upbeat story of an American inventor more in the style of a Frank Capra show. It seemed that Francis accepted Lucas's point of view. Since the loss of Zoetrope Studios and almost a decade of directing experiences where he really wasn't in charge, Coppola had lost his confidence. Where once there had been swagger and bold initiative, now Coppola was filled with self-doubt. On each project he directed for hire, he committed to doing the most professional job he could, but there was a price to be paid. In 1988 Coppola told Robert Lindsey for a *New York Times* magazine profile, "I knew George had a marketing sense of what people might want. He was at the height of his success, and I was at the height of my failure, and I was a little insecure."[2] So *Tucker: A Man and His Dream* was a somewhat uneasy collaboration. Lucas saw it as his responsibility to keep Francis on point: focused on achieving an accessible portrait of an optimistic maverick who did not perceive of himself as a failure despite losing his dream. Coppola decided not to write the screenplay. Instead he approached Arnold Schulman, who admired Coppola enormously. Schulman had a deep and varied résumé including *Goodbye, Columbus, Love with the Proper Stranger*, *A Hole in the Head (for Frank Capra)* and *Funny Lady*. Schulman was anxious to collaborate with Coppola but confessed he hated cars. Schulman met with Lucas, and Lucas made perhaps the most salient observation about the entire venture. Lucas told Schulman, "This film is not about cars. It's about Francis."[3] Lucas saw the parallels between Preston Tucker and Francis Coppola. Both men were dreamers and inventors. Both had experienced the highs and lows, the successes and failures of an adventurous, risk-taking professional life. Both men eventually would land on their feet.

The production had a generous $25 million budget initially financed by Lucas without any studio support. Casting began with the central role of Tucker assigned to Jeff Bridges. Coppola remembered Bridges in one of his first roles in Peter Bogdanovich's *The Last Picture Show*. As a child he had acted with his father, Lloyd Bridges, in television's *Sea Hunt* and was now a solid working actor with considerable physical appeal.

Bridges was extroverted, with a million-dollar smile, and Coppola thought he would do well as Preston Tucker. Joan Allen, who had worked with Coppola on *Peggy Sue*, was cast as Tucker's devoted, effervescent wife. Frederic Forrest came on board as Tucker's loyal key mechanic, and Martin Landau gives a tour-de-force performance as Tucker's financial adviser. Dean Stockwell, who had appeared in *Gardens of Stone*, is quirky and believable as Howard Hughes trying to convince Tucker to defy the overwhelming powers-that-be as Hughes had been able to do with his outsize aircraft the Spruce Goose.

Coppola's crew consisted of a number of loyal regulars. Fred Roos and Fred Fuchs were producers. Storaro and Tavoularis photographed and designed, and Richard Beggs was the sound designer. As a production, the essentials went smoothly. The film is narrated to familiarize the audience with the character of Preston Tucker. Coppola was able to complete shooting in 13 weeks. The preproduction had been a challenge. The design of the film was exacting, and Coppola and Storaro had an intense visual plan for color and look. The result is glossy, color-saturated images reminiscent of the pages of postwar magazines like *Life* and *Look*. The design is out-scaled and heightened. Coppola was visually inventive in advancing from scene to scene, starting a scene in one venue and seamlessly proceeding to another location in a dynamic movement. The entire film travels at a rapid pace as if a Tucker were revving its engine throughout the storyline. The climax of the film is an enthralling coda: Tucker Sedans of all colors appear on display in a moving, circular cavalcade. The colors and unique style of the individual Tuckers are breathtaking and elicit a poignant emotional response and sense of what might have been.

Comparisons to Coppola did not escape the attention of the critics. Critic Peter Travers writing for *People* magazine noted: "What makes this unapologetically up movie work is Coppola's infectious idea-mongering. No matter if Tucker the man sold only fifty cars, or if *Tucker* the movie sells only fifty tickets. Coppola, like his maverick mentor, has made a thing of beauty."[4] Actor Bridges felt *Tucker* was about a renegade who pushed back at the system. Bridges played Tucker as a man with confidence that he had something better to offer, and even though he is defeated, his spirit survives. The spirit lives on. He wondered about Coppola's similarity to Tucker.

Tucker, however, was not another *Peggy Sue*. Despite some positive critical reaction, as with his other films of the 1980s, initially it failed at the box office. Perhaps if Lucas had trusted the American audience a bit more, Coppola could have shaped Preston Tucker's narrative with less hoopla and more perspective. Coppola dutifully rode the circuit promoting the film, but his own ambivalence was revealed. When he told Robert Lindsey that Lucas "wanted to candy-apple it up a bit—make it like a Disney film,"[5] the artistic differences between Lucas and Coppola were evident. Despite their differing artistic perspectives, in the long run, the film made money in international release. Especially in France and Japan, the audiences revered a Coppola picture.

Coppola did, however, achieve one priceless objective. At the film's conclusion is the loving dedication, "For Gio, who loved cars."

Coppola was worn out. He started to make public statements that he was retiring. Nearing 50, and after spending close to a decade undoing the financial fiasco of *One from the Heart*, Coppola wanted to switch gears. His hope was to resolve his debts, which he was closer to doing, and then exit quietly. Then he would consider his life choices, but they would not include making more mainstream films within the current Hollywood system.

Almost immediately he was approached by director Woody Allen, who wanted to develop an anthology film with stories about contemporary New York directed by New York film directors. Allen would do one 30- to 40-minute segment, and two other directors would follow suit. Martin Scorsese, an ultimate New York director, committed. Coppola was approached. Although he had spent most of his childhood in New York, once he attended UCLA he was really identified as a West Coast director. He wasn't Sidney Lumet or Mike Nichols or Bob Fosse. Nevertheless, Coppola agreed. He had maintained an apartment in the Sherry Netherland Hotel since the mid-1970s, and he would use the hotel as home base for his segment. Coppola decided he could provide an opportunity for his teenage daughter Sofia to participate in the segment in the kind of internship situation he had offered Gio and Roman in the past.

Scorsese was pleased to have Coppola as a member of the series. He was a great Coppola admirer and looked to him as the leader of the film-school generation. Both Scorsese and Coppola shared a love of film history and a breadth of knowledge about world cinema and all genres of film. Scorsese talks about when he first met Coppola at the Sorrento Film Festival:

> He was writing *The Godfather* at the time and we got along very well. . . .
> we went sightseeing to Pompeii. And when I finally did *Mean Streets*,
> I had to pay $5000 to the San Gennaro Society. . . . I didn't have
> $5000, so I asked Francis to help me and he did. And as soon as we sold
> the picture, he was the first person I paid back and the first person to see
> the film. I went to San Francisco and screened a print for him.[6]

Even as Francis Coppola agreed to the project he had an argument with himself—he just didn't want to do it; he wanted to retire. Again he was in the public eye, facing New York reporters interviewing him about *Tucker* and about his future plans. Invariably the possibility of a *Godfather* sequel arose. Coppola always vetoed it.

Sofia Coppola's role in the production was substantial. She would cowrite the screenplay with her father and function as costume designer and title designer. Silverfish trailer in tow, in June 1988 Sofia and Francis settled into their Sherry Netherland apartment to realize the segment.

Coppola's segment was titled "Life without Zoe." It is the story of a prepubescent girl who lives in the Sherry Netherland Hotel. While her wealthy parents (who are separated) pursue their extravagant lives, Zoe is lovingly cared for by the hotel staff. Zoe's father (Giancarlo Giannini) is a world-famous flautist—clearly a reference to Carmine Coppola (who has a cameo as a street musician and wrote the music for the segment). Zoe's mother, played by Talia Shire, is a journalist. Zoe is a child of privilege, precocious and inventive. While her parents are away she and her friends attend a lavish birthday party for a new friend, a young boy purportedly the richest in the world, but very lonely. Zoe is able to shop where she wants, eat what she wants, and has access to whatever money she needs. The costumes and titles Sofia designed are fun and funky, but the overall sense in observing Zoe and her friends is one of superficiality and the height of overindulgence. After some plot point shenanigans involving a robbery Zoe witnesses, Zoe is ultimately able to reunite with her parents, and the last scene depicts the whole family at the Acropolis, where her father is performing an open-air charity concert.

The character of Zoe probably made perfect sense to Sofia Coppola. She was without doubt a child of privilege and had experienced much more in her young life than the average teenager. Because it was Coppola's habit to bring his family with him to any location that kept him away more than two weeks, Sofia had traveled extensively and was exposed to many cultures. She also needed to adapt and learned to entertain herself. Needless to say, creativity was encouraged in the Coppola family, and Sofia spent time sketching and drawing. She had already spent two summers in Paris interning at Chanel with Karl Lagerfeld.

At Sofia's level of maturity, a teenage girl with artistic promise, it was up to her father to decide the appropriateness of this endeavor, recognizing that her wares would be on the large screen for all to see. Whereas the boys had apprenticed behind the scenes in gofer jobs and second unit and with welcoming professionals to oversee their tasks, Sofia was asked to formulate a story and make a major contribution to its visual look. It was an awkward and ill-advised judgment. In *Life without Zoe* responsibility for such poor decision making must be assigned to Francis Coppola himself. Even with the best intentions as a loving father, Sofia's efforts are out of proportion to the professional situation in which she was placed. The talents of Coppola's devoted crew (likely devoted to Sofia as well)—producers Roos and Fuchs, Storaro, Tavoularis, and Barry Malkin—are simply wasted. *Life without Zoe* is the weakest link in the anthology trio. It is particularly embarrassing to view immediately after Martin Scorsese's *Life Lessons*—a top-notch character study of an aging, egotistical, and manipulative artist played to perfection by Nick Nolte.

As the decade ended, Coppola continued to seek quietude he had not achieved since he purchased Hollywood General Studios. As he approached 50, he felt the full brunt of the decade's grueling director-for-hire schedule and the ever-painful loss of his first-born son. He claimed his desire was to free himself from the Hollywood grind and find a place where he could create his personal films without interference. It harkened back to his days making *The Rain People*, *The Conversation*, and *Rumble Fish*—the films he continued to cite as his favorites.

Immediately after the success of *The Godfather Part II*, the drumbeat began for a sequel. In the ensuing years, Coppola was endlessly cajoled, questioned, and begged to continue the *Godfather* saga. He always responded in the same way: he didn't want to direct another *Godfather* movie. He had no inclination to go back to gangster territory. Coppola contended that the two parts were self-contained; the Corleone family had moved from succession in *Part I* to the pure evil of Michael Corleone in *Part II*. Any empathy audiences might have felt for the Corleones as a loving family in *Part I* was eradicated when Michael Corleone ordered the murder of his oldest brother, the banishment of his wife Kay, and the violent execution of his enemies in *Part II*. Coppola and Puzo were unequivocal in their condemnation. The mafia was a powerful and destructive undercurrent in American society.

For Paramount Studios the motivation for another sequel was simple: it was strictly monetary. The 1980s had not been as fruitful for Paramount as the *Godfather* years of the 1970s. The Studio saw *Part III* as a cash cow and had tried to make it happen any way they could. Paramount's intended concept was to continue the story with the focus on Michael's son Anthony. Over the years other directors and screenwriters were considered to replace Coppola and Puzo as the two were unwilling.

Paramount commissioned treatments and screenplays and contemplated Scorsese or Sylvester Stallone to direct. They thought of John Travolta for the role of Anthony. Nothing panned out. Puzo eventually was seduced by a quarter of a million dollars and 6 percent of a potential gross to write a 50-page treatment. Although some of the elements were there, even a treatment written by the actual author of *The Godfather* didn't gel. In 1986 Puzo tried again. The current Paramount chairman, Frank Mancuso, encouraged Puzo to refocus on Michael Corleone and the dynamics of the Corleones that had so enthralled audiences. The result was more workable, and Nicholas Gage, who had been hired to executive produce the property, did a rewrite that developed a new character—the illegitimate son of Sonny Corleone and Lucy Mancini, who were so evident as grunting lovers during Connie's wedding scene in *Part I*. The character, Vincent Mancini, would seek ascendancy as the next godfather, Michael's replacement.

Armed with what they believed was a credible plot line, Paramount determined that production should begin on *The Godfather Part III*. The missing ingredient, of course, was a director. Through an emissary, Talia Shire agreed to deliver the Puzo/Gage script to Coppola. His reaction was heated; he threw it in the fireplace.

If we didn't know that Coppola was the director of record on *The Godfather Part III*, it would be logical to assume after Coppola's response that the case was closed. There arose, however, a compelling intervening variable. Coppola's protracted efforts to rise above the specter of his financial reverses took another turn for the worse. Although on paper it appeared that Coppola's net worth was clearly in the black, a demand note for substantial cash would not be easy to meet. It looked as if one of his Zoetrope creditors was about to win a court battle for millions of dollars plus interest.

Under these circumstances, Coppola reasoned that a *Godfather III* director-for-hire job would be more palatable than most forced choices. Paramount needed him, and he could leverage that need—pressing for a substantial salary and artistic control. Coppola and Mancuso struck a deal, and then Paramount took months to iron out the particulars. The final agreement was an amalgam with the Studio and Francis each making concessions. *The Godfather Part III* would continue to concentrate on the remaining key characters from parts I and II and most specifically on Michael Corleone. Francis firmly believed that the tragedy of *The Godfather* centered on Michael Corleone; he wanted the film, which he referred to as an epilogue, to be called *The Death of Michael Corleone*, but the studio disagreed. Coppola no longer wielded the power to prevail. Reprising the characters employing the same actors, who now commanded star-level compensation, would automatically increase the budget, along with a hefty fee for the writer/director and Puzo. Coppola would have to adhere to the agreed-upon budget and bring in the completed project ready to open Christmas Day, 1990—an extremely tight schedule. Further, it was stipulated that the film's length could not exceed two hours and twenty minutes.

Puzo and Coppola set about the task of formulating the screenplay; Coppola focused on themes of Shakespearian proportion, especially those of *King Lear.* Instead of their typical six-month allotment for script develop-ment, the team was constrained to a six-week turnaround. Coppola often worked in Vegas or Reno, taking advantage of the 24/7 environment. They began in that mode and then switched to their routine of writing separately and reconvening to review their versions. On April 7, 1989, Coppola's 50th birthday, the first draft of *The Godfather Part III* was completed.

Pulling together a production of this scope, where much of the cast was pre-determined, was not easy. Everyone from the previous *Godfathers* made salary demands. Eventually, Al Pacino, Diane Keaton, and Shire were in place. Robert Duvall as Tom Hagen was a key component, and Coppola was anxious to use him as the negotiator with the Vatican, an important plot point, but they simply could not settle on terms. He was written out as the Corleone law-yer and replaced by the suave George Hamilton as the family's adviser. John Savage was a newly created character, a priest who was Tom Hagen's son, but the role does not call for much. New characters are introduced to support the story line. Joe Mantegna and Eli Wallach are cast as members of rival fam-ilies. For the critical role of Vincent Mancini, Coppola chose Andy Garcia. He seemed to fit into the Corleone family. Coppola notes, "He's a great looking guy and a skilled actor. He's also an actor who can bring out the emotional and irrational stuff that's hard to put your finger on. People like him when they see the film. Everyone remarks on how good Andy is."[7] Mary Corleone, daughter of Kay and Michael, was to be played by Winona Ryder. In Eleanor Coppola's *Further Notes*, a continuation of the diary she began during *Apocalypse Now*, she relates the situation that changed the contour of *The Godfather Part III* at least for the Coppola family. Shooting was in Rome at Cinecittà Studios. Sofia was visiting from California for the Christmas holidays, and on December 28 a call came from the set. It seemed that actress Ryder had become ill and would not be able to perform the role of Mary. Immediately, Francis decided to cast his daughter Sofia in the part. He asked Sofia to come to the studio immediately for a costume fitting. Eleanor recalls relating Coppola's decision. "I told Sofia as evenly as I could, but tears of emotion were welling up in my eyes. She was very excited at first. Then it sank in, she became anxious. I could see how worried she was about letting her father down. I said I was sure he would never have cast her if he didn't believe she could do it."[8] The cast and crew erupted, and so did Paramount.

Coppola's sister Tally tried to talk him out of it. Paramount offered him any choice he wanted, but production would have to shut down until the actress was found, and the pace was already frantic. For Paramount, the operative word was *rush*. Besides, Coppola believed Sofia could do it. He saw her as an innocent, ethnically Italian girl who was the prototype he had imaged as he wrote the role. Coppola had artistic control, and the decision was his own. His daughter would not refuse her father, and production continued with Sofia cast as Mary. Eleanor reported that well-meaning people were accusing her of a form of child abuse. Ellie stayed close to the set. Her brother Roman was there. In the end, although many wished otherwise and felt Sofia was in for critical razzing, with whatever moxie she had the role of Mary was hers. Costume designer Milena Canonero was of special assistance to Sofia, not only in her role as costume designer but as a caring, competent woman. Many years later, she would work with Sofia on *Marie Antoinette* and win an Academy Award for costume design. Then too, Jacqui de la Fontaine was on the set as wardrobe assistant. Thankfully, Sofia was surrounded by family. Sofia says of the experience, "The critics tore me apart, but I didn't want to be an actress. If I had, then it would have been harder." She notes that after *The Godfather Part III* she avoided the movie business. "I became a dilettante. I wanted to do something creative but I didn't know what it would be."[9]

Hindsight being 20/20, it's easy to speculate on Coppola's decision to cast Sofia. Knowing he has a hot Italian temper and that in part he didn't want to be involved in the project at all; was feeling some anger, rational or not, that Ryder had withdrawn with such incredibly short notice; and was unwillingly to sacrifice his creative control as he was plainly sick of conceding, one might understand his resolve. Coppola completely loved his daughter. He had lost one of his sons. Perhaps he really needed her there. He claimed on his commentary on *The Godfather Part III* DVD that whenever he watches, he is pleased to see an 18-year-old Sofia on the screen. He calls it a "home movie" and appears to have warm feelings about it. As for the considerable negative criticism Sofia endured as a young girl with no acting credentials or training, Coppola claims any blasting was really meant for him and not Sofia. Astutely he observes that since *The Godfather Part III* Sofia has developed into a successful young woman with a considerable résumé. Eleanor concurs. In a May 1995 entry in her diary she notes, "I realize now that during the production of *Godfather III*, I watched Sofia grow from a sheltered child into a young woman on a very difficult project. She recognized she couldn't quit and worked through all the challenges until the film was completed. That creative and strengthening experience gave her a firm foundation for work in the arts."[10]

The Godfather III focuses on redemption and reconciliation. In 1979, Michael Corleone is not a well man. He suffers from diabetes and is wracked with guilt for the sins he has committed since becoming the Don. Michael Corleone divests himself of all illegitimate businesses. He gives an enormous amount of his wealth to the Catholic Church. He shies away from the mob families who want to pull him back in. He reconciles with his children, Mary and Anthony. He had allowed Kay to educate the children, and with them now as young adults and with coaxing from Kay, he gives his blessing to Anthony to be an opera singer. Mary will run his charitable foundation. Michael Corleone wants to be a legitimate businessman on a large scale. To do this he moves to purchase majority shares of an international conglomerate whose ownership extends to the deep recesses of the Vatican. There are many intrigues as far up as the Pope, and Michael learns that corruption in the Catholic Church is as destructive as it is in the mafia. Michael may want redemption, but he will learn it cannot be bought.

The existence of Don Michael Corleone had already been fated. His beloved daughter Mary is in love with Vincent Mancini, who will become the heir apparent to the family business. Michael's *quid pro quo* for the power he will invest in Vincent is Vincent's commitment to let Mary go. Michael wants Mary to be safe, and life in the family is not safe. Michael's sister Connie does not really agree with Michael's efforts to eradicate the true family business and is more closely aligned with Vincent than Michael. The last act of the film is a dramatic interplay of son Anthony's inaugural operatic performance at the Palermo Opera House intercut with the family's attempt to eradicate all existing enemies that challenge Michael's supremacy, including the Catholic Church. It is a one-act opera from 1890 called *Cavalleria Rusticana*, composed by Pietro Mascagni. The opera is conducted by Coppola's uncle Anton, whom he had seen conduct Broadway shows as a child. The intercutting technique used to such great effect in the first *Godfather* epic is every bit as stimulating here. In the climactic final scene on the majestic steps of the opera house an assassin's bullet intended for Michael merely nicks him but kills Mary. Michael was in too deep to ever be redeemed. And so we have the true death of Michael Corleone, who will live out his years in solitude in Sicily and die alone a broken man.

Although it is generally concluded that *The Godfather III* is the least effective of the three parts, there are elements to commend it; as described, the last act is riveting. However, the film seems, at times, to suffer from the use of the Cinecittà Studios as opposed to real location work. And yes, some scenes where Sofia has prolonged dialogue do grate. One can only wonder how the film would have been served as a whole if Ryder had been Mary. It is difficult not to wonder when we see how magnificent and nuanced she is in the role of Mina in Coppola's next film, *Bram Stoker's Dracula*.

It is fair to say the entire venture would have benefited from more time. Coppola has said he was rushed, and this seems undeniable. Having a release date certain of December 25, 1990, influenced many creative decisions. If there had been more flexibility it is surely possible that some wrinkles, inconsistencies, and even Sofia's performance might have worked to everyone's advantage. But Paramount had commerce to think about, and therein was the rub.

Carmine Coppola worked for the last time with his son Francis on this movie. He died on April 26, 1991. Francis makes a few observations on the DVD audio track of the *Godfather Part III*. He says that while Carmine was conducting in rehearsal for the party scene he missed a cue. Francis pointed it out to Carmine, and Carmine denied it. Francis said his father had never missed a cue. It made him feel Carmine didn't have much longer. Then at the Academy Awards on March 25, 1991, Carmine's end credits song was passed over for an award. Francis said he had a stroke, and a month later he was dead. Carmine Coppola had a great career. He wrote and orchestrated for many of Francis's films and was also hired independently. To achieve recognition during the last decades of his life was a gift. Earlier in his career he deserved recognition on his own merits but had never gotten it. Francis Coppola was the facilitator.

There is an additional performance of note in *The Godfather Part III*. That is the brittle but assured characterization of Connie Corleone played by Shire. We are left with the impression that Connie will remain with Vincent and carry out the tasks she performed for her brother when he was godfather. She believes in the life of the family. Shire's perception of the role of Connie as she moves from young bride to caregiver for Michael is that when their mother died she took her place—the queen is dead, long live the queen.

In her acting career Shire believes she came into her own when she was cast in *Rocky* as Adrianna Pennino (Pennino was Italia Coppola's maiden name). Shire identified totally with Adrian and gained confidence through the years just as Adrian did in each subsequent *Rocky* sequel. She credits her getting the role in the first place to her ability to relate to Stallone so easily. To her, he was just like one of her brothers. It took Shire many years to overcome her reticence and insecurity about her acting skills. She attributes those feelings to her classic upbringing as an Italian girl who is conditioned to be one step behind any man. With her marriage to Jack Schwartzman, lawyer and producer, that changed. He had a different philosophy than the Italian men in her family. Sadly, Schwartzman died of pancreatic cancer in 1994.

The Godfather Part III wasn't quite the blockbuster Paramount had hoped for, but it steadily earned money and conformed to the two prior sequels to round out the *Godfather* saga. The press continued to badger Coppola. Apparently he was their favorite big target. The *New York Times* wrote an article in March 1991 about film sequels that flopped, and *The Godfather Part III* was included. Coppola was enraged (and likely hurt), so much so that he wrote a letter to the editor. In it he pointed out that the film had a substantial gross, which was only domestic, and had already been nominated for Academy Awards. By Coppola's lights he could not accept labeling *The Godfather Part III* a flop. This incident reinforced Coppola's belief that the mainstream press invariably targeted him unfairly.

The Godfather III was nominated for seven Academy Awards: Best Picture, Best Director, Best Supporting Actor (Andy Garcia), Editing, Cinematography, Art Direction, and Original Song. It did not win any awards. To date the worldwide gross for the film is $136,766,062 dollars.[11]

As Coppola's responsibilities for *The Godfather Part III* wound down, he and Eleanor made a decision to protect their financial future. There were two elements. Whereas Coppola had always used his own lawyers and functioned without an agent, he joined Creative Arts Agency (CAA). Foremost, the Coppolas went to bankruptcy court and filed under Chapter 11 so they would have an orderly way to finally resolve the debts that plagued them for over a decade. Their assets were listed at $52 million with liabilities at $98 million. On November 13, 1992, the following statement was issued to the press:

> The bankruptcy filing closes the book on a complicated decade-long series of financial and legal problems arising from the making of *One from the Heart*. It will finally let us resolve all remaining debts and obligations stemming from the film and enable me to focus my attention on projects.[12]

Despite claims he wanted to retire, Francis Coppola was never without plans. In development at different stages was his long-gestating epic *Megalopolis*, a television series based on *The Outsiders* (which aired on Fox and lasted for eight episodes), a film on J. Edgar Hoover, and Carroll Ballard's film *Wind* about the America's Cup.

Seemingly out of the blue a project about one of his childhood favorite characters came to his attention. Ryder approached him, anxious to make amends for her costly failure to perform in *Part III*.

She had received a script from James V. Hart, a young writer whose only known credit was *Hook*, directed by Steven Spielberg. This script was titled *Bram Stoker's Dracula* and was developed by closely following the author Bram Stoker's version of the Dracula tale. Coppola was immediately enthused. As a boy he and his brother August saw every film horror story available and especially relished *Dracula*, *Frankenstein*, and *The Wolfman*. Of course, over time, these film stories became part of the Saturday matinee line-up with version after version and spinoffs of these scary stories. The most authentic was the silent film directed by F. W. Murnau titled *Nosferatu*. Tod Browning's *Dracula* with the iconic Bela Lugosi is a respected version of the *Dracula* tale. John Carradine's *House of Dracula* was one of the boys' favorites. Director James Whale's *Frankenstein* with the esteemed Boris Karloff is considered a classic. Spinoffs that diluted some of the principal elements of the stories appeared: *Dracula's Daughter*, *Son of Dracula*, *House of Frankenstein*, and *Abbott and Costello Meet Frankenstein*, but the horror genre continued to attract a mass audience. Francis and his older brother were members of the horror genre audience. They did not fail to see any of the tales of these captivating creatures.

Francis talks about his love for children (which is obvious) and the period when he was a camp counselor in upstate New York. His bunk was a group of eight- and nine-year-olds, and each night he read them a story at bedtime: it was Bram Stoker's *Dracula*. So Coppola's passion for this authentic version began very early. When the James V. Hart's screenplay came to him and he read it, he was thrilled at the prospect of bringing it to the screen. As a boy Coppola's curious mind led him to research Count Dracula in the Coppola family *Encyclopedia Britannica*. There he found the ancient story of Vlad Tepes—Vlad the Impaler, who is the basis for the tragic story of Count Dracula.

On February 15, 1991, Francis Coppola wrote in his diary, "Here we go. I'm going again and it's *Dracula*."[13]

To prepare for *Bram Stoker's Dracula*, as it would be called, Coppola screened *Citizen Kane*, Eisenstein's *Ivan the Terrible*, and Orson Welles's *Chimes at Midnight*. He made copious notes for the art director and copious notes for himself. His writing was energized, and when he felt he was close to a shooting script he took the family on vacation to Mexico, including Gia. He was in a reflective mood with thoughts going to his son Gio. He writes: "My son Gio is gone, but his memory is not. And his laughter lives on in his daughter Gia. It is amazing how much she is like him when she laughs. The main thing is to remember how much I loved going to horror films with my brother. . . . This film ought to be called *Francis Coppola Meets Dracula*."[14] Coppola understood the perpetual circle of life. He felt the presence of his beloved son in the laughter of his granddaughter and lightheartedly reminisced about his movie-going joys with August.

The casting for the film was partly set. Coppola knew that Ryder would play the crucial role of Mina. He described her as "Snow White." For the demanding role of Dracula Coppola first considered Daniel Day Lewis. He was unavailable, filming *The Last of the Mohicans*. Gary Oldman was seen as an intense actor with emotional reserves that could be tapped. Although Columbia Studios was concerned that Oldman did not have enough sex appeal, they deferred to Coppola. In fact in virtually all decisions Coppola was at the helm. This was of great psychological value to Francis. As if to counter Oldman, Keanu Reeves was cast as Harker, the present-day love of Mina. Anthony Hopkins is cast as Van Helsing and also narrates the tale so audiences are clear as the story unfolds. Newcomer Sadie Frost plays the incredibly sensual Lucy. Coppola made savvy decisions regarding the crew. Another key decision was not to shoot on location but to use sound stages.

German-born Michael Ballhaus was chosen as director of photography. He had shot in diverse situations with many directors. In Germany he worked with Werner Fassbinder. In the United States he shot several Scorsese films, including *The Last Temptation of Christ*. Thomas Sanders was the production designer. For the all-important score, Coppola chose Wojciech Kilar, a well-respected Polish composer who had been composing movie scores for the finest Polish directors since 1960. The score to *Dracula* was the first American film for which he would write. Subsequently, Polish director Roman Polanski had Kilar score several of his films, including the award-winning *The Pianist*.

The costumes were designed by Eiko Isioka, who had designed the costumes for Paul Schrader's *Mishima*, a film that Coppola and Lucas had executive produced. Roman Coppola was responsible for the second-unit work on the film. The complex action and fight choreography made the second unit contribution invaluable.

The shoot began on November 14, 1991, with a budget set at $40 million. Coppola was determined to come in on time and under budget.

As was habitual for Coppola there was a rehearsal period in Napa. Most of the actors thought it was of great value. Coppola let the actors make contributions to the script as it related to their character. Hart was present and remembered it as one the best days of his life. Anthony Hopkins was the exception. He didn't like the idea of rehearsals and felt uncomfortable and claustrophobic, yet he had taken the role for "the fascination of working with a genius like Coppola. I would have killed for the chance."[15] When this phase was completed, Hopkins said, "It was the best experience I've ever had on a movie. It proves that the rehearsal was worth it."[16]

Coppola employed the use of an electronic storyboard throughout the shoot to great effect. The color of scarlet, representing blood, effused the environment. There is a sensual quality and also one of dread as the horror tale of the once-honorable Vlad/Count Dracula moves through the centuries from Transylvania to Victorian London and back. On February 2, 1992, the shoot wrapped on budget and ahead of schedule. Postproduction was ahead. There was a lot riding on this for Francis Coppola. When Francis was finished with postproduction he was so nervous about the ultimate fate of the film he took Ellie and went to Guatemala so he wouldn't have access to the weekend box office numbers. Five days after the film had opened he coaxed Ellie to find a phone in town to get the results. Ellie returned, and according to Francis's journal the following exchange ensued. " 'Well, how did it go?' Without a word, she dropped a few scraps of paper in my hand. . . . I was getting very nervous—which was it? She looked at me as though I was a moron. 'Add them up', she said. . . . Finally *she* did: thirty-one and a half million in the first weekend. It was a success and it saved my neck."[17]

The ultimate box office numbers on *Bram Stoker's Dracula* are $215,862,692.[18] It was time for Coppola to exhale.

Home Free: Coppola as Producer, *Jack, The Rainmaker*

The enormous worldwide success of *Bram Stoker's Dracula* positioned Francis Coppola as an artist who could make decisions based on choice rather than necessity. With the pressure of paying off debts removed, Coppola was free to allow his creative mind to take priority. For Coppola this was the blessing of all blessings. Since graduating from UCLA his major priority was to be an artist who could control his destiny by writing, directing, and producing his own projects. This was the original purpose for the 1969 establishment of Zoetrope.

In 1993 his initial desire was not to direct another film but to be involved as a producer on worthy projects where he thought he could make a contribution. This was not a new idea. Most public focus and certainly the press's attention had been on Coppola as a director; it was much more colorful, and the intrigues on the set and power plays with the money men were constant fodder for *Variety, The Hollywood Reporter*, and the Los Angeles daily columns. The reality was that Coppola had always been committed to the community of artists. They were his extended family. From the beginning he had lent support to creative ideas that needed assistance in order to see the light of day. Coppola was a lover of film and film history. His producer credits are extensive and varied. From Coppola's earliest days in the film industry he used either his clout or his money or both. Pre–*Star Wars* George Lucas could not finance *American Graffiti*; Coppola's earnings from *The Godfather* underwrote the project. In 1979 he produced *The Black Stallion*, directed by his classmate Carroll Ballard. Coppola and a post–*Star Wars* Lucas underwrote Akira Kurosawa's masterpiece *Kagemusha* when he was not able to obtain financing in Japan. Lucas and Coppola made certain the film had worldwide distribution. In 1982 Coppola produced *The Escape Artist*, directed by respected cinematographer Caleb Deschanel. That year he also produced *Hammett*, directed by Wim Wenders, and in 1983 he produced *The Black Stallion Returns*, directed by Robert

Dalva, who had edited the first *Stallion*. Coppola's producing efforts in the late 1970s through *The Black Stallion Returns* were not without problems. They came at a time when Coppola was consumed with Zoetrope Studios, and his decision-making capacities were compromised. There was often friction between the directors and Coppola, and most of these ventures were not commercial successes, with the exception of *The Black Stallion*. As his circumstances stabilized, his commitments became well defined and other-directed.

In 1985 writer-director Paul Schrader was desperately trying to obtain funding for his project *Mishima: A Life in Four Chapters*. This was to be a Japanese American production based on the writings of the enigmatic Yukio Mishima. Schrader, a UCLA graduate, author of *Transcendental Style in Film*: *Ozu, Bresson, Dryer*, screenwriter of *Taxi Driver*, and director of *Blue Collar* and *American Gigolo*, was passionate about this project. When Coppola was flush he wanted Zoetrope to produce the film. Now he was no longer in a position to provide funding but could still give his name to the endeavor. Lucas was able to underwrite the film, and Coppola and Lucas are credited as executive producers. Coppola would now begin a period where he provided producing support without the meddling that characterized some of the earlier endeavors. For the next 10 years, until he was offered *Jack* as a directorial opportunity, Coppola produced about a dozen films.

The story of the Children's Crusade, about a group of orphans who join Richard the Lionheart's Crusade, was a tale that was of interest to Coppola. At one point he thought about directing it. Apparently it also caught the attention of Franklin J. Schaffner, who was toward the end of his career. Schaffner went into preproduction. Coppola and Schaffner had a history. As a young screenwriter Coppola and Edmund North had written the screenplay for the Academy Award–winning *Patton*. Schaffner won the Oscar for Best Director and *Patton* was best picture of the year. Caught up in the sweep, Coppola and North shared an Oscar for the screenplay.

Producing *Lionheart*, also known as *Lionheart: The Children's Crusade*, became a family affair. Coppola's sister Talia Shire was now married to Jack Schwartzman, a New York lawyer turned producer, and they had established an independent production company. Their first venture was a complex and costly James Bond film, *Never Say Never Again*, in which Sean Connery agreed to reprise his James Bond role for a very hefty fee. It was a big gamble, but it paid off. The film made a fortune, and the production company was immediately in demand. In 1984 Schwartzman announced plans for four big-budget films; the first was *Lionheart*. Schwartzman indicated that Shire would be the producer on this first venture.

For Shire, her relationship with Schwartzman allowed her to blossom. She states, "I don't want to partner a powerful man as Irene Selznick did. I didn't want to pick another man like my brothers. This relationship with Jack is very exciting for me because it shows I've achieved something coming from my background. I'm finally allowing a man to give me an egalitarian relationship. . . . He doesn't ask me to forfeit my power."[1] Coppola had helped Schwartzman in the final hours of *Never Say Never Again* negotiations. For *Lionheart*, he and Schwartzman are credited as executive producers. The film did not go into distribution until August 1987. Apparently, Orion Pictures had little confidence in the picture. It had only a limited release and did not fare well. Schaffner made one last picture, a Vietnam film titled *Welcome Home*, before his death in 1989.

Coppola executive produced the 1987 film *Tough Guys Don't Dance*, directed by Norman Mailer, arguably one of the finest American writers of the twentieth century. Unfortunately, his expertise did not extend to filmmaking. The story of Coppola's participation on Mailer's project is a strange one. Mailer had written the novel in 1984. Mailer was cajoled into writing a script for the iconic French film director Jean-Luc Godard. It was a contorted version of *King Lear*. It was not his intention to see the script realized, but he had struck a deal with Menahem Golan, then the chairman of Cannon Films, to deliver a script. The arrangement was forged in a restaurant in Cannes. Godard contacted Tom Luddy, the film archivist and cineaste who was such a valuable figure as liaison for Coppola on many occasions. Luddy knew that Mailer wanted to develop a film based on *Tough Guys Don't Dance*, and a trade-off deal was made where Mailer would commit to a *King Lear* script for Godard and Canon would support both projects. There was a condition: Coppola and Luddy needed to oversee the projects. Therefore, both are credited as executive producers. It is difficult to know Coppola's participation on *Tough Guys Don't Dance*, starring Ryan O'Neal and Isabella Rossellini. The picture failed miserably. As for *King Lear*, Godard virtually blew off Mailer, and Godard's version of *King Lear* is considered one of the most bizarre and forgettable features he made in his illustrious career. The film industry is rife with such stories; executive producers may have financial involvement, creative involvement, may have once owned rights or be willing to relinquish rights for a producing credit, or may babysit a project, as was Coppola's assignment in the case of *Tough Guys*. Coppola and Mailer were known to be friends, and in 1991 while Coppola was filming *Bram Stoker's Dracula*, American Zoetrope purchased the rights to Mailer's gargantuan spy novel *Harlot's Ghost* with John Milius intended to write the screenplay. Fred Fuchs explains, "We got to see the galleys very early on. Francis and Norman are good friends. In fact, they met to talk about the book while Norman was still writing it. I think Norman felt all along Francis was the right person to direct the film."[2] In 1994 Francis Coppola and Columbia Pictures commissioned Eric Roth (*Munich*, *Forrest Gump*) after Roth had read *Harlot's Ghost* and was intrigued by it. But Coppola rejected Roth's script and abandoned the project, unable to relate to the unemotional characters. Columbia offered the script to a number of directors. Columbia personnel kept changing hands. Eventually, John Frankenheimer was to direct, with Robert De Niro acting in the film. When Frankenheimer died, Roth did rewrites that moved from the original inception of the script to create a Cold War drama. That had been

De Niro's interest for many years. The result was *The Good Shepherd* (2006), which De Niro directed, produced, and in which he acted. It was a highly successful film about the inner workings of the CIA. The film is a serious and well-crafted vehicle, and because Coppola was involved with the initial property he is listed as one of six executive producers on the film.

When Coppola first screened Godfrey Reggio's *Koyaanisqatsi*, an experimental film with the subtitle *Life Out of Balance*, he was deeply moved and believed the film needed to have a wide distribution. The documentary film was the first of what would become known as the *Qatsi* (Hopi for life) trilogy. It was lyrical, with a full score written by avant-garde composer Philip Glass. Zoetrope struck a deal with Reggio for worldwide distribution of the film. The documentary was received enthusiastically. The advertising poster read, "Francis Ford Coppola Presents" in small print above the title of the documentary. Coppola lent his support to the subsequent films, particularly *Powaqqatsi*. To Coppola, the documentaries represented the power of pure cinema.

In 1989 Francis Coppola championed Belgian filmmaker Dominique Deruddere's film *Wait until Spring, Bandini*. It was another instance of Luddy's matchmaking.

Coppola's UCLA classmate Carroll Ballard had been directing film documentaries and had developed *Wind*, a story about yachting races and the America's Cup in 1987. Coppola and Fuchs were executive producers, and Luddy was a producer. It was produced through American Zoetrope.

In 1993 Francis Ford Coppola Presents sponsored the adaptation of the infamous William Burroughs short story *The Junky's Christmas*—a claymation/live action short released to DVD and directed by Nick Donkin and Melodie McDaniel.

Coppola and American Zoetrope next sponsored Frances Hodgson Burnett's classic English tale *The Secret Garden*. Warner Bros. had brought the property to him in the 1980s, but it did not arrive at the filming stage. Francis had been drawn to a talented Polish director, Agnieszka Holland, who was mentored by the revered director Krzysztof Kieślowski. In the United States she was best known for *Europa, Europa*, which had been distributed widely in America. Coppola asked her to direct the film. In 1999 American Zoetrope had Holland direct *The Third Miracle*, written by Richard Vetere, a serious film with a religious theme. Holland continues to work steadily and has shown her versatility by directing two episodes of the cable hit *The Wire*. Both were written by Richard Price.

Coppola lent the American Zoetrope name to a film titled *Don Juan DeMarco*, directed by Jeremy Leven. Marlon Brando was to play a psychiatrist with Johnny Depp as his patient. This was in 1994. As a follow-up to Coppola's authentic version of *Bram Stoker's Dracula*, Coppola was intrigued by the notion of a treatment of Mary Shelley's *Frankenstein*. Superb British actor and director Kenneth Branagh had decided to build the project and would direct and play Dr. Frankenstein. Coppola would act as producer and was quite an active participant in the development of the production. Robert De Niro played Dr. Frankenstein's monstrous creation. The film's title of record was *Mary Shelley's Frankenstein*. With a $45 million budget, its showing in the United States was disappointing, but it achieved success with its worldwide distribution.

In 1995 Coppola was one of the executive producers of *My Family/Mi Familia*, directed by UCLA film school graduate Gregory Nava. That same year he was one of several executive producers on the British production *Haunted*. Also around this time the script called *Jack* was given to Coppola. He considered it a warm story and thought it might be time to direct. The story is about a boy who has an unusual disease that causes him to age at four times the rate of a normal human being. Coppola related to the theme on a number of levels. He considered how isolated this boy would be, having no friends and relating only to his parents and tutor. It reminded him of his feelings during the year he had polio. He also thought of his son Gio and how short his life had been, contemplating that if Jack's life would be cut short like Gio's, the important factor would be to live his shorter life fully and happily.[3] His cherished granddaughter Gia was always asking her grandfather to make a movie *she* could see. This childlike story would fit the bill. Finally, he knew the perfect actor to play Jack—his San Francisco friend Robin Williams. A deal was struck; in September 1995 filming commenced. As Coppola has done on virtually every film project, he set up a theatrical rehearsal schedule. This time he set up a youth camp for the cast so they could begin to relate to each other. Diane Lane was cast for a third time in a Coppola film in the role of Jack's mother. Bill Cosby played a pivotal role as Jack's tutor, who convinces his parents to send him to school so he can be among his fifth-grade peers. Because this was a star turn for Williams, who is a versatile comic and serious actor, the film has poignancy. There is, however, an awkwardness attached to Jack's overwhelming physical presence paired with kid-size kids. Probably based on Williams's charisma, the film did well at the box office. Coppola dedicated the film to his granddaughter Gia because she could see it. The dedication read, "For Gia—'When you see a shooting star . . .' "

In 1996 Francis Coppola was travelling, and in an airport bookstore the number one bestseller caught his eye. It was John Grisham's *The Rainmaker*. Coppola had never read a Grisham novel and wanted to see what all the fuss was about. *The Rainmaker* appealed to him, and he could visualize it translating to film. The dialogue engaged, and he felt he could build on the characterizations. American Zoetrope purchased the rights, and Coppola wrote the screenplay with voiceover assistance from Michael Herr, who had done the narration for *Apocalypse Now*. The cast was colorful and spot-on. In the role of the young ambulance-chasing lawyer, 26-year-old Matt Damon is superb. That same year (1997) Damon had his breakout role in Gus Van Sant's *Good Will Hunting*. He and his close Boston buddy Ben Affleck won an Academy Award for best screenplay. Coppola included stalwarts Dean Stockwell and Mickey Rourke in the cast, and Teresa Wright gives the final performance of her career in the film. Roman Coppola did second unit. Francis Coppola directed the film with expertise and finesse; it crackles, and the pacing is superb. Perhaps many professional journeymen could have directed *The Rainmaker*, but the film artist Francis Coppola did.

The Rainmaker was released around Thanksgiving 1997, and Coppola had much to be thankful for. The John Grisham plot translated successfully to the film medium. Coppola had read *The Rainmaker* to get a better idea of the public's taste and found he was part of the public, too. He recalls, "I became a sucker for Grisham just like everyone else. I couldn't put it down."[4]

The success of the film mattered to Coppola on a personal, emotional level. Since *Bram Stoker's Dracula* eliminated the nagging debt that had hung over him for years, he was determined to live a creative, fulfilling life. He wrote in his journal in 1993, "I plan only to work on what my heart is in—simple to say, but difficult to do."[5] Coppola knew he had demons; he could be anxious, moody, and depressed and volatile. These were emotions he needed take care about—they were part of his complex nature.

Entrepreneur, Father of the Filmmaker

Francis Coppola has an incredibly fertile mind. As the 1990s wound down Zoetrope Studio had no difficulty identifying projects of interest. There was new attention to the medium of television. In 1997 Coppola executive produced a miniseries for NBC, *The Odyssey*, with an all-star cast featuring Armand Assante, Isabella Rossellini, and Greta Scacchi. It was directed by famed Russian director Andrei Konchalovsky. He won an Emmy for direction. Also beginning in 1997 Coppola executive produced a science fiction series for the Sci-Fi Channel. A Canadian/American production, *First Wave* ran for 64 episodes.

A significant portion of Coppola's energy was gravitating toward the establishment of a major winery in the Napa Valley. The Niebaum Estate property (now called Niebaum-Coppola) was secure. He could focus on building a solid base in the wine and hospitality business. Although the industry of film had been an agitating and sometimes cruel experience for Coppola, even when there was a positive financial yield, this would not carry over to a new venture in a different environment. Francis could be entrepreneurial, he was the great impresario, and he knew how to surround himself with colleagues who had the corporate skills he lacked. He had wonderful taste and panache along with the ability to make a presentation on a grand scale. The Coppola name was a draw. To apply a circus analogy his family often uses, he was the ringmaster.

In 1994 Coppola entered into a joint hospitality venture with two high-profile friends and actors associated with Coppola-directed films: Robin Williams, who would soon act as the lead in the Coppola directed film *Jack*, and Robert De Niro, who had been extraordinary as young Don Corleone in *The Godfather Part II*. The trio invested in Rubicon, a San Francisco restaurant in the financial district very near Union Square where the lovers in *The Conversation* have their clandestine exchange. The Rubicon was conceived by Drew Nieporent, a master restaurateur who continues to collaborate with

De Niro in the Tribeca section of New York. The Rubicon was highly successful in a competitive location until closing in 2008.

Francis and Eleanor Coppola had moved to the Napa Valley in 1975. Their original intention was to explore the region to find a retreat as a getaway from their oversized San Francisco mansion by the bay. Francis thought it would be nice for Gio and Roman to be able to climb trees in the country. They would look for a property with some grape vines so they could maintain the family tradition of making wine for the family. As chance would have it, while they were scouting the area, the well-known Niebaum Estate came on the market for auction. The estate was totally out of their price range, but the Coppolas' real estate agent thought it would be pleasant for the Coppolas to see this beautiful section of Napa—part of the historic Inglenook Estate, which had been divided into parcels and had various owners. The estate was magnificent, but purchase was out of the question; they would be in way over their heads. Eleanor and Francis looked elsewhere, but nothing could satisfy them after Niebaum. In classic risk-taker fashion, Coppola impulsively bought the estate for $2 million—it had about 1,600 acres of vineyards and a glorious home. The purchase put Coppola between a rock and a hard place. In order to obtain financing for *Apocalypse Now*, he immediately had to use the newly purchased Niebaum Estate as security along with many other assets. In the jungles of the Philippines, Coppola had this additional stress to pile onto an already harrowing filmmaking situation. When the shoot was finally completed, Coppola returned to San Francisco, where the advance word on *Apocalypse* was not reassuring. The press had been ferocious and would continue its "Apocalypse When?" campaign for the lengthy postproduction period. The idyllic Napa estate was in constant jeopardy, but by hook or crook, they managed to hold onto the property while Coppola worked all film jobs he could get.

Flashforward to after *Dracula*, and Francis had $10 million in hand, which he gave to Eleanor to invest. Over time, the estate had become their main residence. The Coppolas had money in the bank and newfound security. And then lightning struck twice. The adjoining parcel to their property became available for purchase, and Coppola saw a once-in-a-lifetime opportunity. He asked Ellie for the money back and then needed another $2 million to meet the $12 million asking price. Coppola felt certain it was an investment that would pay off; indeed, it was a serendipitous acquisition that allowed Coppola to rejoin the original prized Inglenook vineyards. The real estate was an additional 95 acres and the stunning Inglenook château. Eleanor and Francis began to create an overarching vision for the substantial vineyards they now owned.

In 1997 Zoetrope, which was now virtual (www.zoetrope.com), launched an online quarterly magazine named *Zoetrope: All-Story*. Its mission is stated on its website: "a quarterly magazine devoted to the best new short fiction and one-act plays."[1] The stature of the magazine is evident from the caliber of its submissions and the numerous awards it has garnered. The magazine has a guest artist who designs each issue and a classic reprint—a short story that inspired a film, with the notion of illustrating the connection between the two mediums. A sampling of the participants to the magazine includes David Mamet, Mary Gatskill, Woody Allen, Salman Rushdie, Don DeLillo, Elizabeth McCracken, and countless others. A sampling of guest illustrators and designers includes Laurie Anderson, David Bowie, Gus Van Sant, Mike Figgis, Tom Waits, and countless others.

In an interview with *Bloomberg Businessweek* Coppola was asked how all his businesses—food, wine, literature, film—connected with each other. Coppola explained, "I know that to some people it seems diverse. But to me, there's an underlying theme. . . . These are all projects at least vaguely associated with show business. They're all involved with presenting an idea, show, or story to people for their pleasure and orchestrating all the elements to some total result."[2] Coppola believed that all these pleasurable, stimulating enterprises engaged people in a kind of audience participation.

Adding to his enterprises, in 1999 Coppola opened Café Niebaum–Coppola in the North Beach section of San Francisco where as a young filmmaker he spent many mornings in modest cafés typing screenplays. It was a stone's throw from the historic City Lights Bookstore, famed stomping grounds of Allen Ginsberg, Gregory Corso, and Jack Kerouac, author of *On the Road*, a film project still on Francis's radar.

To extend his reach even further, Coppola opened a luxury resort hotel named Blancaneaux Lodge in the rain forest of Belize (formerly British Honduras). Coppola had a fascination with Belize not only for its beauty and culture but because he envisioned the location as an ideal hub to expand intercontinental communications and initiatives throughout the Americas. Coppola's enterprises would grow in number and sophistication. In the 1990s, Zoetrope.com and the restaurants, cafés, resort accommodations, *Zoetrope All-Story*, and the wine collection were in their growth phase; these would mature and prosper as twenty-first-century propositions.

Francis and Eleanor Coppola observed with gratification the maturation of their two children, Roman and Sofia. Each was involved in artistic endeavors. Roman had attended New York University's film school, the Tisch School of the Arts, to prepare himself academically for a career in film. He was fortunate to have had practicum through the years on Francis Coppola's film sets. When he returned to the West Coast, he worked closely with his father in charge of the second unit on *Bram Stoker's Dracula*, *Jack*, and *The Rainmaker*.

Roman was also forging his own path working with friends and family of his generation. In 1996 he acted in and cophotographed a short directed by his sister Sofia, Andrew Durham (who would become a high-end photographer),[3] and Ione Skye, who also wrote the short. The other cinematographer on the shoot was Spike Jonze, Sofia's longtime boyfriend and future first husband. Also in the cast were renowned singer-songwriter Donovan Leitch, Ione

Skye's father, and Jacqueline de la Fontaine, the late Gio Coppola's girlfriend and Gia Coppola's mother. In Hollywood and environs, it was not unusual for the offspring of famous people to establish close bonds with one another. Sofia Coppola and Zoe Cassavetes, daughter of independent filmmaker John Cassavetes and renowned actress and muse Gena Rowland, had been close friends for several years. And, of course, the Coppola dynasty itself was growing by leaps and bounds. Roman was the executive in charge of production for *Gunfighter* (1999), written and directed by his cousin Christopher Coppola, brother of Nicolas Cage.

Roman branched out, making full use of newer technologies. He founded The Director's Bureau, a compendium of directors working on music videos, commercials, and films. Roman directed numerous music videos for major entertainers such as Green Day, the Strokes, Fatboy Slim, and Phoenix. He is in demand directing commercials on an ongoing basis. His corporate clients have included Orbitz.com, Levis, Honda, GAP, and Coca-Cola. It is abundantly clear he inherited his father's comfort with technological innovation and penchant for invention. Equally adept in a variety of media, Roman shifts with the dictates of creativity and business demand. Invariably he is available to support Sofia Coppola's projects. When she was developing her first feature, *The Virgin Suicides*, he was on board as second unit and more importantly as a safety net.

Sofia spent her years after attending California Institute of the Arts exploring her artistic options. She had interests in photography, music, and design but wasn't sure exactly how to blend them. In the early 1990s Sofia produced a short video with her friends Zoe Cassavetes and Andrew Durham titled *Ciao L.A.* Zoe and Sofia were also in the cast along with Adam Horovitz, who is playwright Israel Horovitz's son. Sofia also appeared uncredited in another video short titled *Beastie Boys: Sabotage*. Both shorts were directed by Spike Jonze. Sofia and Spike became very close. In 1994 Sofia, her friend Stephanie Heyman, and Sonic Youth alternative-rock group member Kim Gordon founded MilkFed, a clothing store in Japan. The major draw was a t-shirt line, but the store also included some dresses, pants, and accessories. The impetus for the clothing line was casual attire with a bit of flair not ordinarily found in t-shirts and other reasonably priced apparel. The demographic appeal was young women. The impression is that the designs are for small-figured bodies. MilkFed was a success, and its brand is Heaven 27. There is a Heaven 27 boutique in Hollywood. Sofia explains the fashion philosophy: "You know, most clothes in this price range are pretty generic. The Gap all looks the same. My clothes are definitely different. Now my father wants to know when I'm going to do my perfume!"[4]

Sofia and Cassavetes teamed up for a short-lived Comedy Central show called *Hi Octane*, which had a fun-filled run on cable in 1995. It was the first series shot entirely on digital video and was characterized by entertaining skits and off-beat guests. When Jon Stewart interviewed the two hosts on his show, one gets a glimpse of Sofia's persona.[5] While Cassavetes is animated and vocal and makes eye contact with her interviewer, Sofia is retiring and appears somewhat nervous, at times looking off in another direction. Her voice is soft and has a tendency to trail off at the end of a sentence. It seems hard for her to keep a rhythm with Stewart in their exchanges, yet when they cut to a break and you can still see her, she leans in and appears engaged with Stewart in a much more relaxed manner. Simply put, she is shy and reticent yet has a sweet quality that makes people like her. She has acknowledged that she has stage fright, and in truth it shows.

Sofia continued to photograph professionally, and her work appeared in high-end glamour magazines. Not only is she a talented photographer, she is also a photographic model and over time became Marc Jacobs's photographic muse. In 1997 Marc Jacobs became the creative director for the Louis Vuitton men's and women's apparel collections. Arguably, he was and continues to be the most influential designer of the day. His diverse women's ad campaigns appeal on the one hand to the Marc Jacobs signature or on the other to Louis Vuitton's. Sofia Coppola is an integral part of Marc Jacobs's line and continues to be a major photographic model for his brand. She may not have been able to act, but despite a crooked nose and a mouth that can look a bit snarly, the camera loves and transforms her. Jacobs is in awe of Sofia. He described her as "young and sweet and innocent and beautiful. The epitome of this girl I fantasize of."[6]

Before meeting Sofia, Jonze had been developing his own filmmaking career. Spike Jonze is a pseudonym for Adam Spiegel. Spiegel was born on October 22, 1969, in Maryland, and grew up primarily in Bethesda. His parents were divorced early, and, by accounts, Adam was often left to his own devices. He had an early passion for dirt bikes and skateboarding. He attended high school but showed no passion for learning. He is described as nonintellectual and unschooled even in film, although he attended San Francisco Institute for the Arts and met several classmates who would be future collaborators, notably Lance Acord, who photographed his breakout film *Being John Malkovich*.

Sofia worked with Spike on some of his many projects, but he was on his own with *Being John Malkovich*, which took years to be greenlighted. The Charlie Kaufman script had been travelling around Hollywood studios and almost everyone loved it, but no one would commit. The business environment in Hollywood was risk averse, possible even more so than in Francis's day. On occasion Francis Coppola intervened on Jonze's behalf. Jonze and Kaufman struggled to get a studio commitment and an okay from John Malkovich, who needed to agree to appear in the film. Malkovich got a call from Coppola asking that he meet with Jonze. Malkovich recalls Francis saying, "In 10 years we'll all be working for him."[7] They met in Paris.

Jonze is notoriously introverted and rarely makes himself available to the press for interviews. His close friend and associate Mark Lewman says Jonze

avoids interviews, cancels press conferences, fabricates biographical information, and does not correct erroneous reports that circulate about him.[8]

Spike Jonze, as he is most often known professionally (although he has also
used the name Richard Koufey [spelled variously]), is an inventive, quirky,
prolific, and exceedingly successful director of music videos for groups such
as the Beastie Boys, Sonic Youth, singer Björk, Weezer, R.E.M., and Beck.
He was a founder of *Dirt* magazine and edited *Freestylin'* magazine. He directs
clever, cutting-edge commercials for clients like Adidas, IKEA, and GAP. He
cocreated the television series *Jackass* and *Jackass: The Movie*.

As he geared up for his first feature, executive produced by Michael Stipe, the
unique artist of R.E.M., Sofia was in the planning stages for her debut feature,
The Virgin Suicides. After directing her first short, *Lick the Star*, in 1998, she felt
ready to commit to a filmmaking career. She realized how much she had
absorbed from years on Francis Coppola's movie sets. Francis now gave her specific counsel: "Sit right next to the camera so the actors see you; see you're in
control. Remember that the actors' hands are almost as important as their faces.
Hands are very expressive. If you cut hands out of the frame you're losing
30 percent of the performance."[9] Sofia's father, the experienced director, was
trying to impart all the tricks of the trade to his fledgling director daughter.

On June 26, 1999, Sofia Coppola and Jonze married at her parents' Napa
Valley estate. The wedding was elegant, with friends, family, and colleagues
in attendance. Francis served wines from 1971, the year of Sofia's birth, and
explained the wine's special bouquet to guests at every table. Film director
Lucas was present, which must have been a thrill for Jonze, who is rumored
to have seen *Star Wars* hundreds of times.

At the time of their marriage both the bride and groom were in postproduction on their films. *Being John Malkovich* was released in October 1999.
It was an unpredicted success, achieving almost universal raves. The film circu-
lated for many months and grossed in the vicinity of $22 million worldwide. It
was nominated for Academy Awards for Best Direction—Spike Jonze, Best
Original Screenplay—Charlie Kaufman, and Best Supporting Actress—
Catherine Keener and received many other accolades. So there was not one
happy couple, but two. Kaufman and Jonze would definitely team up again.

Virgin Outing as a Director: Sofia Coppola's *The Virgin Suicides*

"I do have my own way of working, my own style."

Sofia Coppola

Sofia Carmina Coppola spent much of her childhood on movie sets as her father Francis directed some of his most significant film works. She was in front of the camera in a matter of weeks after her birth on May 14, 1971, appearing as a baby boy in the pivotal baptism sequence in *The Godfather*, her first of many cameos in her father's films.[1] Sofia gravitated toward an artistic life but not screen acting. Her one substantial acting role in *The Godfather III* was sparked by a daughter's loyalty when Winona Ryder was forced to withdraw from the role of Mary. Sofia's performance was generally considered a father's misguided indulgence. Eleanor Coppola notes in her journal that she and Francis advised Sofia not to read the critics' reviews and to let time pass before she evaluated her performance, but she did read the mostly negative reviews, and it was painful. Eleanor notes that "Francis said he felt those criticisms were meant for him, and that Sofia received them the way Mary Corleone got the bullets intended for Michael."[2] With the passage of time, Sofia, noting that she is camera shy, reflects, "I never wanted to be an actress. It's not my personality."[3]

In 1998 Coppola co-wrote[4] and directed her first film, *Lick the Star*, an 18-minute short about a seventh-grade girl clique, adolescent cruelty, and adolescent hysteria. To a degree, *Lick the Star* became an unintended dry run for Coppola's inaugural feature, *The Virgin Suicides*.[5] For the short, Sofia invoked a solid Coppola tradition, enlisting family members and friends on the production. Her cousin Christopher Neil (Eleanor Neil Coppola's nephew) was a producer, her cousin Robert Schwartzman (Talia Shire's son) acted, and Zoe Cassavetes acted and assisted on second unit. Casting family and trusted friends in her films and employing them as production and crew members would become standard operating procedure for Sofia as it had been for her father.

Sofia Coppola read Jeffrey Eugenides's 1993 debut novel *The Virgin Suicides* and immediately labeled the book a "classic." She was enthralled by the beauty of its narrative and the ethereal atmosphere of the story. She began envisioning its filmic possibilities and decided to adapt it as a screenplay. Completed script in hand, Coppola reached out for the rights and, as luck would have it, they were held by Muse Productions (Roberta and Chris Hanley.) Sofia knew Roberta Hanley through Jacqui de la Fontaine, fiancée of her late brother Gian-Carlo Coppola, and Hanley lobbied for Sofia's manuscript.

Coppola's next hurdle was whether she would be the screenwriter/director. Chris Hanley originally wanted independent film director Nick Gomez (*Laws of Gravity* [1992], *New Jersey Drive* [1995], *Drowning Mona* [2000]), but Gomez had written a script that Hanley felt didn't quite work. Roberta Hanley pressed for Sofia as screenwriter/director, and Sofia was hired to embark on her first feature film with Chris Hanley on board as one of the producers.

The Virgin Suicides is set in an upscale suburb of Detroit in the 1970s. Five teenage sisters, the Lisbon girls, reared by a strict, oppressive Catholic mother and loving but ineffectual father, commit suicide. At 13, the youngest sister Cecilia is the first suicide, slitting her wrists in a first attempt then impaling herself on the house fence in a second, successful try. Unaware, the rest of the girls are participating in a stilted boy/girl party orchestrated and chaperoned by their mother in the basement of the house.

As a result of Cecilia's suicide, Mrs. Lisbon allows the cloistered girls their first taste of freedom; they attend a high school dance. School heartthrob Trip matches up each sister and, totally infatuated, he chooses 14-year-old Lux for himself. They spend the night in sexual rapture. When Lux arrives home at dawn, there are dire consequences. The girls are withdrawn from school, isolated and confined to the house. As they linger in an endless malaise in their bedrooms, they maintain clandestine phone contact with the boys using pop recordings played into the telephone receivers to express their emotions. The boys are observing the sisters through a telescope from a house across the street. Trip disappears from the scene, and an unhinged Lux has random sex with all takers on the roof outside her room. Ultimately, the sisters arrange for the boys to visit their house. When the boys arrive, Lux greets them, but they are soon numbed by the discovery that the other sisters have committed suicide, each by a different method. Lux kills herself in the garage by carbon monoxide poisoning. Throughout the film, the impact of these macabre acts is detailed in backstory through a male narrator speaking for the teenage boys who idolize and obsess over the sisters, unable to resolve their suicides even decades later as grown men.

Francis Ford Coppola coproduced the venture through American Zoetrope Productions. The proud papa was on the set only occasionally as a support system for Sofia and gentle mentor if needed. The budget for the film was purportedly $6 million and the shooting schedule just shy of a month. As Sofia assembled the cast and crew, key players emerged. For cinematographer the renowned Ed Lachman was selected. Lachman had a stellar reputation photographing independent films. In 1995 Francis Coppola had executive produced director Gregory Nava's *My Family/Mi Familia*, which was photographed by Lachman. Lachman was well known for superb collaborations with independent filmmakers and had worked with Todd Haynes and Steven Soderbergh. Lachman related to Sofia Coppola's vision of the film. Together, they looked at many photographs from Sofia's extensive collection. In particular, Coppola was influenced by the photojournalism of Bill Owens, specifically his iconoclastic book *Suburbia*.[6] Lachman was keen to develop a visual conception of *Suicides* that meshed with the look Sofia conceived. "The overall approach that Sofia and I discussed is that this is an adolescent world . . . it was very important that I created this childlike world, and even though things were happening that were kind of nightmarish, it was still from a childlike perspective."[7] Sofia also responded to the look of Haynes's 1995 film *Safe*, which takes place in a well-to-do suburb and has an eerie and disturbing storyline. Coppola wanted the style of the film to be simple, like a series of tableaus emphasizing adolescent femininity through pastels and lots of light. The camera is often set back to establish the reverie of the male observers' point of view.

To design the costumes Coppola enlisted Nancy Steiner because of the subtlety she observed in her work on *Safe*. Steiner explains, "We worked to give the girls' identities through outward appearances. The idea is that the Lisbon girls are completely misunderstood. Their perception of themselves is entirely different from how everyone else saw them. That's something I think we all can relate to and it's a big theme of *The Virgin Suicides*."[8] Another collaborator from *Safe* was editor James Lyons,[9] who shared credit with Melissa Kent, who had edited *The Rainmaker* for Francis Coppola. Sofia used sound designer Richard Beggs, who was a constant collaborator on her father's films and had sound designed her short *Lick the Star*. The aural environment was enhanced greatly by the score supplied by Air, a French electronic group that Sofia admired. She listened to Air while writing the screenplay. Coppola perceived that the music had "the feeling of memory because it's very dreamy and ethereal. It's influenced by the 70s but is also very modern."[10] The sound track is rounded out by songs of the period: Heart's "Magic Man" comments on Trip's introduction to the film, "Alone Again (Naturally)" by Gilbert O'Sullivan, "Hello, It's Me" by Todd Rundgren, "So Far Away" by Carole King, and "Run To Me" by the Bee Gees are used in the phone sequences, and "Come Sail Away" by Styx is danced to at the high school.

Roman Coppola was Sofia's right-hand man throughout the production. He was credited as second-unit director but most significantly functioned as

Sofia's alter ego; as Sofia pointed out, they think so much alike.[11] Sofia recruited her cousin Chris as acting coach to instruct the many young and inexperienced extras and supplementary cast members. Eleanor Coppola was on the set to document the making of the movie, which appears on the DVD as a featurette. Needless to say, the presence of her mother was reassuring for Sofia. On the documentary Eleanor marvels at Sofia's unflustered demeanor. Eleanor compares the Coppolas to a circus family where Francis as director has been on the high wire with the family there to support him.[12] Now Sofia was on the high wire and the family's support shifted to her. Author Eugenides was a presence on the set and spoke approvingly of Sofia's approach to transforming the novel to film and of the unique colors and shaping she brought to the screen story. Director Sofia Coppola gained and held the respect cast and crew. She had authority and, unlike her father, a quiet reserve. She brought an informed feminine perspective when it was appropriate to the material.

To cast *The Virgin Suicides* Coppola and the casting team used several methods. Once again she employed certain actors she knew from her father's films and some relatives upon whom she relied. For the crucial role of Mrs. Lisbon, Sofia chose Kathleen Turner, with whom she had acted in her father's film *Peggy Sue Got Married* (1986), playing Peggy Sue's little sister.[13] The role was a stretch for Turner, who was known for her glamour. Coppola felt Turner met the challenge head on. "It was a real risk for Kathleen," observes Coppola. "It's so different from how you usually think of Kathleen, but she has the extraordinary ability to play this very strong, very tough woman with a certain amount of sympathy."[14] James Woods was cast against type as Mr. Lisbon, the inept father who is unable to assert his love for his daughters. When Woods read the script he was committed. "She had written an amazing script," says Woods. "Then when I met with her she was so terrific. She is a very talented, very imaginative, very daring director and writer who is also quite a lot of fun to work with."[15]

For the vital role of Lux, Coppola had many casting calls, but her gut choice was 16-year-old Kirsten Dunst, whose current acting schedule was tight. Sofia discovered Dunst was on another project in Toronto where *Suicides* was shooting, and a deal was struck. Dunst's performance provides just the right nuance as the innocent yet provocative Lux, and the chemistry with Josh Hartnett as Trip is explosive. Other roles were filled by relative newcomers, all of whom carried their weight. The cast also included Sofia's cousin Robert Schwartzman (Talia Shire's son) and Leslie Hayman, who had cowritten *Lick the Star* and was a childhood friend, as Therese.

The role of the narrator was given to Giovanni Ribisi, whom Coppola felt was among the most impressive actors of the 20-something crowd. His off-camera performance is delivered with melancholic resonance.

The Virgin Suicides made the festival circuit rounds, screening at Cannes, opening the San Francisco International Film Festival, and airing at the 2000

Sundance Film Festival. Reception to the film was generally warm and positive, although some viewers were uncomfortable with the subject matter. Sofia Coppola's distinct capabilities were recognized and her directorial skills separated from the towering image of her father. On May 12, 2000, the film opened to general audiences in the United States and enjoyed a respectable art-house run. With her first feature film in the can, Sofia Coppola had cut her eye teeth and could safely contemplate her sophomore effort.

13

Roman Coppola's *CQ, Apocalypse Now Redux,* and Producing *Redux*

In the year 2000 another milestone occurred in the Coppola family. Jacqui de la Fontaine, considered a valuable member of the Coppola clan both for her own qualities and as the mother of Francis and Eleanor's only grandchild Gia, announced her engagement to Peter Getty, eldest son of Ann and Gordon Getty and an heir to the Getty fortune. Jacqui had been close to the Coppolas, and in the early years after Gio's death and Gia's birth, Jacqui and Gia were physically part of the Coppola family. Jacqui worked on *The Godfather Part III* as a wardrobe assistant, and Gia was in tow in Rome and Sicily in accordance with Francis's practice of bringing his family with him on extended productions. Little Gia can be seen waltzing with Al Pacino and Sofia in a dance originally intended only for Michael and Mary Corleone. Gia was on the set as her aunt had been as a little girl, and when she saw Sofia dancing she wanted to join in. Eleanor Coppola noted the incident in her diary. "Today Sofia did the scene where she waltzes with Al. It was so sweet, so reminiscent of Marlon waltzing with Tally. . . . During the shot, Gia ran on the dance floor and grabbed hold of Sofia's skirt. Francis let the cameras roll. I would wager that spontaneous moment will end up in the final cut."[1] Predictably, Gia was memorialized in the *Godfather* saga.

After *The Godfather Part III*, Jacqui was hired as a costume designer for several films during the 1990s. She was a hard-working, independent individual and built a life for herself and Gia in the Hollywood Hills home Eleanor and Francis had purchased for her and Gia. When the Coppolas were told of her impending marriage to Peter Getty they were genuinely thrilled. Getty seemed to embrace the now adolescent Gia, and this was comforting for the grandparents. The Napa Valley estate was chosen as the locale for the wedding, and Francis Coppola walked the bride down the aisle. An admiring Jacqui commented about this gesture. "He's not my real father, and he didn't have to, but he took real responsibility."[2] Coppola is nothing if not loyal and devoted to family. The wedding was elegant. Jacqui wore a $100,000 Oscar de la Renta gown and was escorted on the arm of Francis Coppola as the San Francisco Philharmonic orchestra played in the background. At the time, it seemed like a fairy tale romance for de la Fontaine.

Also that year Roman Coppola decided to try his hand as writer/director of a feature film. *CQ* was to be homage to several films that were part of the French nouvelle vague and the moviemaking scene during the late 1960s radical period in Paris. Roman was actually born in a suburb of Paris in 1965 when his father was there writing a screenplay version of *Is Paris Burning?* Roman could have chosen a serious subject but instead decided on a send-up to some of the genres of the period. The "CQ" translates to "seek you"—part of the film's theme about seeking love. The references most frequently cited in *CQ* are *Barbarella*, directed by Roger Vadim, starring his wife at the time, Jane Fonda, and *David Holtzman's Diary*, directed by James McBride. *Barbarella* is based on a French comic book series and is futuristic—the year is 2001 (the year *CQ* was made), like the film being made in *CQ*, called *Dragonfly*. *David Holtzman's Diary* is a faux cinéma vérité documentary about a film-maker. In *CQ* there is a character making a documentary film within a film.

The movie's obvious strengths are in its visuals and adherence to the essentials of the genres. They are all presented in a lighthearted, playful manner with exacting detail, no doubt with the benefit of production designer Dean Tavalouris. Also referenced is Dino De Laurentiis, expertly caricatured by Giancarlo Giannini. Gérard Depardieu is superb as *Dragonfly*'s radical director. Sofia Coppola has a cameo as Gianinni's paramour, and Jason Schwartzman is smarmy as the replacement director. There is an obligatory chase scene complete with the bells and whistles of a futuristic car reminiscent of James Bond, and the color palette created by Robert Yeoman (Wes Anderson's cinematographer) is true to the period and the excesses of the film.

Apparently when Roman Coppola screened the film outside of competition at Cannes, it was poorly received. Before its general release it was re-edited. *CQ* did not catch on with the general audiences. It had a short run and was not profitable. Nevertheless, it was a learning experience for him. Roman observes, "If you're going to make a movie, especially a first-time movie, you make it about a world you're familiar with."[3] That rings true for a member of the Coppola clan.

In 2000 Francis Ford Coppola made the creative and energizing decision to revisit the film that had cost him three years of his professional life, had compromised his health, had jeopardized the stability of his marriage and livelihood, and had subjected him to ridicule and rancor from the Hollywood press. He decided to reevaluate *Apocalypse Now*. With distance he believed the viewing audience was prepared to absorb the film in what should have been its totality. In an *Esquire* magazine interview he had stated, "ten or fifteen years after *Apocalypse Now*, I was in England in a hotel, and I watched the beginning of it and ultimately ended up watching the whole movie. And it wasn't as weird as I thought. It had in a way, widened what people would tolerate in a movie."[4] Coppola discussed the idea with Kim Aubry, who was at Zoetrope overseeing the digital preservation of its film library. Aubry, vice president for post production and technology, explained, "Initially it was a research project to see if we could cut in some of the old scenes rather than just offering them as bonus extras. We went back to the old dailies and the whole thing snowballed."[5]

In the spring of 2000, Coppola asked his trusted longtime colleague Walter Murch to re-edit *Apocalypse Now.* Coppola envisioned an expanded version of the film to be released as a 25th anniversary edition (of the cessation of the Vietnam conflict) with several scenes that had not made the final cut to appear in the revised edition. These kinds of reissues are generally known as the "director's cut" and show a fuller version than the released film. This version is closer to the director's original intention before time, money, and other constraints require shortening the final product. By 2000 the business of DVD reissues was growing in scope and often included alternate versions, outtakes, commentaries that ran simultaneous to the visual track, and interviews with members of the cast and crew. These special editions provided viewers with a new expanded experience related to a film they had seen in the movie theater or a fresh experience for a viewer who had never seen the film.

When Coppola approached Murch, it may have been this type of rerelease that he had in mind, but rather quickly Murch knew that a more complex and exciting redux would be in the offing. When Murch discussed the necessary ingredients to make a powerful new experience out of the 1979 *Apocalypse Now,* he believed it would be more restoration and reimagining than an expanded version with extras, and Coppola agreed. Coppola asked Kim Aubry to coproduce this new venture, knowing he could rely on Aubry's technological savvy and his knowledge from the 1979 film.

Much had changed with the passage of time. Vietnam and the United States had normalized relations in 1995. The country was no longer as viscerally divided about the painful conflict. Many other films had examined aspects of the Vietnam War: *Platoon, Good Morning, Vietnam, In Country, Full Metal Jacket,* and *Born on the Fourth of July.*

For a generation of filmgoers *Apocalypse Now* had entered the vernacular. "I love the smell of Napalm in the morning" might not have been as recognizable as "Frankly, my dear, I don't give a damn,"[6] but it was a familiar movie reference to a major slice of the population.

As often happens with concise ideas, the execution was not quite so simple. Murch almost immediately discovered that some of the deleted scenes Francis wanted reinstated had never been finalized. They would require sound work and reshoots, dubbing, and other technical massaging. As Murch delved into the assignment Coppola had given him, in order for it to meet Murch's technical standards the task grew increasingly complex. Rather than shut down or pull back, Murch forged ahead. In a business where challenges build exponentially, Murch is one in a million. He approaches each task with intellect, intuition, invention, generosity, and incredible dedication. *Apocalypse Now Redux* would be no different.

The team began assessing the status of the film materials. For the section of the film that had not seen the light of day, known as the French Plantation sequence, much finishing was required. Francis was particularly desirous of including this tableau. The plantation family was French, their home abutting the river. They were vestiges from French Indochina and France's long stronghold in the territory. The family represented a historical perspective regarding occupation of Vietnam and Indochina. The original motivation was to demonstrate that Vietnam was a country that historically had foreign intruders—French imperialism had a long and troublesome story in the region. Including a dinner-table discussion between this French family and an American military interloper underscores the superiority and proprietorship the French feel even at this late date while Americans are in active conflict. When the film was being cut in 1979, this back history seemed to weigh down an already long river trip and disrupt the rhythm and flow of the final journey. The notion had been to always stay on the river. Now, more than 20 years later, the plantation scene had a purpose. The audience was asked to take a longer view of America's presence in Vietnam to see more clearly the futility of U.S. intervention after many previous and futile intrusions. By allowing this interlude off-river, this anachronistic, intelligent, if aloof family unit provides a history lesson through Willard's eyes. And Willard has a brief interlude with young Roxanne, who invokes a feminine life-affirming flicker for Willard as he approaches his destiny. Aesthetically, Dean Tavalouris has created a cocoon-like enclave that encapsulates the group for a brief time. With intimate dream-like lighting and sharp sunlight in Willard's eyes, the moments at the plantation are an uneasy respite before the journey's final thrust. The acting is superb, especially that of Aurore Clément (wife of production designer Tavalouris).

To accomplish the incorporation of this sequence Murch first had to complete the scene, upgrading the prints to state-of-the-art 35mm Technicolor dye transfers. The visual result was saturated color and improved detailing of darker images. Vittorio Storaro was very pleased with the Technicolor dye transfer, which separated the primary colors and physically rubbed them onto the film. For sound, Murch did a remix using the most current digital sound mixing—Dolby sound. Because the decision had been made to recut and remix every scene that would appear in *Redux*, the ultimate challenge was to conform the entire narrative sonically and visually. As producer Aubry explains, "*Apocalypse Now* is mostly known for its seamless, very complex soundtrack with original impressionistic ambiences and unusual score. We had to find a way to 'break in' to this track ten or eleven times with new dialogue and new locations while never breaking the feeling of the old track."[7] Several of the actors made themselves available to redub their dialogue.

The nuances in the re-editing create a different rhythm to the film. There are additions that clarify some of the questions that existed in the original version. We are now able to see the burial of Clean and the Chief's reaction and obvious affection for him. Most significant is a more meaningful conclusion and expanded performance by Marlon Brando, which explains his inner turmoil. He reads news articles aloud to Willard; these *TIME* magazine columns claim that the war is going well and propagandize the American position in Southeast Asia. Brando is seen upright and in sunlight. He reads T. S. Eliot's "The Hollow Men." What is still in some respects an unsatisfying performance by Brando becomes more coherent with these additions.

The overall effect of *Apocalypse Now Redux* is to corroborate Coppola's belief that the film isn't about Vietnam, but that it is Vietnam. *Redux*, created more than two decades after the conflict, sharpens the calamity of that war. Coppola always believed *Apocalypse Now* was an antiwar film. Seen in the *Redux* context, it is clear that Coppola's intention was to reveal the impossibility that the Vietnam War was justified.

Apocalypse Now Redux premiered out of competition at Cannes in May 2001. In August it had a limited release and earned approximately $4.5 million. Both versions are on the record. DVD viewers can see either version or both in the dossier release. Reaction to *Redux* was mixed, but two prominent film critics were more than enthusiastic. Roger Ebert considers it one of the central events of his life as a moviegoer. David Thomson writing for the *New York Times* observes that Murch and Coppola have "finally trusted and freed the proper film"[8] with the reflection of 22 years and an additional 53 minutes. In sum, the filmmaking experience of *Apocalypse Now* could be put to rest. As to Murch's influence, Coppola acknowledges Murch's unique value as a fellow filmmaker and close friend and colleague. On the cover of Murch's book *In the Blink of an Eye*, Coppola is quoted—"Nothing is as fascinating as spending hours listening to Walter's theories of life and cinema and his countless tidbits of wisdom, which he leaves behind him like Hansel and Gretel's trail of bread: guidance and nourishment."[9]

Since directing *The Rainmaker* in 1997, Coppola had not stopped producing and executive producing. That same year Francis executive produced *Buddy*, directed by Caroline Thompson, who had been the screenwriter of *The Secret Garden* that Coppola had executive produced in 1993. Thompson also wrote *Edward Scissorhands* for the Tim Burton. *Buddy* was based on a true story about a wealthy woman and a gorilla she domesticates and cares for.

In 1998 fellow San Franciscan Wayne Wang, who had burst on the scene with *Chan is Missing* in the early 1980s, joined forces with Coppola to form the Chrome Dragon Company. Wang, a Hong Kong native, was attracted to a piece of material titled *Lanai-Loa* (sometimes known as *Lanai-Loa—The Passage*). This was a supernatural mystery that took place in Hawaii. The film was directed by Sherwood Hu. Coppola compatriots Fred Fuchs and Tom Luddy executive produced, and Wang and Coppola produced. Hu was at the start of his career. The film did not find much of an audience. This was the only Chrome Dragon production; no other projects emerged from this coventure.

In 1999 Coppola was a producer for *The Florentine*, directed by Nick Stagliano, an NYU Film School graduate. Coppola worked with Steven Weisman, who had been an assistant on *Jack*, had assisted Fuchs on *The Secret Garden*, and was assistant to the producer on *Bram Stoker's Dracula*. The film is set in a bar in a down-and-out Pennsylvania steel town. There are many recognizable actors from previous Coppola ventures: Chris Penn, Mary Stuart Masterson, and Burt Young (who worked with Talia Shire on the *Rocky*s). Also in the cast was Jeremy Davies, who would appear in Roman Coppola's feature *CQ*. Stagliano continues as an independent filmmaker, directing the 2011 production of *Good Day for It*. Also in 1999 Coppola was one of several executive producers on *Goosed*, directed by Aleta Chappelle. Chappelle had been a casting director on *The Godfather Part III*.

In 1999 Tim Burton directed *Sleepy Hollow*, based on the Washington Irving legend. Coppola was one of two executive producers on the project. The other was Larry Franco, who had been a second assistant director on *Apocalypse Now* and had built a producing career to include *The Hulk*, *Batman Begins*, and *Jurassic Park II*. Coppola's executive producing career is always an interesting "follow-the-dots."

After executive producing *The Virgin Suicides* for Sofia and *CQ* for Roman, in 2001 Coppola assisted a director he had reached out to for many years, Victor Salva, on his newest film, *Jeepers Creepers*. The history of Coppola's relationship with Salva began in the mid-1980s when the young filmmaker won the Sony/AFI award for fiction for the 1986 short *Something in the Basement*. In 1989 Salva wrote, produced, and directed his first feature, *Clownhouse*, a horror genre film. Francis Coppola contributed to the financing of the film, and Roman Coppola, having graduated from NYU, was assigned as executive producer. It was determined that while directing the film, Salva sodomized the 12-year-old lead actor. Salva was arrested and pled guilty to several counts of deviant behavior. He was sentenced to three years in prison and paroled after 15 months. Salva acknowledges his actions and takes full responsibility. He is a registered sex offender. Francis Coppola visited Salva in prison and encouraged him to focus on his abilities as an artist. When he was released, Coppola gave him $5,000 to help him get back on his feet.

Because of Salva's grievous offenses, not everyone in the industry believed he should have the opportunity to continue his artistic career. Coppola observes, "They're entitled to feel that way, but he has a real gift as a filmmaker. The punishment has been completed, and he should be a citizen again."[10]

In 2001 Coppola was one of the executive producers of *Jeepers Creepers*, written and directed by Salva. The film was a financial success, and in 2003 Salva prepared a sequel, *Jeepers Creepers II*, on which Coppola was one of several executive producers. This film was also a major success.

Also in 2001 Coppola was an executive producer for Hal Hartley's *No Such Thing.* Hartley has been part of the independent film movement since 1988 when his first film, *The Unbelievable Truth,* appeared on the scene. That same year Coppola brought *The Legend of Suriyothai,* directed by Chatrichalerm Yukol (aka Yugala) to the United States under the Francis Ford Coppola Presents banner. He was continuing his tradition of bringing cinema from other countries to the United States for exposure. This Thai production was co–executive produced by Coppola and Aubry, Coppola's producer on the *Apocalypse Now Redux* project. This film was an epic production on a grand scale that was enormously popular in Thailand and was presented as an 8-hour television miniseries to Thai audiences.

The story is of Queen Suriyothai, who sacrifices herself during the Burmese-Siamese War of 1548 when she faces the Burmese army on her battle elephant to save the king. Coppola went to Thailand to work with the film's director on re-editing the production for presentation at a shorter length. The film's director attended UCLA film school with Coppola.

Pumpkin, directed by Anthony Abrams and Adam Larson Broder and starring a young Christina Ricci, was an atypical love story. This film, along with *The Virgin Suicides, CQ, Jeepers Creepers, and No Such Thing,* was executive produced by a trio including Coppola, Linda Reisman, and Willi Baer (aka Bär), all related to MGM. In 1998 Coppola was appointed to the MGM Board of Directors. In 2000 MGM and Zoetrope closed a 10-film arrangement for production and distribution.

Robert Duvall's *Assassination Tango* (2002) was executive produced by Coppola and Reisman. Duvall wrote and directed the film in which he, his wife, Luciana Pedraza, and Rubén Blades appear. Coppola was pleased to support his colleague's venture. In 2003 Coppola was executive producer for Sofia Coppola's second feature, *Lost in Translation.* In 2004 Coppola was one of four producers on *Kinsey,* written and directed by Bill Condon. It was then time to concentrate on preproduction for Sofia's *Marie Antoinette.* In 2010 Coppola executive produced Sofia Coppola's fourth film, *Somewhere.*

In many respects it had been a good decade for Francis Coppola. He was finally released from the chokehold of studio financing and control. Always known as a free-thinking rebel, he was now financially independent and could experience the liberation he held so dear. His wine and hospitality industry allowed him to support his family and make choices of personal value. He made two personal films that met his time-honored criteria. And he could see a future that had nothing to do with advancing age. He had things to do.

14

Lost in Translation

Sofia Coppola and Spike Jonze had married at the end of June 1999. In the winter of 2000 *Being John Malkovich* was considered for three Academy Awards, and in mid-May *The Virgin Suicides* was released to general audiences. The newlyweds were both gearing up for their next features. It was not a leisurely time, although maybe that wasn't their style. They were both young and energetic and had financial underpinnings. Jonze began preproduction on *Adaptation*, his follow-up feature with Charlie Kaufman about writer's block. In the starring role as twins Charlie and Donald Kaufman was Nicolas Cage, Sofia's older cousin. And so the Coppola circle expanded yet again to include a cousin-in-law's project.

Coppola was entertaining an idea for her second feature. Because she had done a fair amount of travel for music video shoots, *The Virgin Suicides*, and a clothing line Milkfed, spending time in hotels, she began working out a treatment for a story she conceived and planned to develop into an original screenplay for a film she would direct. The storyline progressed into a reverie about loneliness in a foreign place—specifically a male midlife crisis and a young newlywed on her own while her husband is away on business. This kernel evolved into Coppola's sophomore film, *Lost in Translation*. The foreign setting would be Japan—Tokyo, Kyoto, and environs.

Sofia was no stranger to Japan. She and childhood friend Stephanie Hayman owned Milkfed, a clothing line based in Tokyo, and when they were there on business they stayed at the Park Hyatt Hotel, which serves as home base for the lead characters in *Lost in Translation*. The central male character is Bob Harris, a middle-age movie star perhaps not at the very top of his game. He is in Tokyo to film a Japanese whiskey commercial (Suntory) to appeal to high-end drinkers. The female lead is a soft, tentative young woman accompanying her husband to Japan as he climbs the ladder as a photographer to the stars. He is out on shoots; she is cloistered in the hotel. Coppola's first choice for the female role was Scarlett Johansson, and she accepted immediately. Coppola had seen Johansson in *Manny and Lo*, and her husky voice and introverted demeanor appealed to Sofia. For the male lead Sofia wanted Bill Murray. Actually, she insisted upon Murray. She had written the part for Murray and would not make the movie without him. Thus began the arduous task of getting a commitment from the notoriously elusive Murray. Sofia spoke to his agents, but they hadn't heard from him; she left messages on his answering machine; she asked everyone she knew if they had a way of getting to Murray. Much to her own embarrassment, she even called Al Pacino because he and Murray had houses in adjacent towns. One of her good friends, director Wes Anderson, who had worked with Murray on such films as *Rushmore, The Royal Tenenbaums,* and *The Life Aquatic with Steve Zissou,* was willing to go to bat for her. Anderson and screenwriter Mitch Glazer, one of Murray's good friends, invited Coppola to meet them for lunch. Sofia was totally attentive, and everyone felt Murray would commit. To seal the deal, Murray, Anderson, and Sofia met for dinner in an out-of-the-way Japanese restaurant of Murray's choosing. It was a go. Murray comments on the experience, "I got reeled in from way, way offshore, but Sofia's very good on the phone and she spent a lot of time getting me to be the guy. In the end, I felt I couldn't let her down. You can't ruin somebody's dream."[1] Those who know her are not at all surprised by her persistence and persuasiveness. Jonze observed, "Sofia has such a strong point of view, and really, that's what being a director is: knowing what you would like and what you don't like and standing by that, despite all the pressures."[2] Glazer reveals, "She knows how to be relentless. She's completely genuine, but she is driven and tough as anyone I've met in Hollywood."[3] In summary, Murray states, "Don't let Sofia's littleness and quietness confuse you. Sofia is made of steel."[4] There was a solid, crystal-clear consensus that this soft-spoken young woman was decisive and relentless, and those who crossed her path professionally respected these surprising qualities and gave her their all.

Now with a green light, Sofia assembled her crew to include trusted family members, friends, and colleagues with whom she had a continuing relationship; in this way she followed the Francis Ford Coppola tradition. For cinematographer she brought on Lance Acord, whom she had met on a shoot with fashion photographer Bruce Weber. While Coppola was filming *The Virgin Suicides,* Acord was shooting *Being John Malkovich.* Acord was an up-and-coming cinematographer. Among his credits are Vincent Gallo's indie *Buffalo 66,* music video director Peter Care's feature *The Dangerous Lives of Altar Boys,* and both *Being John Malkovich* and *Adaptation* for director Jonze.

Both her father and Fred Roos were executive producers of the film. Roos had known Sofia all of her life and has been unconditionally supportive of her work. A pivotal producer who worked at her side throughout the 27-day shoot was Ross Katz. Katz is New York based. He preceded her to Japan and then spent the entire shooting schedule working with her to consider all the minute-to-minute challenges of shooting in Japan (including an impending typhoon). Coppola describes *Lost in Translation* as a stealth production; she did not want a lot of advance publicity, knowing that the crowded city with unpredictable weather and shooting constraints might present obstacles, particularly with no possibility for down time. Coppola wanted maximum flexibility within the tight framework and modest budget of approximately $4 million. Coppola was committed to partnering with Katz so they could deal together with any and all issues—the good, the bad, and the ugly. Katz considers the experience of producing *Lost in Translation* one of the most unbelievable of his life. He minces no words describing Coppola's directorial skills. Simply put, he identifies her as a remarkable filmmaker.

Lost in Translation is about two people at different points in their lives who are lost in the same way. Their loss is the aloneness that comes from the sense of detachment from the lives that have been defined for them and the emptiness they experience when they attempt to carry out those assigned definitions.

Charlotte and Bob's presence in Japan only accentuates these emotions. They are all the more vulnerable because they are physically jet lagged, they lack familiar surroundings to anchor them, and there are no external restrictions to prevent them from causing damage to their already unhappy existence. They are unfamiliar with the Japanese language, therefore setting limits on their ability to negotiate for themselves. For Bob, when he is being directed on his commercial shoots he has a translator providing instructions. Bob asks a clarifying question, and its translation seems exceedingly long. The cultural formality of the Japanese communication style and the length of words in the language result in the sense that something is lost in translation.

Charlotte, who has just married and already feels estranged from her self-centered husband, is at a loss to understand what she can do to carve a life for herself or create a meaningful marriage. Bob, a seasoned professional, feels the arc of his life moving in a downward spiral and regrets the diminished relationship he has with his wife, without faulting either of them.

This film has been compared to the old chestnut David Lean's *Brief Encounter* (1945) where a couple meet in a railway station and are tempted to have a liaison. *Lost in Translation* has also been suggested as Coppola's artistic expression of her own current situation with Jonze. Coppola rejects that allusion while acknowledging that the themes in the film can be recognized as situations she has had or that friends have experienced. It doesn't really matter. If one subscribes to the theory that all art is autobiographical, then perhaps it is about Sofia's personal relationship; if that is not the viewer's perspective, the film is simply a poignant coming together of two decent people at a heart-rending point in time. For Charlotte, she is at the beginning of her adult life; she will move through it as she can. Bob, in his midlife crisis, will also come to some resolutions. For the two, they have both gained an invaluable and unconditional bond during their time together. And each learns that there are ways not to be as alone as they fear.

Coppola's decision not to introduce a sexual relationship during this liaison is worth its weight in gold. Further, the introduction of humor and companionship balances the connection between them. They find the value of their friendship and appreciate the experiences they share. This underscores the full potential of their personalities. Using the backdrop of Kyoto, its beauty and culture is another way of watching Charlotte grow. Likewise the karaoke scene shows how much they appreciate each other. Charlotte thinks she is mean, but she is only human. Bob sleeps with the cabaret singer, not a shining moment but not a crime. He's human, too.

The acting is uniformly superb. An 18-year-old Johansson plays a 20-something young wife with intelligence, vulnerability, and humor. Murray is sublime. The supporting cast, especially Giovanni Ribisi (who had narrated *The Virgin Suicides*) and Anna Faris (*Scary Movie*), draw recognizable characters in their brief screen time.

The technical aspects of *Lost in Translation* are superb. The cinematography of Tokyo is captured in neon glory. Acord explains that of necessity he shot with a lot of natural light and practical light. For the scenes where Charlotte is alone in her hotel room (often sitting on the windowsill) Acord, Coppola, and Johansson were often alone. They rolled camera and did most of it handheld. It was a small crew anyway, and the approach created a sense of intimacy. Acord was also able to shoot the large buildings at night with only natural sources because there are so many varieties of light. If adjustments needed to be made, for instance because of oversaturation, they could be addressed in the lab. Likewise the arcade environment and subways were exciting because they are fluorescent. The desired result could be obtained by timing.

Acord explains that the final scene in the film was difficult and mapped out very specifically. He and Sofia discussed it:

> The scene would start with a long lens POV of Scarlett's head bobbing among the crowd, and then using the camera position on a different lens, you have Bill Murray in the shot walking towards Scarlett. Then there'd be a close-up of Bill where the window would go down.... We did one tracking shot from a Western Dolly that moved with them through the crowd.... For the wide master for the entire scene where they're kissing, within that scene we had close-ups of Bill over Charlotte's shoulder and of Scarlett over Bill's shoulder and then the wide shot shows they've separated she walks toward the camera.[5]

Sofia showed her guerilla filmmaking techniques in this effective closing sequence. She did not shy away from the complicated logistics required to make it happen.

Nancy Steiner's costume choices are spot-on and deceptively simple. Coppola was especially appreciative of Richard Beggs's sound design. When the shoot of less than one month was complete, Beggs returned to the Tokyo Hyatt and recorded the ambiance of the elevators and hallways and specific outside sounds such as wind to particularize the aural environment.

And, of course, Roman Coppola was there to run and gun second unit at a moment's notice.

Lost in Translation received a very strong reception in the United States. It was a critical and financial success and was nominated for four Academy Awards: Best Picture, Best Director, Best Actor, and Best Screenplay. On February 29, 2003, Coppola won an Academy Award for original screenplay, acknowledging first her father for all that he had taught her. She was the third generation of Coppolas to win an Academy Award. Coppola also won a Golden Globe for Best Screenplay—Comedy or Musical, and Murray won a Golden Globe as Best Actor—Comedy or Musical.

In December 2003, Coppola filed for divorce from Jonze, citing irreconcilable differences. Coppola's publicist issued the following statement. "It is with sadness that Sofia Coppola and Spike Jonze have jointly announced that they are divorcing."[6]

The Empire: Francis Ford Coppola Presents

In 1995 when Francis and Eleanor Coppola purchased the Napa Valley acreage adjacent to their property, the land that had been the Inglenook Estate, they began to envision the development of a winery that would resurrect the splendid vintages of past days in the valley. The rejoined, contiguous vineyards were now part of the Niebaum–Coppola Estate, which would be home base for the winery where the Coppolas hoped to build a worthwhile business. They wanted the enterprise to satisfy their high standards, enhance the industry, benefit the community, and respect the heritage of the vineyards. During that first year renovation began on the château, which would be the centerpiece of the property, an eventual gathering place for the public to partake of the vineyard's yield.

The notion of a winery was always part of the Coppolas' Napa Valley vision. When they made their initial Napa Valley purchase in 1975 they decided to develop a winery on the property. To do so Francis Coppola applied his tried-and-true philosophy of selecting the right people and then giving them the authority. He selected Rafael Rodriguez to oversee the land, grow the grapes, and make the wine with a staff of his choosing.

In a book titled *A Sense of Place: An Intimate Portrait of the Niebaum–Coppola Winery and the Napa Valley*, by Steven Koplan, the author describes the history of the vineyards in the Napa Valley. John Daniel Jr., who was sea captain Gustave Niebaum's great-nephew, took over the Inglenook Winery in 1936 and ran it until 1954. This was known as the Daniel Era of Inglenook. Under Daniel's direction the winery returned to a level of quality that had been its reputation before Prohibition. One of the key supervisors at the vineyard had been a Mexican named Rafael Rodriguez. Coppola sought him out and invited him to work at the winery once again. Rodriguez explains Coppola's generosity and respect for the tradition of the winery: "When I returned here in 1976, my salary was one of the highest paid in the Napa

Valley. I went from $25,000 to $40,000. Francis said, 'You work for me, you will be part of an ownership program, you will have benefits, vacation, retirement. . . . The dreams that Francis had to begin with were beautiful. He wanted to make a nature preserve here and revitalize what John Daniel had.' "[1]

For the early years between 1975 and 1990 the venture was not profitable. Francis was still working his way out of bankruptcy, but by 1997 the property was on the upswing. During that year Coppola honored Rodriguez with a plaque and named one of the vineyards for him. Rodriguez gave private tours of Niebaum–Coppola, describing the history of the vineyards in vivid detail. Rodriguez and his workers developed a particularly superb section of the vineyard and named it the Gio vineyard after the late Gio Coppola.

As the enterprise continued to grow, and finally flourish, Coppola hired other experts to manage various aspects of the operation. The vineyards are maintained in accordance with the principles of viticulture including control of pests and diseases, proper fertilization, and irrigation. The winery has recently announced it is bee-free. These efforts contribute to the *terroir*, the French term that describes the unique characteristic of the vineyard's earth and what it brings to the overall wine product. Over the years Niebaum–Coppola made acquisitions in Napa Valley. In 2011 Coppola was able to purchase the Inglenook trademark for its exclusive use.

The château that was on the Inglenook Estate was transformed into a magnificent showcase for the wineries. There are guided tours, tastings, and a gift shop. The château itself was refurbished with the assistance of Dean Tavoularis, who designed many of the exteriors and interiors, including a magnificent staircase made from wood imported from Belize. Special events are ongoing. There is a movie gallery with recognizable memorabilia from Francis Coppola's five-decade career. In 2010 the memorabilia section expanded to include two large boats that were props from Sofia Coppola's 2006 film *Marie Antoinette*. Outside on the estate are bocce courts and board and card games available to visitors at no charge. For guests who want to dine there is the Rustic restaurant offering many of Coppola's favorite dishes and an Argentine grill. There is a full Coppola wine list. Always family friendly, there is a park area on the premises. In season there are swimming pools and an outdoor, informal café for light fare. On the premises there are seasonal farmers' markets. As part of giving back to the community, the winery has an annual holiday food drive.

There is a retail shop with a wide variety of tasteful merchandise from around the world and locally, including wine glasses, ceramics, and games, DVDs that are Francis's favorites, and a writer's corner for those interested in storytelling.

And what is the selections of wines? The winery produces over 40 varieties under the direction of winemaker Corey Beck. Not surprisingly, many of the wines are named for family members or reference aspects of Francis

Coppola's career. Examples from the collections include the FC Reserve collection—Francis Coppola Reserve Director's Cut, which is a limited production of wines from Sonoma Valley that include Cabernet Sauvignon, Chardonnay, Pinot Noir, and Syrah. The labels have been art designed by Tavoularis. The next collection is called Director's Sonoma Valley Cinema, another limited production of Zinfandel, Cabernet Sauvignon, and Petit Syrah. This collection is described by the winery as "spicy, full-bodied red wine layered with dark berry fruit impressions and an edge of earthiness."[2] The Diamond Collection includes the magenta label Alicante Bouschat. Coppola's grandfather used Alicante Bouschat grapes to make homemade wine, and Francis yearned for the taste. These grapes were grown in Lodi, California, which now has a vineyard to produce fruit for this wine type. One of the signature varieties is Sofia—Blanc de Blancs, a light sparkling wine bottled with pink cellophane wrapping to suggest a peony. The house produces Votre Santé Chardonnay and Pinot Noir in honor of Francis's father's mother, Maria Zasa. Sonoma County Archimedes wines are in honor of Coppola's grandfather Agostino. The Su Yuen varieties include a somewhat sweet white wine grown in Monterey County and a Syrah to accompany anything grilled. Vintner Coppola has a thriving wine business, and this is only one of his ventures. The flagship wine of the Inglenook Winery is a red variety named Rubicon.

Coppola has a number of restaurants in the San Francisco area. In North Beach is Café Niebaum-Coppola; in the Sentinel Building is Café Zoetrope; and in Napa, Mammarella's Café is named for his late mother Italia. Coppola's mother Italia was called *mammarella*, meaning "little mama."

Italia Pennino Coppola was born in Brooklyn, New York, on December 12, 1912, and died at age 91 on January 21, 2004. Much of the artistic heritage of the Coppola family can be traced to Italia's father Francesco Pennino, who composed songs in Naples, Italy. He imported Italian films to be screened at the Empire Theater in Brooklyn, which he owned. Italia Coppola was an extremely beautiful woman and was offered jobs as an actress, but her father wouldn't allow it. Instead she married Carmine Coppola and became a traditional Italian American housewife. She raised her children instilling music and storytelling in the household. After she married she became an excellent Italian cook and in her later years published *Mama Coppola's Pasta Book*. In recalling his mother, Francis Coppola said, "In a family of artists, she brought the magic to our family's creativity. She had a young girl's style even at 91.[3] As part of the Francis Coppola Presents brand, the company produces pasta, sauces, and related condiments and foodstuffs as Mammarella Foods. Her young, beautiful face adorns the product line. All the foods are organic, with several varieties of both sauces and pastas.

In addition to Coppola the vintner and restaurateur, Coppola is also an hotelier. Coppola discovered Belize (formerly British Honduras) in 1981 when he and Tavoularis travelled together to scope out the newly independent state with the idea of establishing an innovative kind of studio in Central America. Coppola felt that Central America had the potential to be a receptive environment in which to make use of new technologies such as satellites. He and Tavoularis were the guests of the deputy prime minister, who was anxious to promote the nascent country and meet Coppola's potential needs. Coppola quickly became enchanted with the physical beauty of Belize, its diverse characteristics and rich history. He was so enchanted that he purchased a house there after making *The Outsiders.* Although close to personal bankruptcy, he was anticipating a business future in Belize. The house became a haven for Eleanor and Francis on numerous occasions.

Over time, as another element of his business empire, Coppola has developed several resorts in Belize. He conceptualized the resorts in concert with the varied landscapes of the country. The Blancaneaux Lodge is located in the Pine Ridge Mountain area. Turtle Inn is on the Caribbean, and La Lancha is on Peten Itza Lake. Coppola has used his vision to conceptualize vacations that meet the needs of any vacationer. There are options to travel among the three resorts to partake of the geographic diversity and myriad activities. There are archaeological sites, caves, water sports, rain forests, and exotic birds and animals. The resorts are a kind of paradise for many. In addition there is the opportunity for privacy, and the cuisine is produced in large part from organic gardens. The Coppola ownership contributes to environment projects. The accoutrements within individual cabanas are largely imported from Bali.

In classic Coppola tradition, one special offering is a retreat designed for vacationers who want to develop their own screenplay facilitated by professionals. Coppola's newest ventures in hospitality are Jardin Escondido, located in the heart of Buenos Aires, and 714 Gov. Nicholls Street, an inn located in New Orleans's French Quarter.

In March 2012, Coppola opened his first resort in Europe, located in the country and locale of his ancestors. The Italian resort is in the Basilicata region of southern Italy in the town of Bernalda, birthplace of his grandfather Agostino. Named Palazzo Margherita, the hotel has nine rooms and suites. The amenities are luxurious and high-end. With film always in Coppola's DNA, the Palazzo's salon converts into a private screening theater where guests can enjoy Coppola's personally curated collection of 300 classic Italian films and documentaries. Accomplished French designer Jacques Grange reimagined the nineteenth-century Italian villa with interiors that include hand-painted fresco ceilings in Baroque style, furniture designed by Grange, and marble flooring. In these lush and elegant surroundings guests can also experience the simplicity and old-world character of the village of Bernalda itself. The culinary staff is available to guests interested in learning how to cook the local cuisine, and *trattorias* abound in the nearby towns. Physical activities including swimming at the Palazzo's pool, and local beaches, golf courses, and bicycle riding are available. Cultural opportunities such as museums and monuments and exploration of the area's natural spectacles ensure that vacationers will have an idyllic adventure conceptualized with abundant care and specificity by the Coppolas and their expert Coppola Company professionals.

To bring the Coppola brand full circle, the quarterly literary magazine *All-Story*, first established by Zoetrope in 1997, has expanded to include writing workshops, events, and contests. The magazine has always attracted a vast array of known literary talent and now offers learning opportunities for growing talent and skill development.

For ventures of this magnitude, Coppola needs a Harvard MBA—and he has one. Jay Shoemaker is the CEO of Coppola Companies and Francis's consigliore. Coppola could be clearheaded about what was needed to run a megabusiness when he was in charge. Eleanor was also savvy and could see the big picture when it came to their enterprises. Carefully, they chose executive management who were capable of carrying out the Coppola Companies philosophy. It is a far cry from Francis's difficult experiences at the behest of the financial suits in the movie industry.

The businesses outside of film have made Coppola an extremely wealthy man. He is a multimillionaire. Francis Ford Coppola Presents has underwritten *Youth without Youth*, *Tetro*, and *Twixt*. There isn't much chance he will be forced to gamble and take risks of the financial kind in order to be a motion-picture storyteller, and because he now sees himself as an amateur with a learning curve, creatively he is enjoying himself and providing the opportunity for his audience to reap the artistic benefits.

Not a Piece of Cake:
Marie Antoinette

After the major success of *Lost in Translation*, Sofia Coppola was now an Academy Award–winning screenwriter well positioned to contemplate her next filmic effort. Her marriage to Spike Jonze had ended on December 9, 2003, and *Translation* was commonly believed to be autobiographical when it touched on issues that confront a young wife as she questions her marital relationship.

Sofia read the biography of Marie Antoinette by Antonia Fraser—*Marie Antoinette: The Journey*. Lady Fraser, Harold Pinter's widow, was an accomplished historian with numerous books about European royalty. Several basics motivated Coppola to take on the subject. There had been no feature film about this historic figure since MGM's 1938 biopic featuring four lustrous stars of the day: Norma Shearer, Tyrone Power, John Barrymore, and Robert Morley. Coppola felt ready to challenge the notion of a period film by applying her own style to counter a classic Hollywood studio production. Coppola was a Francophile. She had spent time in France as a young girl and loved the French sensibility. Sofia easily envisioned Kirsten Dunst as Antoinette for her physical attributes and her ability to grow with the character from a 14-year-old princess transplanted from Austria to a 20-year-old queen and mother. Coppola loved Versailles and was able to broker the use of actual locations for the filming of *Marie Antoinette*. Having the historical venues at her disposal was a huge draw for Coppola. Her love of costume design enticed her all the more, as there was ample opportunity to develop a wardrobe of unparalleled beauty. This, along with the chance to art decorate what were now the Versailles museums and to meticulously adorn the royal environment, were all tantalizing eye candy for Coppola's well-established artistic mien.

Lady Fraser gave Sofia Coppola her permission to adapt the book. This ambitious project had a budget greater than her first two films combined.

The budget was estimated at $40 million with a production schedule from January 2005 to April 2005. Coppola began to gather her cast and crew.

For cinematographer she chose Lance Acord, who had shot *Lost in Translation* and her short *Lick the Star*. Acord shot Jonze's *Being John Malkovich* while Sofia Coppola was directing *The Virgin Suicides*. Acord was comfortable with Sofia's directorial flair and committed to pictorially accomplishing her eclectic vision of the essence of Marie Antoinette and the story of her reign. Sofia used the tried-and-true Coppola family decision-making process by approaching the Academy Award–winning Italian costume designer Milena Canonero to lead a team of designers in the huge task of outfitting the cast of *Marie Antoinette*. Not only had Canonero worked with Francis Coppola on such films as *The Cotton Club* and *Tucker: The Man and His Dream*, Canonero had personally dressed Sofia in *The Godfather III*. Coppola knew the costume designer could make a unique contribution to the physical look of the characters and that fashion was serious business. Coppola is quoted as saying, "You're considered superficial and silly if you are interested in fashion, but I think you can be substantial and still be interested in frivolity."[1] For the daunting task of redressing Versailles, Coppola relied on K.K Barrett with whom she had worked on *Lost in Translation*. Barrett has also production designed Jonze's films.

Francis Ford Coppola was executive producer, and Sofia's brother Roman continued in his role as second unit director. Her cousin Jason Schwartzman was cast as the dauphin who ascends to king.

Sofia Coppola's *Marie Antoinette* is a visually stunning, loosely biographical rendering of the life of the ill-fated Marie Antoinette. Coppola's focus is on Marie as a young girl set adrift in hostile surroundings and her efforts to forge her own identity. The historical facts of Antoinette's life are minimally outlined in the first half of the film and then communicated only in chronological snippets as the film progresses. The milieu of eighteenth-century France functions more as backdrop, and the political detail and reality of the time is given short shrift. Coppola is intentionally comfortable bypassing accuracy. She is not interested in educating the viewer about the court of Louis XVI and its place in European lore or in the arc of Antoinette's life (and death)[2] once Marie appears to have achieved personal authenticity. Acting styles, uniform accents, and other conventions applicable to historical drama are absent here; Coppola employs a musical sound track comprised primarily of twentieth-century postpunk and electronic guitar. Even the costumes and sets that appear so authentic, in fact, lack accuracy for the period. As Canonero indicates, consistent with Sofia's vision, the costumes are a "stylization" and "psychological." The camerawork leans toward handheld and rapidly moving shots that are true to Marie's uncontrolled character but do not inform the viewer of the palatial scope of the environment or the mannerly behavior of an eighteenth-century court as compared to the cinematography in Stanley Kubrick's *Barry Lyndon*. Acord describes the lighting as "embracing high key "and "pop." Coppola chose to suspend period-piece requirements in favor of communicating an "impressionistic," intimate, timeless story. For this reason the Antoinette character is comparable to Lux in *The Virgin Suicides* and Charlotte in *Lost in Translation*. These are three wandering girls struggling to develop into young women. In this way they also mirror Coppola herself as she emerges as an artist in her own right. In the making of *Marie Antoinette*, her father counseled her to "make it totally the way she wanted it and the more personal it was, and the more it was her impression of what this was all like, the better it would be. That she should be throwing a Marie Antoinette party and invite everyone to come to it in costume."[3]

Dunst as Marie Antoinette is compelling in every respect. Schwartzman as Louis XVI is effective in his portrayal of the unprepared young dauphin who gains quiet confidence as his brotherly relationship with Marie matures. All the character actors—Rip Torn, Asia Argento, Marianne Faithfull, Judy Davis, and Danny Huston—take good advantage of their brief opportunities to shine, each acting in the security of his or her own style. In the end, it is not Coppola's eclectic approach to historical drama that results in a sense of dissatisfaction with the film but the weak screenplay that sags as the film progresses. By the time Marie and Louis leave the Versailles palace confronted by mobs of the French proletariat, the film is virtually without dialogue or nuance. The story ends with this departure and an image of a palace room in ruins. It is left to the viewer to invoke the final days of the king and queen and surmise their ultimate fate. Coppola explains her rationale for the ending: "In the early draft, I wrote to the end of her life and then I realized that I was really rushing it . . . " Coppola continues, "I decided to just focus on her time in Versailles and start the film with her arrival in Versailles and end it with her departure at the Revolution. For me, the end of the story is her personal evolution and the scene on the balcony of her coming into her own and implying what happens."[4]

Reception to *Marie Antoinette* was mixed. At Cannes some members of the French press booed. At the 44th New York Film Festival, cosmopolitan New Yorkers were more accepting. Some critics considered it on the level of a music video, while others defended its approach. Ultimately, from the film's opening run on October 20, 2006, to the end of its international screening life, *Marie Antoinette* grossed over $60 million. Canonero was recognized for her costume design, winning her third Academy Award at the 2007 Oscars.

For Sofia Coppola life moved forward. She was living in Paris, and on November 28, 2006, she gave birth to a baby girl, Romy, named in honor of her brother Roman. The father was Thomas Mars, the lead singer of the French rock band Phoenix.

Youth without Youth

After 1997, with the successful release of Francis Ford Coppola's last film for hire, *The Rainmaker*, the rhythm of life changed for him. He was busy producing and executive producing other filmmakers' projects, lending his name and support to other ventures, and developing his empire outside of the film industry. He was always available for advice when Sofia and Roman began developing their films. Coppola was engrossed in his potentially mammoth film *Megalopolis*. He continued to work on material. He researched and read and worked on a script/novel but hadn't been able to iron out all the storyline issues; he didn't believe he had the complex totality in place. Still the plan was moving forward. Coppola had the freedom to explore this endeavor for as long as needed because he had financial security. It seemed he couldn't get past doubts about his writing abilities, although he had written original screenplays from the time he was in high school. Coppola's confidence would ebb and flow. Nevertheless, by 2001 Coppola and his team were scouting locations in New York City, where much of *Megalopolis* would take place. American Zoetrope had a satellite office in Brooklyn. In May 2001, he announced his intent to begin filming before the end of the year, looking toward a release date in 2003. While the team was in Brooklyn, Kim Aubry directed a 10-minute short documentary called *Francis Coppola's Notebook* showing for the first time his "prompt book" for *The Godfather* and explaining how he used it to adapt Mario Puzo's novel in preparation for directing the film. For *Megalopolis*, it seemed all systems were go.

The course of development, preproduction, and perhaps the project itself took a major and unfathomable turn for the worse on September 11, 2001, when the Twin Towers were attacked and demolished and New York City was changed forever. In terms of *Megalopolis*, Coppola panicked. He could not conceive of a way to refashion the utopian theme that was set in New York City without acknowledging September 11 and its wrath. He was stalled. As time passed, although he did not immediately abandon the project, he also could not make much headway.

Over the years as he worked and reworked aspects and sketches of the epic, he stayed in touch with his Great Neck High School friend Wendy Doniger. Doniger was Mircea Eliade Distinguished Service Professor of Religions in the Divinity School at the University of Chicago. Knowing Coppola was ready to proceed with making a film and recognizing he wasn't able to address the *Megalopolis* issues, when she and Francis Coppola communicated, Doniger suggested he read the writings of Mircea Eliade, especially his novella *Youth without Youth*.

Here is how Francis Coppola explains his decision to make *Youth without Youth*, the first film he would direct in a decade:

> I had spent the last several years laboring over an ambitious original screenplay that was defying my efforts to complete it. The project was intended to be the crowning moment of my career; it was ambitious, with grand themes and scope, and even aspired to contribute new ideas to the present state of cinematic language. I decided that my film could go further in exploring two areas, Time and Interior Consciousness. When I showed my ambitious, unfinished screenplay to a high school friend, Wendy Doniger (who as a young girl was not only pretty, but brilliant . . .) she helpfully sent back notes, including some quotes from the writings of her mentor, Mircea Eliade: "The question 'what do we do with Time?' expresses the supreme ambiguity of the human condition.[1]

Coppola read *Youth without Youth* and other writings of Eliade and realized this story could unleash the hold that the unfinished screenplay of *Megalopolis* had on him. For Coppola this would be an opportunity for the 66-year-old film director to create in the manner that the young director of *The Rain People* had created—to direct without inhibition and explore filmmaking as a budding artist. Coppola told Alex Simon in the *Hollywood Interview*,

> It was like I had been hit by lightning and I thought "Gee, I could just go off and make this. I could fly off to Romania, use my own money, and the kind of technology that I had done when I was young . . . just have all the equipment in a truck and ship it there." And although this is a big picture, I approached the production in such a logical way, that I could afford to make it exactly as I wanted to. In the process, I was able to fix this part of my life that was so frustrating.[2]

Coppola began adapting Eliade's novella and prepared to go into production in Romania in late 2005. Romania is the main location of the story. To understand the intricacies of *Youth without Youth* it is worthwhile to offer a fundamental plot synopsis for the reader.

On its textual level *Youth without Youth* is the tale of a 70-year-old linguistics professor, Dominic Matei, who in 1938, on the eve of World War II, is despondent and alone. At his advanced age, he has been unable to achieve his life-long goal of deciphering the origin of language. Waking from a nightmare on Christmas Eve, he goes into the cold, snowy street still dressed in his pajamas to take refuge in a nearby tavern, the Café Select. Because he is confused and not dressed he is turned away. No longer able to persevere, at Easter he travels to Bucharest, the city of his youth, intending to commit suicide. He is inconsolable, thinking of Laura, his lost love who left him when they were at university because she felt second to his studies. He considers his life a failure. In a thunderstorm in the streets of Bucharest, he is struck by lightning and suffers severe burns. In the hospital, his body fully wrapped in gauzy bandages, he is treated with little likelihood of survival. He is unknown to the medical staff, and initially they have no verbal way of communicating. As time passes they find a way to communicate nonverbally, and the medical team begins to observe his unusual recovery. As his wounds heal, Dominic appears not old but younger and younger. He loses his old teeth and develops strong new ones; he grows a robust head of hair; and his body has strength and vigor. Thus begins the mysterious transformation of an old, feeble man into a young, intellectually astute being. With this transformation the story exposes an increasingly complex evolution of meanings. As Coppola observes the levels of complexity, text, and subtext, he notes, "The story of *Youth without Youth* is exotic and certainly a lot of crazy things happen, not unlike an episode of *The Twilight Zone*, in some ways, but it's not difficult to understand what it's about."[3]

As Matei changes into a vital, brilliant man, the threat of current events puts him in jeopardy. Word has spread of this amazing reversal of the aging process, and Matei's physician, Professor Stanciulescu, who has documented his recovery, recognizes that the Nazis who have occupied the city will abduct Matei to learn more about his miraculous regeneration. To pursue this phenomenon, the Third Reich begins experimenting with lightning, electricity, and its powers; confiscates all of the professor's data about Matei; and subjects Matei to an examination. Stanciulescu shelters Matei. While in seclusion, Matei begins to experience inexplicable abilities he cannot interpret. He does not know if he is in reality or some other level of consciousness. He discovers he has knowledge of many languages not previously known to him: German, French, and ancient Sanskrit. He also has intense sexual encounters with the "woman in room six" in the enclave where he is staying and does not know if these trysts are dreams or real. Matei also begins to encounter another self, physically in his image—his double, a counterpart that he often sees in a mirror. To prove to himself the existence of this other persona, Matei asks the double for material evidence. Seemingly out of nowhere, two roses appear, one placed in his hand and one on his knee, as Matei has requested. The professor, who has witnessed this exchange, interrupts before the double can ask where he should place a third rose. The professor prevails upon Matei to leave Romania to escape the Nazis. After fleeing he discovers he now has the capacity to forge passports and creates a new identity for himself as Martin Audricourt. He arrives in Switzerland. There he discovers that the woman in room six was a Nazi spy and is there with the German doctor conducting the electrical experiments. There is an altercation during which the woman is killed protecting Matei. The doctor tries to convince Matei that his abilities are qualities of a super race and that only he and others like him will survive coming catastrophes, including nuclear warfare. Matei's double agrees, but Matei wants no part of these supermen and uses his extraordinary mental strength to telepathically turn the doctor's gun around; the doctor is killed by his own hand.

Time passes and the war ends. Dominic continues life with his new skills, creating a secret language that will only be understood in the future when there are sophisticated computers to interpret it—in 2010 after a nuclear Armageddon.

Years later while Matei is hiking in the Swiss Alps, he encounters a beautiful woman. His double says she is Laura's reincarnation. Her name is Veronica. The mountains are hit with a sudden severe thunderstorm, and Dominic rushes to find the woman and rescue her. He finds her, struck by lighting, in a cave speaking Sanskrit. He is able to reassure her by speaking in her language. In the hospital she identifies herself as Rupini, a Buddhist from India. Although the doctors believe the woman has amnesia, Dominic thinks she is in a similar condition to his own. He contacts scholars to determine if Rupini was a real person in India. The scholars conclude that centuries ago she existed and would go to a particular cave to meditate. They embark on an expedition to India in hopes that Rupini will lead them to the cave. In India Rupini is identified by a holy man who guides them to the cave. There they discover the remains of Rupini. Once the remains are found Veronica returns to her current incarnation.

Dominic and Veronica fall in love and go to live in an idyllic setting in Malta. While Veronica sleeps Dominic tells her he has always loved her. In her sleep she becomes agitated. She begins to chant in another language, and over time she exhibits multiple past incarnations that take her closer to the origin of language. Dominic records the many languages she speaks, some of which are unknown to him. His double encourages him to continue to study Veronica's past lives, but Dominic can see that these explorations are causing Veronica to age and become unwell. He decides to leave Veronica so she can live in peace; Dominic's double wants him to continue experimenting so he can successfully complete his life's work by discovering language's origin. Not willing to sacrifice Veronica's well-being, he explains to her what he has been doing and that he must leave her.

In France, years later Matei sees Veronica disembarking from a train with two children. Without her knowledge he snaps her picture. As she passes she does not recognize him, and he begins to cry.

He returns to the Romanian town where he had been a linguistics professor. His alter ego tells Dominic he is the first man of a future superhuman species and as man evolves he will survive, but millions will die, including

Veronica. In a fit of rage, Matei smashes the mirror in which he sees his double. The double begins moaning—"Dominic, what have you done?"—and slowly disappears, shouting in an unknown language.

Matei returns to the Café Select he tried to enter when the story first began. In the tavern are old friends and colleagues, all of whom are long dead. In a state of agitation Dominic begins to age and tries to explain that all this is a dream within a dream. His colleagues do not understand. Matei staggers out into the snowy night. When he is found the next day, his aged, dead body is discovered at the bottom of a staircase where the students and colleagues met so often in his youth. The identification on his passport is Martin Audricourt. The final scene includes Veronica's voice asking, "Where do you want me to place the third rose?" Dominic is holding it in his grasp. He has forsaken knowledge and died for love.

Coppola was determined to direct *Youth without Youth* so it could be appreciated on many levels. He was approaching the experience as a novice director wanting to learn and benefit from a methodology he had last used in its purest form on *The Rain People*. His intention is echoed in the title of the film. He would be young in his approach but would be directing at age 66. Coppola communicated about the physical production with as little fanfare as possible. He wasn't interested in getting involved with the press and publicity. He took his granddaughter Gia, still a teenager, to Romania with him, in part because it was the habit of his career for family members to travel with him and, in part perhaps, for the influence true youth would have on him. The two traveled throughout the country, tracing the steps of Eliade in his native land.

Coppola assembled a crew from the local environment, and the majority were young, with little experience. The main exception was to bring Walter Murch to Bucharest for the final edit after an assembly had been prepared by another editor. Invariably a master at selecting cast and crew, Coppola chose 28-year-old Romanian-born Mihai Malaimare Jr. as cinematographer. He wanted the camera to see the images with young eyes. For the challenging role of Dominic Matei, Coppola chose an experienced and capable actor, Tim Roth. Roth's career has cut a wide swath, including roles in *Reservoir Dogs*, *Pulp Fiction*, the television series *Lie to Me*, and Vincent Van Gogh in director Robert Altman's *Vincent and Theo*. As Dominic Matei, his challenges included playing a part where the character's age range is 26 to 101 and also interpreting the role of his character's double. Roth's physical look is particularly European and fits the timeframe to a tee. He is capable of intensity, melancholy, a professorial quality, and great gentleness and vulnerability. As his double he communicates authoritatively, with hubris and menace.

In the role of Laura/Veronica, Coppola cast Romanian-born Alexandra Maria Lara. Lara was raised in Germany. Coppola had seen her in the 2004 German film *Downfall*, about Hitler's last days in the bunker. Lara played Hitler's secretary. Coppola was so impressed he wrote to her and asked her to take the female lead in *Youth without Youth*. Coincidentally, Bruno Ganz had played Hitler in the film, but in *Youth* they had no scenes together. Ganz was born in Switzerland but has spent most of his career in Germany. He is a highly respected theater and film actor and brings great sincerity and humanity to the role of Matei's doctor. Lara shows her inner beauty and versatility in the disparate roles of Laura and Veronica. Actor Matt Damon does a cameo as a CIA type trying to help and protect Dominic during the war years. It's a long way from his lead role in *The Rainmaker*.

The triad of director Coppola, cinematographer Malaimare, and production designer Calin Papura resulted in an extraordinary visualization of the novella *Youth without Youth*. To read this novella is a private experience where one can imagine the real and surreal elements of the story, contemplating the concepts of time and space established by the author. The reader can move at a self-determined pace and mull over the complicated elements the novella puts forth. The reader is able to read the story in parts, contemplate its meaning, and pick it up and put it down at will. When transformed into a cinematic visualization, all that changes.

Transforming from literature to a filmic medium, Coppola was always at the helm; he was first on the set in the morning and last to leave at night. Nevertheless, he has always exercised the philosophy of allowing full participation and considerable freedom when it comes to his collaborators. His belief is to make the right selection and then allow the collaborators to have artistic choice. In the case of *Youth without Youth* he could not have been more prescient. The youth, enthusiasm, and raw talent of his cinematographer resulted in, by turns, naturalistic and surreal imagery. He was flexible and could use whatever equipment was available. He was confident enough to suggest solutions when they were needed. His respect for the director was beyond measure. Romanian production designer Papura had collaborated with Romania's major directors. Unfortunately, most Americans have not seen much of his work product because of the paucity of international distribution. Papura is adept in both drawing and film. He has deep knowledge of his country and its locales. His collaborations with directors from other countries in coproductions include *Captain Conan* (screened at the New York Film Festival), directed by the esteemed French writer/critic/director Bertrand Tavernier, and *Eyewitness*, directed by renowned Greek film director Costa Gravras. The resulting effect of this triumvirate is a remarkable visual imagining of the novella.

Remarkably, the Romanians' knowledge of their country allowed for location selections that simulated Switzerland, India, and Malta within the country of Romania. Except for one sequence, the entire production was filmed on Romanian soil. This contributed significantly to the limited budget of an independently financed film.

Although Coppola was a producer for the motion picture, he was supported by several trusted colleagues. Anahid Nazarian had been a member of

Coppola's coterie since *One from the Heart*. Functioning as the research librarian for Zoetrope, her responsibilities grew as the years passed. She created a tape library and has freelanced in art and costume research on projects such as *The Road to Perdition* and *Artificial Intelligence*. Nazarian had been on the set with Coppola on every film since *The Outsiders*. Anxious to expand her skill base, Nazarian produced some low-budget independent films, and Coppola agreed to have her on board as executive producer for *Youth*. Also executive producing was Fred Roos. Costumes are expertly designed by Gloria Papura, and the make-up team contributes immeasurably to the aging and rejuvenation processes and attendant challenges. Finally, Osvaldo Golijov's musical score and suite are inestimable. Along with the sound design, Golijov's deep and varied musical knowledge translates to the aural richness of the film. Golijov's roots are Eastern European. In his 30s he moved to the United States and has been involved in teaching, composing, and conducting in musical compositions as diverse as opera, Klezmer, symphonies, and contemporary arrangements. Because of his unique exploration of the world of music, Golijov received a prestigious MacArthur grant.

To interpret the subtext, symbolism, and mystery of *Youth without Youth*, viewers will bring their own philosophical, religious, and life experiences to the fore. Some viewers will be satisfied with a somewhat cryptic but engaging story that doesn't explain everything but that inspires emotion and contemplation. Those viewers allow the experience to wash over them, and that is enough. Others feel compelled to see the film more than once, seeking the "answers" to the unexplained occurrences the motion picture presents. Multiple viewings of *Youth without Youth* are not essential in the manner of screening a film such as M. Night Shyamalan's *The Sixth Sense*, where clues become more evident as they are re-exposed. *Youth without Youth* is not a mystery to be solved, yet there can be satisfaction in deeper understanding of the symbols and happenings that may confound the viewer.

Should the audience wish to expand its knowledge, there are plausible interpretations for the phenomena. For others it may require a leap of faith. Being struck by a lightning bolt can in some mythologies and religions symbolize rejuvenation or rebirth. Some religions believe that God has actually prevented death because there is a reason for the person to live. Or some viewers may believe that Matei is willing to make a Faustian pact so he can complete his life's work and be successful instead of dying a failure. However, he must accept the nuclear catastrophe that will befall mankind, except for those who have been labeled as the super race.

To induce Matei to keep his bargain, he is provided with a double or doppelganger to offer feedback that will reinforce his pact. Doppelgangers are prevalent in literature and film as well as in mythology. The doppelganger is often the more sinister form of the living person. There are doppelgangers in Rainer Werner Fassbinder's *Despair* and Krzysztof Kieslowski's *The Double Life of Veronique*.

The use of electricity often suggests the creation of a new, transformed, and powerful entity. A simple, nonesoteric example is the creation of Frankenstein's monster. The conundrum of what is real and what is a dream or supernatural and where we are on the continuum of time and space is a theme that appears over and over in literature, most notably in H. G. Wells's *The Time Machine*. In film a classic example is *The Wizard of Oz*. Films that deal with time travel include Coppola's own *Peggy Sue Got Married* and Robert Zemeckis's *Back to the Future* series. In *Youth without Youth* Coppola helps his audience visually to understand the dream state by introducing dream sequences upside down. Apparently, the fictional writings of Eliade include the mystical teachings associated with shamanism, of which there are many varieties. For those who are interested, it is another area of exploration.

Coppola finished the production of *Youth without Youth* in March 2006. It had been an 85-day production shoot. The film was released at the end of 2007 in several countries on limited screens. Coppola did not have money for advertising and distribution nor was his motivation to have a commercial success or please the critics.

Coppola's intention for this film was to realize a work of art to the best of his ability. The film has numerous indications that a perpetual master of film art is at work. Coppola has employed an old methodology with a life's worth of creative experience. From the opening aural ticking of a clock to the motion picture's final frame, the elegant compositions of this unusual and unexpected tale encapsulate the viewer in an intimate and rare trance.

Tetro: Signed, Sealed, Delivered

After the release of *Youth without Youth* Francis Coppola could relish the accomplishment of producing and directing an independent film on his own dime and for his own satisfaction. He felt impelled to do it again and add the component of an original screenplay, his first since *The Conversation*. This would become *Tetro*. As Coppola stated, "I always hoped, even when I was younger, to do films that were original screenplays and more personal. My career changed a lot when I made *The Godfather* because it was so successful. Now, at this age, I'm doing what I wanted to do when I was 22."[1] He began writing *Tetro* while *Youth* was being edited.

Coppola talked about creating personal films that grew out of his dreams. There are other directors who have used their dreams or unconscious as the genesis of a film idea. The film *Three Women*, directed by Robert Altman, was based on one of his dreams. *Eyes Wide Shut*, the final film directed by Stanley Kubrick, was based on an Arthur Schnitzler novel, *Dream Novella*, with the entire film predicated on not knowing what is real and what is not real. Kubrick felt that the film audience was perpetually in a dream state. The films of Ingmar Bergman are often interpreted as dreams, especially *Persona*. *Tetro* certainly has many elements that appear personal and autobiographical, but as in dreams and nightmares the familiarity that seems autobiographical is not likely. If you are looking for accuracy and verisimilitude you are not going to be satisfied. There are multiple references that resemble aspects of Coppola's life and genealogy, but they are mixed up and jumbled just as they would be in a fantasy or dream.

To plot *Tetro* as if it were a linear, realistic story is to misidentify its genre. This is a story of seeming reality in parts and of psychological and referential improbability in equal mixture. The fundamental story of *Tetro* is the love between two brothers. The younger brother, Bennie, idolizes his older brother, Angelo, known as Tetro, short for Tetrocini, the family surname. Tetro rejected his family when Bennie was a little boy and left him a letter saying he would come back for him, but he did not. Tetro is living in Argentina in a bohemian section known as La Boca. Bennie, at 17, is desperate to seek out his brother. He gets employment on a cruise ship that will dock in Argentina and appears at Tetro's home unannounced. There he meets Miranda, Tetro's live-in girlfriend, a warm, beautiful, and generous woman who is thrilled to welcome Bennie. When Tetro discovers Bennie in his Buenos Aries home, there is an immediate sense of tension. On the one hand he loves his brother; on the other he has chosen to abandon his family, and Bennie's presence sharpens all the agony he has left behind. The subtext for that complete rejection is not yet known. Miranda acts as a liaison between the two, encouraging Tetro to embrace his brother. She tries to explain to Bennie his brother's volatile personality. The brothers begin to explore each other and the environment where Tetro lives. Bennie is introduced to Tetro's artistic life and the companionship he has with performing troupes. Tetro has told Bennie he can stay until his ship sails in a week, but the audience intuits Bennie will not sail. It will take much longer to unravel the mysteries of Tetro's past, which is the key to understanding his family. Once having found Tetro, he will not leave.

What unfolds is the cruelty of their father Carlo, a renowned composer and conductor, who will not accept any success but his own. He tells Tetro there can be only one genius in the family, and that is Carlo. He stifles his own brother, who is also a composer. The father's intense rivalry and malice have forced Tetro to abandon his family and seek an alternate life where he can try to function. The storyline has many twists and turns. Tetro has written a play that will be performed in competition. Tetro will win the competition that takes place in the Patagonian Mountains but will reject the award to remain outside the superficial, strings-attached system. There is a hidden book of Tetro's written in mirror language and a suggestion of madness in that artistic act. Unbeknownst to Tetro, Bennie is determined to unravel the book's content and allow Tetro's genius to emerge. In flashback, we observe an even more sinister underbelly between Tetro and his father. We learn that Tetro has witnessed his mother's death in a car accident and that his father has seduced his girlfriend. There are dreamlike sequences that may or may not reveal truths.

Tetro is photographed in a contrast, widescreen black and white with flashback and dream sequences photographed in color to distinguish them. Coppola wanted black-and-white referencing the European directing masters of the 1960s—in particular, Luchino Visconti's film *Rocco and His Brothers*. Coppola has also referred to *On the Waterfront*, directed by Elia Kazan. This film was shot in black and white with a theme about love and conflict between two brothers, starring Marlon Brando in an iconic role.

Whether or not *Tetro's* conclusion is reality or just a dream is not especially relevant. What rises to the surface are the issues that matter for the brothers. Their love for each other becomes unconditional, and Tetro surfaces as an unencumbered artist who only needs to answer to himself.

Tetro has many visual pleasures and metaphoric images. Coppola is known for the long list of newcomers who owe their breakout opportunity to his artistic instincts. In *Tetro* Coppola chose as cinematographer Romanian-born Mihai Malaimare Jr., whom Coppola discovered in his home country while preparing for *Youth without Youth*. Born in 1975, Malaimare was one of many cinematographers to shoot casting tests for Coppola. When he needed to hire a director of photography, he chose Malaimare because his skill and talent were apparent to Coppola. He said about hiring him for *Youth*, "The movie was about becoming young again. I liked the fact that Mihai was so young, had a gentle personality, and was tremendously talented."[2] This was the first time Coppola was responsible for discovering a cinematographer. Coppola considers Malaimare a perfect collaborator who can shoot in a minimalist style. For Coppola to realize *Tetro* he needed to return to the kind of philosophy he used on *The Rain People*. It gave Coppola great pleasure to make a film as he did in his 20s before he was enveloped in the Hollywood studio system as director of *The Godfather*. He considers this his second career, the one he expected to have as a young man.

In casting the two brothers Coppola found another newcomer for the role of Bennie. This was Alden Ehrenreich, whom Coppola first saw when he was still attending Crossroads High School in Los Angeles, a school for students in the arts. Coppola asked Ehrenreich to read for him at his Napa office. This became a series of auditions and screen tests over several months. At their first meeting Francis asked Ehrenreich to read passages from J. D. Salinger's *The Catcher in the Rye*. Ehrenreich's performance in *Tetro* is poignant and compelling. Still at the beginning of his career, he is attending the Tisch School of the Arts at NYU and has been cast in several roles since *Tetro*.

For the title role Coppola had originally thought of Matt Dillon, but ultimately the part went to Vincent Gallo, an enigmatic, thoroughly independent filmmaker responsible for the well-respected indie film *Buffalo 66* and the controversial *Brown Bunny*. Gallo is an excellent counterpoint to Ehrenreich's innocence. In the role of Miranda, Spanish actress Maribel Verdú adds great passion. She notes that, "From the start he [Coppola] was clear in telling me that I had to provide the heart, to bring a bit of light between these two brothers and their tormented relationship."[3] The world-renowned Austrian actor Klaus Maria Brandauer (*Mephisto*, *Out of Africa*, *Hanussen*) does double duty as the malignant father Carlos and also plays his brother. Spanish actress Carmen Maura, who has had a continuing collaboration with director Pedro Almovador, offers a welcome cameo as an Oprah-like mistress of ceremonies at the Patagonia art festival.

There are references of all kinds in *Tetro*. The most obvious relate to Coppola's family tree. There are some professional similarities, but the resemblance stops there. We can assume that Bennie is an unformed Coppola, at least in terms of his adoration of his older brother and the gentleness of his demeanor, which Coppola's mother Italia described. Coppola was in awe of his older brother August. His father Carmine was a composer and conductor. His uncle Anton conducted opera (including conducting *Cavalleria Rusticana* in *The Godfather Part III*) and is still conducting music at an advanced age. As often is the case with artists, they absorb their own backstory and use the skeleton as invention and fantasy for creative ideas.

The other main reference in *Tetro* is to *The Tales of Hoffmann*. *The Tales of Hoffmann* was an opera by Jacques Offenbach. In 1951 it was adapted into a highly successful film by the British directorial team of Michael Powell and Emeric Pressburger. This film is cherished in Coppola's memory. He saw it as a young boy with his brother August on one of their many excursions to the movies. In addition, Powell is a director revered by many film directors, and Coppola asked him to be in residence at Zoetrope Studios when he was developing and directing *One from the Heart.*

Some critics and Coppola himself have made reference to Coppola's other black-and-white film, *Rumble Fish*, also filled with visual symbols (clocks) and about the devotion of brothers. Perhaps this is why Dillon was first considered for the part of Tetro; he would be like Motorcycle Boy. Coppola observes in an interview with *The Independent* in 2010, "Well, maybe *Tetro* is kind of the sibling to *Rumble Fish*. I made *Rumble Fish* because it reminded me of my own brother. In fact, the film is dedicated to him."[4]

Throughout the film there is a visual metaphor of circular lights and flickering light and fluttering of moths' wings. We see this in flashback when Tetro is in the car accident that kills his mother. At first the flickers and flares affect only Tetro (who runs the lights at the theater as Coppola did in his theater days) and then Bennie also experiences the flickers and flares. Ultimately, after their father's funeral, Bennie runs into traffic and the headlights surrounding him and his brother saves him. The film ends with discs of light serenely moving across the screen (this final image was second unit, shot by Roman Coppola.)

Coppola asked his trusted colleague Walter Murch to edit the film. Murch had the particular challenge of transitioning from black-and-white sequences to color. The color images are reduced to two-thirds the size of the black and white to maintain the full clarity of the black-and-white images.

Tetro was reasonably well received critically when it opened in the spring of 2009, but it was perceived as an art film and did not attract a wide audience. Nevertheless Coppola had met his objective. He made the film by his own standard to be appreciated by any audience that found it.

At age 70, Coppola is quoted in the *New York Times* as saying, "I don't have a lot of time left, but I'm so in love with the cinema that I want to learn all I can about making movies. I just want to write another screenplay and make another movie."[5]

As fate would have it, on October 27, 2009, just a few short months after the release of *Tetro*, August Floyd Coppola, beloved older brother of Francis Ford Coppola, died of a heart attack at age 75 at his home near Los Angeles.

Francis has stated many times that August was his role model in all things, and, indeed, August's life was remarkable. He had extensive academic credentials, attending UCLA where he received a bachelor's degree in philosophy; he went back east to Hofstra for a graduate degree in English and then earned a doctorate in comparative literature at Occidental College. For many years he taught comparative literature at California State–Long Beach and then relocated to San Francisco where he served as dean of creative arts at San Francisco State University. August Coppola was an out-of-the-box thinker responsible for many educational innovations. He also wrote a novel, *The Intimacy* (1978), and had a second novel in progress, *The Nymbus*. He worked with his brother Francis at American Zoetrope on special projects, among them Abel Gance's *Napoleon*. August Coppola founded the San Francisco Film and Video Arts Commission and chaired Education First! which sought support from Hollywood studios for education. He developed a weekend college program for working adults to pursue advanced education. In 1981 Governor Jerry Brown appointed August Coppola to the Board of Trustees of California State University. Of his passing, Brown said, "Augy was a brilliant man. He was a man of letters and ideas. I learned from him."[6]

Of his father, Nicolas Cage said, "He was one of the most remarkable characters anybody's ever going to meet. When I was a kid, the other kids were going to see Disney, and he was showing us movies like Fellini's *Juliet of the Spirits.*"[7]

Fascinated with the sense of touch, August Coppola helped create the Tactile Dome at the San Francisco Exploratorium, where attendees move through darkness using touch as their guide. Touch was also the main theme of his book *The Intimacy*. In the mid 1990s he moved to Savannah, Georgia, for four years so he could work on a second novel in a quiet atmosphere.

Professor Gregory Frazier invented a process where readers describe movie action so the blind can better understand it. When Professor Coppola learned of it, the two opened the AudioVision Workshop and brought the idea to the Cannes Film Festival.

At Cal State–Long Beach the Comparative World Literature and Classics Conference Room has been named in his honor.

19

Somewhere

Marie Antoinette, Sofia Coppola's third feature film, opened in the United States on October 20, 2006. The next month her daughter Romy, was born in Paris. For now, Paris was to be the family's home. Sofia was a working mother but not officially planning another feature film. Like many film directors of her generation, she is diverse. For directors who want to keep their hand in between features, there are two major areas of creative activity that are rewarding and also relatively short-term commitments—music videos and commercials. Sofia was successfully involved in both undertakings.

Francis Coppola and his American New Wave film school colleagues devoted their energies to directing feature films and an occasional short. Some also pursued producing, and others wrote screenplays. A few were able to do all three. In Sofia and Roman Coppola's generation of filmmakers there were exciting new options. In addition to making features, there were opportunities shooting high-end commercials and music videos. This broadened the artistic spectrum for the filmmakers of the twenty-first century.

Directors of music videos fall into several categories. They may be talented individuals for whom this is their primary stock and trade. A prototypical example is the incredibly prolific British director David Mallet, who is responsible for the famed David Bowie–Mick Jagger version of *Dancing in the Street*, many long-form videos, and event films and spectacles. Music videos he has directed include work for performing artists Queen, Def Leppard, AC/DC, and Kiss. He has created long-form videos for Blondie, Jethro Tull, U2, and Elton John. Mallet has directed concert recordings, including one for Sarah Brightman and an event film for Cirque du Soleil. He does not direct commercial feature films.

Other film directors may use music video work as an entrée to feature films. David Fincher is an excellent example of this approach. For most of his childhood, self-taught film director Fincher lived with his parents in Marin County in George Lucas's neighborhood. As a young man one of Fincher's first jobs was for independent filmmaker John Korty, who had been an early member of American Zoetrope and had discovered the Folsom Street location where its members gathered in the 1960s. Fincher eventually took a job at Lucas's Industrial Light and Magic (ILM) and then in 1987 along with other film director wannabes joined Propaganda Films, a major production house for music videos. Fincher became a highly successful director of music videos, doing shoots for artists Madonna, Aerosmith, Nine Inch Nails, George Michaels, and The Wallflowers. In 1992 Fincher directed his first film feature, *Alien 3*, followed in 1995 by the wildly successful film *Se7en*. From that point Fincher's major focus has been features including *Fight Club*, *Zodiac*, *The Social Network*, and *The Girl with the Dragon Tattoo*.

Other successful feature film directors who transitioned after their music video experience with Propaganda films are Michael Bay (*The Rock*, *Armageddon*, and the *Transformers* series), Gore Verbinski (*Pirates of the Caribbean* series), and Antoine Fugua (*Training Day*).

Swedish director Lasse Hallström shot all the music videos for ABBA from 1974 to 1982 before his breakout feature *My Life as a Dog* was nominated for an Academy Award in the foreign film category. He then went on to feature filmmaking—*What's Eating Gilbert Grape*, *Once Around*, *Chocolat*, and *The Cider House Blues*.

Pioneers in the music video industry included already-established film directors who skillfully tried their hands as the industry grew. William Friedkin, director of *The Exorcist* and *The French Connection*, directed singer Laura Branigan's *Self Control*. Brian De Palma, director and contemporary of Francis Ford Coppola and famous for *Carrie*, *Dressed to Kill*, *The Untouchables*, and *Scarface*, directed Bruce Springsteen in *Dancing in the Dark*. Iconic film director Sam Peckinpah, who shot the classic *The Wild Bunch*, directed Julian Lennon's *Too Late for Goodbyes*. Director Martin Scorsese shot Michael Jackson performing *Bad*. Film director Gus Van Sant (*Milk*, *Good Will Hunting*) directed David Bowie in the music video for *Fame*. Spike Lee, director of *Malcolm X*, *Do the Right Thing*, and *Jungle Fever*, created *This Is It* posthumously for Michael Jackson and directed music videos in the jazz vein for Miles Davis and Anita Baker.

Other film artists commingle music videos and feature films. Sofia Coppola's ex-husband Spike Jonze is an exceedingly prolific director of music videos and continues to be, but he also has directed films: *Being John Malkovich*, *Adaptation*, and *Where the Wild Things Are*. In addition he directs commercials. The Hughes brothers, Allen and Albert, also commingle their professional choices. The Hughes brothers directed films *Menace II Society*, *From Hell*, and *The Book of Eli* and also direct music videos.

Other recognizable film directors shoot commercials for hire. Spike Lee has directed commercials for Levi's 501 jeans, Nike, Ben and Jerry's, Snapple, and Absolut Brooklyn. Academy Award–winning director Catherine Bigelow (*The Foot Locker*) has directed a Pirelli Tire spot starring Uma Thurman and a lipstick commercial starring Jessica Biel. Darren Aronofsky, director of *Requiem for a Dream*, *The Wrestler*, and *Black Swan*, shot actor Vincent Cassel in an Yves Saint Laurent (YSL) commercial. And sometimes there are directors who appear in commercials. Martin Scorsese and Robert De Niro have both advertised American Express. And in magazine ads Francis Ford Coppola has appeared with his daughter for Louis Vuitton photographed by Annie Leibowitz.

Sofia Coppola has functioned productively in all these genres throughout her adult career. In 2003 she was approached to direct a music video for the duo White Stripes singing their cover version of Burt Bacharach's "I Just Don't Know What to Do With Myself." She conceptualized her idea for the video in a manner she often uses. She thought of a visual image that she would be interested in seeing and then suggested it. In the case of "I Just Don't Know What to Do With Myself" she imagined supermodel Kate Moss doing a pole dance to the song. The video moved ahead and was shot in the basement of the Mercer Hotel close by where Sofia was staying as she wrapped up *Lost in Translation*. Coppola and Moss had known each other since their teenage years, and Moss was ready to give the adventure a whirl.

The music video runs under three minutes. It was photographed by Lance Acord, who was the cinematographer on *Lost in Translation*. It is in black and white. The physical staging is minimal. Moss wears a bra and bikini underwear; her shoulder-length mane of hair is full and blunt cut. Her two props are a solid cube large enough for her to lie and pose on and a metal pole used to dance on. She alternates between these objects, starting on her back on the cube and moving up, down, and around the pole in various positions. Her movements are sensual but not overly provocative. Acord, using chiaroscuro, often envelops Moss's image in black, but sometimes changes the background to a murky gray, and occasionally flares spotlights behind and above the subject. The overall impression of the video is a beautiful but distant woman moving her body in languid random poses expressing visually that she doesn't know what to do with herself. There is no sense of playfulness or eroticism but rather a feeling of ennui.

Toward the end of 2008 Sofia began directing perfume commercials for Miss Dior Cherie. These would become a series of commercials for the fragrance. It was natural to situate a perfume commercial in Paris, and Sofia's familiarity with the city, its culture, and its language made her a superb choice for the campaign. The first 30-second spot features a young, perky girl dressed in a pink sun dress (Dior) walking in Paris and riding a bicycle around the city. Balloons and confections abound (the luscious-looking pastries recall scenes from *Marie Antoinette*). The aural background is a Brigitte Bardot song, "Moi Je Joue." The ingénue floats upward with her balloons and a dab of Miss Dior Cherie. The commercial has obvious appeal for the female youth market and premiered in the United States on November 8, 2008, in *Gossip Girl* and other outlets in the United States.

Romy was now a toddler, and Coppola began conceptualizing her next feature. The subject matter was within her sphere of influence. She contemplated the notion of celebrity and its trappings. Clearly, she was equipped to examine this subject; she had been around the celebrity world her whole life. The premise of *Somewhere* would be a slice-of-life mood piece centered on actor Johnny Marco, at the top of his professional game but aimless as a person. Sofia would work in minimalist style as she had for *The Virgin Suicides* and *Lost in Translation*. A key location for the film would be the famed Chateau Marmont, hotel to the stars, right off Sunset Boulevard in West Hollywood. Johnny Marco, between movies, was residing at the Chateau. The film was designed to be more modest in scope, and the shooting schedule was planned for six weeks as opposed to six months for *Marie Antoinette*, a more realistic timeframe for the mother of a young child (who was often on set as her mother had been with Francis).

The plot, such as it is, has few elements. While at the Chateau Johnny trips and breaks his arm. He copes with the injury initially with the help of painkillers and booze. His 11-year-old daughter Cleo arrives for a day visit. Marco is divorced, and Cleo lives with her mother. Shortly after, Cleo appears unexpectedly, and Marco's ex-wife says she is going away, leaving Cleo in Marco's care until she goes off to camp. Without expecting it, Marco is now the custodial parent. The remainder of the story is the unfolding relationship between Marco and his daughter.

Somewhere opens with a pretitle sequence that starts in black. We hear the sound of a powerful car engine revving and accelerating. The picture comes on to reveal an extreme long shot of a sports car circling an isolated racetrack in the desert. The camera is locked off. The driver repeats the laps and ultimately drives into frame in a medium shot. Marco gets out of the car and looks around briefly; we fade to black, and then the title sequence appears.

The next scene positions the viewer at the Chateau Marmont and then inside the hotel with Johnny and his cohorts. Johnny trips down the stairs and breaks his arm. In his room he is entertained by a set of twins who pole dance for his enjoyment. (Sofia Coppola invoked the image she used in the Kate Moss video.) Loaded with painkillers, he simply falls asleep as they perform. Marco seems to allow his environment to wash over him. His room is appropriated for a loud, boozy party where he is not really the host but merely a conduit. Whether he approves or not, he passively allows the festivities to occur. He appears to have one friend among the large group of hangers-on, Sammy, who relates to him more directly and personally.

Within his behavior is a gentleness and polite demeanor. He doesn't pull rank or offend anyone, yet these qualities seem almost to be waiting for a worthy direction. With Cleo the direction will be found. When Cleo comes for her day visit father and daughter go to an ice-skating rink where she practices. She is obviously talented and tells him she has been taking lessons for a long time—information of which he seems unaware. The viewer can see Cleo entering Johnny's life. As Johnny's time at the Chateau passes he meets his obligations to go to press conferences, photo shoots, and a special effects make-up session for his next film. He has some sexual liaisons that lack any sense of intimacy. There is simply a feeling of ennui.

From the point when Cleo becomes a regular presence, there is a subtle but perceptible shift in Johnny. Sammy visits in their quarters, and they play *Guitar Hero*. Sammy, who is more comfortable around kids, sets the stage for Johnny to engage more actively with his daughter. Johnny needs to go to Milan to receive an award, and Cleo attends the ceremony, glowing in the first row of the theater. They stay at a magnificent hotel, the Principe de Savoia (where the Coppolas stayed when Sofia was a young girl). There is an opportunity to see Cleo in formal evening wear, age-appropriate but clearly communicating her adolescent beauty. They eat every flavor of gelato in bed, thoroughly enjoying each other's company. Johnny has his missteps, sneaking out to sleep with a woman while Cleo is asleep in their suite, but slowly his decision making becomes more focused and responsible. They are bonding. Cleo makes wonderful breakfasts for her father, and their roles shift back and forth—each taking care of the other.

At some point Johnny removes his arm cast, symbolically casting off what is broken about him. As the two prepare for Cleo to leave for camp, they carefully shop so she will have all that she needs. There is an underlying tug as the two know they will be separating. In Johnny's Ferrari they drive part way to the camp location. Cleo begins to cry and says she misses her mother. Johnny is able to comfort her quietly. They make an unintended stop in Las Vegas, where Johnny teaches Cleo how to play craps in a casino. To arrive on time, their last leg of the journey is via helicopter. As Cleo settles into her camp cab, Johnny, with the whir of the copter blades above him, shouts out to Cleo—"I'm sorry I haven't been around." It is a transformative moment for Marco.

Johnny checks out of the Chateau Marmont with no plan to return. He drives his Ferrari toward the same desolate track outside L.A. where the story began. When he reaches the destination he does not drive the Ferrari around the track. There is no need for him to drive in circles anymore. Instead he parks the car on the side of the road, gets out, and with purpose and a soft smile on his face, he begins to walk.

The choice of Stephen Dorff for the role of Johnny Marco was an excellent example of Coppola's intuition. She had known Dorff from his many years acting in eclectic roles and as an industry kid, as she was. His father is Steve Dorff, who is a Hollywood composer. Dorff worked with director Mary Harron in *I Shot Andy Warhol* and John Waters's *Cecil B. Demented*. He was in the vampire film *Blade*, the comedy *Bucky Larson: Born to be a Star*, Michael Mann's *Public Enemies*, and the *Immortals* in 3D. His breakout role was in 1994 in *Backbeat* portraying Stuart Sutcliffe, who played with the Beatles early in their career in Hamburg, Germany. Although Sofia didn't write the script specifically with Dorff in mind as she had for Bill Murray in *Lost in Translation*, she thought of Dorff and the feeling she had about his gentle, sweet demeanor. When she sent him the script he was thrilled. He was ready to do a role like this one after the many villains and outlier parts he had played. His mother had passed away the year before and had always hoped he could show another side of his acting talent. To Dorff, the role of Johnny Marco was it.

For the role of Cleo, Johnny's 11-year-old daughter, Coppola cast Elle Fanning, younger sister of Dakota Fanning. Coppola met her first at Roman's office at the Director's Bureau. The interview was basically talking and becoming comfortable with each other. Elle was immediately taken with Sofia and wanted to work on her movie without knowing much about it. Sofia had Stephen meet with Elle, and they began to improvise the story of a father and daughter who were not especially close. The rehearsal period was the tried-and-true Coppola family method, and by the time they were ready to go into production Elle understood that her character was in need of a father figure and someone to look up to and, at the same time, was anxious to take care of him, in a kind of role reversal. Elle has worked steadily since she was two years old (playing Dakota as a younger girl). Her performance in *Somewhere* has such poise and precision it is hard to believe she is a child actor. Jodie Foster, who began her career as a child, remarks after seeing Elle in *Phoebe in Wonderland*, "I was blown away by that performance—blown away. She should have been nominated for an Oscar. Elle Fanning is just so amazing."[1]

Both actors recognized this was a story that would have minimal dialogue and move at a languid pace, a journey over a summer to a meaningful relationship that would bring security to an adolescent and maturity to a grown man.

The role of Sammy was played by the irrepressible Chris Pontius of *Jackass* fame. He is able to show his versatility in this supporting part.

In *Somewhere* the "character" of the Chateau Marmont is often in juxtaposition to Johnny Marco's development, but it holds its own form of protection as he slowly moves forward in his life. Built in 1927, the Chateau, under new ownership since the early 1990s, is identified as a tolerant haven in the Hollywood community even when some of its occupants display outrageous excess and unacceptable behavior. It affords a unique kind of privacy for myriad Hollywood elites and has done so for generations.

When Coppola was directing the Miss Dior Cherie commercial, the director of photography was Harris Savides. Savides is a highly respected and experienced cinematographer with a diverse résumé. Savides, who studied at New York's School of Visual Arts, has shot several Van Sant films, including *Milk* and the experimental *Gerry, Elephant*, and *Last Days*. He also photographed Ridley Scott's *American Gangster*. He and Sofia shared views on minimalist style and natural lighting. When they talked further Savides felt he could create an intimate visual environment for *Somewhere* using a small crew and natural lighting in the hotel. His contribution to the visual look is apparent. The film is characterized by long takes and no unnecessary camera movements. Richard Beggs creates a sound mix that makes Los Angeles recognizable. The musical score created by Thomas Mars and Phoenix subtly supports the story and combines with the other aural elements.

Somewhere was shown in competition at the Venice Film Festival and won the coveted Golden Lion. In general release in the United States it received mixed reaction and was not a financial success. Perhaps the Michelangelo Antonioni influence that is evident in the pace and spare dialogue was too taxing for American viewers more attuned to action and intricate plot devices. Nonetheless, Coppola achieved her writing and directorial goals. She told a simple story about people she knew in an environment with which she was intimate.

20

On the Road

In 1968 Francis Ford Coppola purchased the rights to Jack Kerouac's 1957 iconic novel of a generation, *On the Road*. Over four decades later the film adaptation of *On the Road* was finally released in spring 2012 by MK2 Productions and American Zoetrope. Its long journey to the screen demonstrates the sometimes convoluted path a project can travel from book to film. Always tenacious, Coppola would not let go of the rights to *On the Road*, nor would he compromise about the seminal novel of the Beat Generation and its potential artistic life on film.

When Coppola bought the rights to *On the Road* his own artistic life was centered in San Francisco. Coppola spent many mornings writing scripts in cafés in the North Beach section of San Francisco, including parts of *The Godfather*. It is likely he was in spitting distance of City Lights Bookstore, where the San Francisco Bay Area Beats congregated and where Lawrence Ferlinghetti agreed to publish Allen Ginsberg's epic poem *Howl*. This storefront, a modest yet dynamic structure, is responsible for publishing many literary works that would likely not have found a home elsewhere; it was heady inspiration for a young, literate filmmaker.

From the beginning Coppola had unwavering demands for realizing the film. He believed the lead characters, Sal Paradise and Dean Moriarty, should be played by unknown actors and that the film should be in black and white. Both of those demands were not likely to attract studio backing.

The story of *On the Road* is largely autobiographical. The narrator, Sal Paradise, is the voice of Kerouac. Kerouac's main buddy Neal Cassady is portrayed in the adventurous, anything-goes maverick character Dean Moriarty. The backdrop of the story is after World War II and centers on a group of free-wheeling, hard-drinking, drug-taking adventurers soaking up the jazz of saxophonist Charlie Parker and trumpeter Miles Davis while carousing with girls and experiencing an alternate lifestyle that came to be known as the Beat Generation. Paradise is divorced and Moriarty is in a rocky marriage to Marylou. Sal works his way cross-country, meeting an eclectic group of characters including Carlo Marx (based on Allen Ginsberg). Sal is heading for San Francisco and making detours, meeting up with Dean periodically along the way. The subtext of *On the Road* is a generation in search of self and spiritual meaning. Kerouac's novel became the literary anthem of a generation and continues to resonate and influence artists into the twenty-first century.

In an article in *The Telegraph* in 2004 Coppola is quoted as telling author David Gritten in 1997 in Paris, "I tried to make it, but couldn't get the money. Now it keeps becoming more important."[1] Coppola knew it was critical to have a nuanced screenplay that would translate the spirit and intensity of the autobiographical novel. A number of highly respected screenwriters attempted writing a script that Coppola would greenlight. Michael Herr, who had contributed to the narration for *Apocalypse Now* and for Stanley Kubrick's *Full Metal Jacket*, made an attempt, but Coppola passed on his script.

The next treatment came from poet/author/screenwriter Barry Gifford. He had written several well-received novels about two characters, Sailor and Lula, with personalities that fit the Beat lifestyle. The first book of the series, *Wild at Heart*, was made into a film by David Lynch. He also wrote the script for Lynch's *Lost Highway*. Gifford had written an oral history of Kerouac titled *Jack's Book* and an essay called *Kerouac's Town*, so he had great familiarity with the author and his themes, but Coppola did not pick up the script.

In the 1990s father and son Roman tried their hand, but Coppola moved on. The next writer under consideration was esteemed author Russell Banks. His novels include *The Sweet Hereafter* and *Affliction*, both made into movies. His characters often have social difficulties and live out unusual existences. Banks had met Jack Kerouac when he traveled to Chapel Hill where Banks was teaching. A friend of Banks asked if they could stop by. Kerouac and a band of friends took over his house for about a week. It was 1967, and Kerouac was in poor health and an alcoholic stupor, but Banks still considered it a remarkable experience. Kerouac was an idol and near the end of his life. It seemed that Francis was ready to accept Russell Banks's adaptation, but development did not progress forward.

Then in 2004 a film from esteemed Brazilian film director and producer Walter Salles titled *The Motorcycle Diaries* came on the scene and received positive acclaim. It was the autobiographical story of a young Che Guevara's motorcycle road trip in search of himself. Coppola was enthralled. He asked its screenwriter, Jose Rivera, to prepare a script for *On the Road* with the intention to use Salles as director. Coppola would executive produce. The film was in development as far back as 2008. Salles collaborated with trusted colleagues from *The Motorcycle Diaries*: playwright Rivera, whose screenplay adaptation for *The Motorcycle Diaries* was nominated for an Academy Award; cinematographer Eric Gautier; production designer Carlos Conti; composer Gustavo Santaolalla; and members of his producing team.

Before directing *The Motorcycle Diaries*, Salles had reread *On the Road*, which he read originally in his early 20s. To help prepare for the film, Salles and a small film crew traced the trip that Kerouac took and talked to old Beats who were still alive as he travelled the route. Salles, who is revered in Latin America and is a graduate of University of Southern California Film School, believed that tracing Kerouac's road map informed him about the man and the decade in which he emerged. He recognized the enormous responsibility of filming a novel that affected an entire generation and is being rediscovered by a new one.

In 2010 *On the Road* was in production. As Coppola had envisioned, the two lead actors were just at the beginning of their careers. Other, more seasoned actors surround them. British-born Sam Riley was cast as Sal Paradise. He has received positive recognition in several British independent films, but this is clearly his breakthrough role. Garrett Hedland was cast as Dean Moriarty. He first appeared in *Troy* and *Friday Night Lights* in 2004. *On the Road* takes his career to another level. Kristen Stewart, well known for the *Twilight* saga, plays Moriarty's wife Marylou. Kirsten Dunst, who has worked repeatedly with Sofia Coppola, is cast as another love interest in the film. Tom Sturridge, born in England, began his career as a child actor and appears in the key role of Carlo Marx. Viggo Mortensen, Steve Buscemi, Terrence Howard, Amy Adams, and Elizabeth Moss, all established and award-winning actors, provide a strong supporting ensemble. *On the Road* had its world premiere at a familiar Coppola venue. The film opened as an official entry at the Cannes Film Festival and received a warm reception and solid reviews.

21

The Kids Are All Right: Colleagues

In the second decade of the twenty-first century, it is not unusual for the many artistic members of the Coppola family to be referred to as a dynasty. Recognizing the creative contributions of the Coppolas for three generations, they are on par with the Hustons, the Fondas, and the Barrymores. The Coppola clan continues to grow and flourish as the family tree extends its branches.

Since the release of *CQ* in 2001, Roman Coppola has had an extraordinarily busy and productive decade. He continues to lead The Directors Bureau, located in Los Angeles, which functions as an artists' clearinghouse and support group for directors of commercials, music videos, short films, and feature films. Both he and Sofia Coppola are now the owners of American Zoetrope, the company having been gifted to them by their father late in the decade. Roman appears to have inherited his father's inventive propensities. In 2004 he created the Photobubble, which now has its own company. The Photobubble is a custom-made production tool designed to simplify a complicated shooting situation. It is particularly useful for photographic challenges during commercials. Photobubbles are inflatable structures that create a soft-box enclosure that is reflection free. The director of photography and perhaps director is encased in the Photobubble and can essentially shoot 360 degrees in a given circumstance. The idea for this invention came to Coppola in response to a need, proving that necessity is the mother of invention. He was shooting a Toyota Prius commercial. He needed a mechanism to allow for filming a car being driven at speed in a totally white atmosphere and eventually conceived the notion of building an inflatable stage lit from the outside. He thought it might work. Coppola brought on a team to design, produce, and market the product. To date, the Photobubble has been used successfully in commercial situations, and its applications are growing.

Roman Coppola has been a sought after second-unit director for his entire adult career. Of course, he provided second unit for Sofia whenever she asked for it. With his father directing films again, he photographed on both *Youth without Youth* and *Tetro*. Roman has developed a professional relationship with director Wes Anderson. He was second-unit director on *The Life Aquatic with Steve Zissou*. They became further connected on the film *The Darjeeling Limited*, which was released in October 2007. Roman was one of the producers, did second-unit directing, and wrote the screenplay with Anderson and Roman's cousin Jason Schwartzman, who was also in one of the leading roles. Roman's collaboration with Anderson continues, and together they wrote *Moonrise Kingdom*, which opened the prestigious Cannes Film Festival in May 2012.

During this period Roman directed countless music videos, many of them for the indie rock group The Strokes and later for Phoenix, Thomas Mars' group. Most exciting in terms of his career growth, he is writing, directing, and producing (Francis's trifecta) *A Glimpse Inside the Mind of Charles Swan III*, with Charlie Sheen in the title role and also starring Bill Murray, who has worked repeatedly with Anderson and starred in Sofia's *Lost in Translation*. His cousin Jason Schwartzman will appear in the film as well. The film is billed as a comedy. Also listed in the cast is Patricia Arquette, his cousin Nicolas Cage's ex-wife.

Since the release of Sofia Coppola's most recent picture, *Somewhere*, she has had joyous events in her personal life. In the spring of 2010 she and Mars welcomed their second daughter, Cosima. On August 27, 2011, Coppola and Mars married in a low-key ceremony in southern Italy in Bernalda, a historic city where Francis Ford Coppola was in the midst of renovations to transform a nineteenth-century villa into the Italian resort Palazzo Margherita. It was an outside wedding on the palazzo. About 100 people, friends and family, attended the ceremony.

In addition to raising her family living in both Paris and New York, Sofia has directed another Dior Perfume commercial. This one is for Miss Dior Cherie and stars Natalie Portman. Her "French" lover in this brief encounter is Alden Ehrenreich, who was Bennie in Francis Coppola's *Tetro*—yet another example of actors becoming part of the Coppola stable. The background music is an iconic French song, "Je t'aime . . . moi non plus," written by Serge Gainsbourg and performed by Gainsbourg and Jane Birkin. It is more sophisticated than the bubbly commercial Sofia made in 2008, appealing to a more chic young market.

In June 2011 designer Marc Jacobs received the Council of Fashion Designers of America's Geoffrey Beene Lifetime Achievement Award. Sofia had long been considered Jacobs's muse, and she had the honor to make the presentation.

At the end of 2011 Sofia curated an exhibit of Robert Mapplethorpe photographs at the Galerie Thaddaeus Ropac in Paris. Sofia chose the photographs from the Mapplethorpe archives in New York, and they reflected her particular aesthetic. Gallery owner Thaddaeus Ropac conceived the concept of pairing an artist with the subject of a show and allowing the artist to select art pieces that reflected his or her response to the artist whose work was being displayed. Some of the photographic choices Sofia selected were lesser-known portraits of children and animals and many of Mapplethorpe's still-life flower photographs and landscapes. That was her aesthetic.

Toward the end of 2011 rumors started that Sofia Coppola was in the planning stages of her next film. The film *Burglar Bunch* (working title) was listed as in development for 2014. It is based on the audacious gang who robbed Hollywood celebrities of millions of dollars' worth of first-class possessions. As the film progressed from development to early production its title became *The Bling Ring*. Sofia is writing, producing, and directing, with Roman Coppola also producing and stalwart Fred Roos on board as executive producer. The cast includes many young actors, most notably Emma Watson of the Harry Potter franchise.

In January 2012 it was reported that Sofia entered into an exclusive arrangement with the Swedish retail brand H&M to prepare an all-out advertising campaign for their Marni Collection. The multifaceted project is set in Marrakesh, Morocco, and includes a film that will be shown in movie theaters and on television. There also will be print advertising. Of the collaboration Coppola observed, "I enjoyed doing this film for the Marni at H&M collaboration, I think it's great how they make fashion accessible and I wanted to show the fantasy fashion can bring."[1]

Actor, musician, and screenwriter Jason Schwartzman, son of Talia Shire and the late Jack Schwartzman, has had a highly successful career that blossomed when he was cast in director Anderson's *Rushmore*, a surprise hit that has cult status. Jason maintains a close relationship with Anderson and has appeared in many of his films, including *The Darjeeling Limited* (which he also co-wrote) and *Moonrise Kingdom*. Schwartzman appeared in his cousin Sofia's *Marie Antoinette* and in his cousin Roman's *CQ*. He wrote the soundtrack for his cousin Bill Neil's film *Goats*, which premiered at the Sundance Film Festival in January 2012. Schwartzman is a talented musician who was the 14-year-old drummer of indie rock group Phantom Planet. He now has a solo act titled Coconut Records. Other movie roles he has played are in *Slackers*, *Shopgirl*, *Scott Pilgrim vs. the World*, and the not-yet-released *A Glimpse Inside the Mind of Charles Swan III*, where he will again perform for his cousin Roman. On HBO he played the lead in *Bored to Death* for three seasons and wrote the theme song for the show.

Jason's younger brother Robert is also a musician and actor. He formed a band called Rooney when he was a junior in high school. He is the lead vocalist. The band signed a contract with Geffen/Interscope Records in 2002. The band has opened for indie rock bands Weezer and The Strokes. Schwartzman had supporting roles in *The Princess Diaries* (in which he also sang) and worked for his cousin Sofia in *The Virgin Suicides*.

Jason and Robert have an older half-brother, John Schwartzman, who is a successful cinematographer. Among his many credits are *The Green Hornet*, *The Bucket List*, *Seabiscuit*, *The Rookie*, *Pearl Harbor*, and *EDtv*.

Marc Coppola is best known as an extremely successful disc jockey (DJ). He is the late August Coppola's oldest son. At an early age he acted in film and television, but his true forte has been as a radio music personality. Broadcasting rock along with intelligent commentary, he was a popular and respected DJ with a strong following on several New York radio stations. He now can be listened to via Clear Channel in extended format broadcasting "Big Classic Hits."

August Coppola's second son Christopher has had an unusual career path within the arts. He is a digital entrepreneur and is president of CRC Productions. In 2006 Christopher inaugurated a digital film festival in New Mexico. One of his missions is to make moviemaking more accessible to the general public by developing methods that make it easier to distribute the product and by developing interactive platforms. His film festival was subtitled Project Accessible Hollywood (PAH). Coppola has also directed eight features between 1998 and 2007, most in the horror genre. Among them are *The Creature of the Sunny Side Up Trailer Park*, *G-Men from Hell*, and *Dracula's Widow*.

Nicolas Cage (*nee* Coppola) has appeared as an actor in well over 50 feature films with some of the finest film directors, including his uncle Francis, Martin Scorsese, John Woo, Werner Herzog, Ridley Scott, Oliver Stone, David Lynch, and Norman Jewison. He has four films in various stages of production and commitments through 2014. He has also produced a number of films.

Chris Neil worked for George Lucas as a dialogue coach. His dream was to direct a feature, and at the 2012 Sundance Festival he was able to showcase *Goats*, a film about an eccentric extended family and an adolescent boy's rite of passage. Neil was able to assemble a remarkable cast—David Duchovny, Vera Farmiga, Keri Russell, Minnie Driver, and Will Arnett. This labor of love began when Christopher optioned the rights eight years ago.

Jacqui de la Fontaine, had married with Francis and Eleanor Coppola's blessing in 2000. In fact, Francis walked her down the aisle at the Napa Valley estate as she wed billionaire Peter Getty. But a decade later the marriage was in shambles as Jacqui discovered Getty's adultery and cocaine addiction. The result was a highly publicized divorce with a protracted battle over spousal support.

Francis and Eleanor's granddaughter Gia is now a successful model who has appeared in the major fashion magazines and was chosen as the Spring 2012 *Whetherly Look Book* model. She is also a budding director and shot a video for *Opening Ceremony* (OCTV) titled *22*. At this point, she is clearly trying to follow in her aunt's footsteps.

And so the majority of the current generation of Coppolas are contributing to the arts and technology. They are involved in filmmaking, video artistry, digital innovation, acting, communications, cutting-edge technology, screenwriting, music, and fashion. As artists, they are moving the twenty-first century forward. Many of them already have children of their own. Clearly, the kids are all right.

22

Francis Ford Coppola's Unrealized Projects

Many film directors with long careers have planned projects that do not come to fruition. Sometimes the projects just don't get off the ground. At times, the director cannot get financing. Some seemed like a good idea, but the concept turns sour; and then there are projects that are long-time dreams, yet they are not realized. Like Francis Ford Coppola, some of the world's most renowned film directors have had this experience. Iconic film director Stanley Kubrick had a project for which he had great passion that was never realized. For most of his directorial career, Kubrick intended to direct a major epic on the life of Napoleon. There are script versions, casting plans, volumes of research, location scouting reports, costume samples, and all manner of preproduction details, but the maker of *2001: A Space Odyssey, Dr. Strangelove—or How I Learned to Stop Worrying and Love the Bomb* and *Paths of Glory* could not get studio financing. It falls into the category of an unrealized dream.

Danish director Carl Th. Dreyer, responsible for the magnificent films *The Passion of Joan of Arc* and *Vampyr*, planned to make an epic on the life of Jesus. Although a script exists, Dreyer was never able to secure backing for the film.

Josef Von Sternberg, who directed six films starring Marlene Dietrich, including *The Blue Angel*, was in production of *I Claudius*, produced by Alexander Korda and starring Charles Laughton and Merle Oberon, when Oberon was in a car accident. There had been conflicts between the director and Laughton, and during the delay the studio abandoned the project. The BBC produced a documentary entitled *The Epic That Never Was* using footage from the unfinished film.

Not every unfinished project has a dramatic explanation for failing to see the light of day, but for Coppola the unrealized *Megalopolis* had been a major part of his creative process since the early 1980s. The inability to develop it into a finished feature film was a painful experience for Coppola. Coppola began to conceive *Megalopolis* around the time *The Outsiders* was released. He was writing it in two forms, part novel and part screenplay. As the title implies, it had to do with an urban environment. He was just beginning to map out a larger storyline, one he conceived would be epic in scope. After writing about 400 pages, the requirements of a new commitment, *The Cotton Club*, pulled Coppola away from the gestating idea. Once again a director for hire, his attention was elsewhere, and the emerging conception was on hold.

After the popular and financial success of *Peggy Sue Got Married*, Coppola summoned the energy to grant his first interview in two years. The years since the death of his son and the continuous demands of directing for a paycheck had taken their toll on Coppola; he had become increasingly weary. The scheduled interview was about wine, not motion pictures, and was conducted by a neighbor and wine writer from Napa. In the course of their discussion, Coppola mentioned he was at work on two scripts. He called one *Secret Journal* (which may have been *Megalopolis*), and the other was *Elective Affinities*.

As the decade of the 1980s wound down and Coppola completed *Tucker, The Man and his Dreams*, he returned to *Megalopolis* with rigor. The plot began to emerge. Characters from ancient Rome at the time of the Catiline Conspiracy[1] would merge with contemporary New York City's corruption and the evils of modern urban life. The resultant film was purported to be on the scale of a Cecil B. DeMille epic. In an interview with *Mother Jones* in September 1988, Coppola told Jill Kearney,

> the thing I'm writing now, which is a long film—maybe 3 hours and 45 minutes, I've been writing it for four years. At the end of *Zoe* I'm not doing any publicity, any film festivals. I'm just going to be free to implement this idea. It's not just about writing—it involves actors, and music, and art, and all the other things except the production level. I have a lot of new theories about composing film that represent a different way of working that's possible now because of computer and video revolutions.[2]

The urge to focus on this independent project was enormous, but Coppola was not really a free agent, and so again he moved on and directed *The Godfather Part III*. Other elements of the epic were unfolding. It had a utopian theme, and one of the major characters in New York City was an architect, so it was likened (not by Coppola) to *The Fountainhead*.

When Francis agreed to direct *The Godfather Part III* he kept the *Megalopolis* plan going by beginning to visually conceptualize it while in Rome. Dean Tavoularis and his team rented space at Cinecittà Studios, and detailed storyboards of the proposed film were prepared. Coppola's plan was to concentrate on *Megalopolis* after completion of *The Godfather Part III*. However, after *Part III* Francis Coppola was forced to declare personal bankruptcy, and he proceeded to map out *Bram Stoker's Dracula* to pay the bills. Once again *Megalopolis* was on the back burner.

After filming *The Rainmaker* in 1997, Coppola embarked on executive producing and producing projects. His businesses outside of film were burgeoning, yet his commitment to *Megalopolis* moved forward. His intention was to complete the script and begin production in 2001. In July 2001 ABC News reported a potential all-star line-up for the film. Coppola told Army Archerd of *Variety* that Russell Crowe, Robert De Niro, Nicolas Cage, and Paul Newman were under consideration. There was already a preproduction crew in Brooklyn, and Coppola was there tweaking the script. Coppola projected the cost of the film at $60 to 80 million.[3]

When Coppola appeared at Cannes in May 2001 to present *Apocalypse Now Redux,* he announced he was "working on an even larger project than his cult Vietnam epic. The film is entitled *Megalopolis* and it is the story of one man's battle to build an ideal world." Coppola told *Reuters* the film was "bigger and more ambitious . . . because it deals with a vision of the future . . . with that unspeakable word 'Utopia.' "[4] It would be self-financed. After September 11, 2001, Coppola was stymied. He did not immediately say he would not proceed with *Megalopolis*; in fact, he suggested that 9/11 motivated him even more. However, as time passed and the schedule was not met, it seemed apparent that the film was on hiatus. Ultimately, he began making plans for a much less ambitious project—*Youth without Youth.*

After Gio Coppola's death, Coppola began thinking of the story of *Pinocchio* as he knew it from Carlo Collodi's nineteenth-century book. Coppola's version would be a departure from the sanitized, animated Disney version that tinkered with the story. Coppola considered the project homage to Gio. Coppola approached Warner Bros. about the project, and they preliminarily discussed a three-film relationship to include *Pinocchio, The Secret Garden*, and *Hoover (*based on the life of J. Edgar). On Coppola's part there was dissatisfaction about Warner's money offer, and he set the negotiation aside. In 1992 Warner Bros. announced that Coppola (Zoetrope) and Jim Henson Productions would collaborate on a live-action production of *Pinocchio* with Fred Fuchs executive producing.[5] Coppola still did not agree with Warner's financial package, and he approached Columbia to gauge their interest. Coppola had researched Collodi and already written a screenplay along with series of songs for the venture. Columbia did not choose to proceed while there was an open issue at Warner Bros. The development went dormant. Kim Aubry notes that he worked on the unrealized *Pinocchio* project for Coppola. "It was to have a computer generated human operated photorealistic puppet living in a live action universe with human actors."[6]

In 1996 *The Adventures of Pinocchio* was released without Coppola's involvement. Ultimately, Coppola sued Warner Bros., arguing he had lost the ability to freely negotiate with Columbia Studios and, therefore, was blocked from making the movie. In a jury trial in 1998 Coppola was awarded $60 million in punitive damages and $20 million in compensation by a sympathetic jury. On appeal the judgment was overturned. In 2002 an Italian actor/director made a version of *Pinocchio* that was financially unsuccessful and viewed as an artistic failure.

Around 1980 when Coppola was in Japan meeting with Akira Kurosawa regarding *Kagemusha* and its release, he read Johann Wolfgang von Goethe's novella *Elective Affinities*. The story involves a married couple, the liaison each has with another person, and the attendant consequences. Goethe's work attaches the affinities of men and women in love to the possible chemical nature of these relationships. Coppola's concept was to meld the cultures of East and West in an enormous project involving four films over ten years. The concept, which does not appear to align with the basic dynamics of the story, may have been attached to his recent visit to the East. In any event, it was unworkable. Coppola was in way over his head with Zoetrope, the backlash of *Apocalypse Now*, and friction in his marriage. Francis was in an emotionally fragile and precarious state after taxing himself psychologically and physically for over two years in the Philippines. Interestingly, the essential plot outline plays itself out in Zoetrope Studios's inaugural production, *One from the Heart*.

23

Epilogue

The American film industry has felt the continuous presence of Frances Ford Coppola for five decades. In the twenty-first century, since he resurrected his directing career in 2007 filming *Youth without Youth*, he has listened to his own mantra. There are three cardinal rules: (1) write and direct original screenplays, (2) make them with the most modern technology available, and (3) self-finance them.[1] In the case of *Youth* the screenplay was adapted, but he was able to adapt the material independently. It took the majority of his professional life to realize this dictum. When he directed *The Rain People* (1969), Coppola was on a trajectory to auteur status, the United States equivalent of the French nouvelle vague directors of the late 1960. And he was happy. Then at age 30 commercial success intervened with *The Godfather* (1972), and the rest is history. That history has been varied and unique and was likely unavoidable, given Coppola's complexity as a person and an artist. His personal and artistic nature prescribed the unpredictability of his career at least as much as his early success. He had a love/hate relationship with the Hollywood film industry, revering the Golden Age of Hollywood and appreciating the moguls at the height of Hollywood's power. He would mention to his film school–generation colleagues, of whom he was the oldest, that he was the only one of his generation to have known Jack Warner, Samuel Goldwyn, Darryl Zanuck, and Adolph Zukor. He deemed it a meaningful link. He was moving forward, wet behind the ears, and they were in the twilight of their careers.

After honoring the art of cinema within the system with *The Godfather*, Parts I and II, *The Conversation*, and *Apocalypse Now*, he made the audacious move of establishing Zoetrope Studios with the intention of upholding the best from the Golden Age and modernizing its legacy with an innovative and technologically cutting-edge cinema system that would carry the art form to the next level. But by the 1980s the studios were "in name only" and were occupied by businessmen looking only to turn a fast profit in an era of double-digit percentage rates; the moguls were gone and the suits called the shots. There was no room for modest art films or trial and error. Risk for the sake of art was anathema. It was the age of the blockbuster and the sequel and films the audience recognized in the trailer because the themes were retreads. The financial bottom line was all-important.

In this environment Coppola was caught in the cross hairs. Zoetrope Studios failed in the short run, and Coppola deferred his artistic dreams to meet financial obligations to his family. Even in the long director-for-hire period that followed, Coppola the artist was unable to give *de minimus*; he committed the best he had to each venture. And when that was done, he built an empire of his own outside of the film industry so he could approach his life apart from corporate Hollywood. He endured the unimaginable—the death of his eldest son Gio. He glories in the success of his two filmmaking children, Roman and Sofia, who are personal filmmakers outside the reach of corporate Hollywood yet functioning in peaceful coexistence with the industry on their own terms. They have carried forward their father's legacy of innovation and are conversant and comfortable with the technology of the day. Eleanor and Francis have found a life-affirming rhythm after their many years together. Eleanor is traveling with her art installation, Circle of Memory. The Circle of Memory is installed in museums throughout the world as a memorial to her son Gian-Carlo and is an exhibit designed for healing and reflection. Eleanor is also deeply involved in the numerous ventures in which the Coppolas spend much of their time both in Napa and Belize. She has continued to write and in 2008 wrote *Notes on a Life*. In part Eleanor was prompted to write *Notes on a Life* after observing her elderly mother. For years her mother had written informal notes on index cards in early mornings but had never consolidated them. There were thousands of index cards, and although Eleanor encouraged her, she would say she would do it the next year. Her mother is now is very elderly and has dementia. Eleanor realized it would be meaningful for her own children to have the many snippets of her writing over the years, so she consolidated them for her children. The result was her journal, which covers a 30-year period.[2]

As for Francis Coppola, he is now creating a film every two years following his cardinal rules, and although by the calendar one might think it is time to slow down, there is no evidence that is the case. In 2011 Coppola wrote, directed, and produced *Twixt*, a horror thriller. The film was shot in and around California, partly on the Coppola estate. Coppola indicates its plot was the result of a dream/nightmare he had, which he used as the basis for the story. The dream seemed to Coppola reminiscent of Edgar Allan Poe, and so Poe appears as a character in the film. The main character is a writer whose career is not thriving. On a book tour he becomes involved in a murder investigation, and while he sleeps he believes a young ghost appears. The writer's role is played by actor Val Kilmer, and the youthful ghost is Elle Fanning, who acted in Sofia Coppola's film *Somewhere*. Bruce Dern, David Paymer, Tom Waits, and Alden Ehrenreich, Coppola's latest find from *Tetro*, also appear. The film has 3D sequences. Scenes from the movie previewed at Comic-Con in San Diego and at the Toronto International Film Festival. Coppola traveled with the film, presenting it with musical accompaniment from one of *Twixt*'s composers who is also a performance artist, Dan Deacon. The notion is to bring the film closer to live performance. It is an innovative approach for Coppola, designed to bring the audience into the experience of cinema. Always the showman, instead of 3D glasses he gave the viewers Edgar Allan Poe masks. Coppola has said that 3D isn't difficult anymore because of computer animation technology. The live audience participation is a fresh idea, and if ultimately it succeeds or fails, Coppola will be pleased to have explored it. Will there be more Coppola films? Perhaps next year, if he stays on cycle.

Coppola is using these experiences to learn more about the filmmaking process. Taking the long view, he reminds us that the moving picture industry is in its infancy and will continue to cycle and evolve. There is no pressure on Coppola to turn a profit as his films are self-financed and he knows the budget they can sustain. He is answering only to himself. He is, in fact, making films for himself and then hoping there is some audience that will enjoy them. It is an unusual situation. Most filmmakers, even those with stellar careers, find it more and more difficult to obtain financing for their projects as they get older. The studios are reluctant to invest. Coppola's status comes by virtue of his independent wealth, another circumstance he could not have foreseen during his post–Zoetrope Studio period of financial struggle and instability.

One quality Coppola possesses is accountability. He has made mistakes in his career and personal life, but he tries to clean things up. He does not regret any risks he has taken as he considers risk part of life's creative force. Regardless of its toll, which was mighty, Coppola is through and through an artist. This is his destiny, and he will forever apply his art to all his endeavors and share it to the utmost with the world around him. There is a generosity of spirit and a core belief that art will nourish the world. As Coppola reflects,

> You have to jump off a cliff. I don't think things through. I feel them through. And I know that half the time I might not land right, but in my life I have to say, that's served me well. When you're this old guy dying, you don't wanna say "I wish I had done that and that." In my case I did it. I did all the things other people would just regret that they didn't try. Because in the end, you die. You don't get any award for just being conservative.[3]

Coppola has always been on the cutting edge of technology. In high school one of his nicknames was "Science" because he could grasp the scientific-technological concept of invention. Coppola has tried to use the latest technological tools to make films. He used his Silverfish, video assist, and electronic (digital) cinema before the crowd. He ignored the snickers and watched as they became state of the art. He is not surprised to see the masses creating short films placed on YouTube for public consumption; he expected it and applauds it.

Coppola respects the many talented personal filmmakers of the current generation. He particularly admires those who work mightily for financing without compromising the quality of their cinematic art. In addition to Roman and Sofia, he frequently mentions David O. Russell, Alexander Payne, Wes Anderson, P. T. Anderson, Todd Solondz, and Tamara Jenkins. He invariably mentions Woody Allen!

Coppola has been responsible for the successful careers of countless actors. He has often cast inexperienced actors because seasoned professionals are out of reach financially. In other cases the project simply dictates it.

Between *The Outsiders* and *Rumble Fish* there is a long list of actors who appeared in their first film for Coppola or who were unknown until after the Coppola films. Coppola, working from his theater background, rehearsed with these inexperienced actors and elevated them, preparing them for long, illustrious careers. These include Diane Lane, Tom Cruise, Matt Dillon, Mickey Rourke, Emilio Estevez, the late Patrick Swayze, the late Chris Penn, Rob Lowe, Vincent Spano, Ralph Macchio, and Tom Waits.

James Caan and Robert Duvall acted under Coppola's direction from the earliest points in their careers. Undeniably, Coppola resurrected Marlon Brando's career and jump-started Al Pacino, Diane Keaton, and John Cazale. Teri Garr had her first nondancing role in *The Conversation*. Laurence Fishburne was 14 when he appeared in *Apocalypse Now*. Alden Ehrenreich appears bound for a positive career after Coppola cast him in *Tetro* and *Twixt*.

Coppola has a worldwide reach. He is interested in many cultures, loves Kabuki theater, and has traveled much of the globe attending film festivals in the farthest reaches and exploring the peoples and cultures of many lands.

Coppola has been the recipient of countless awards and honors. In addition to his Academy Awards for screenwriting, directing, and producing his own films, in 2010 the Academy of Motion Picture Arts and Sciences presented him with the Irving Thalberg Memorial award. The award is for lifetime achievement as a producer. In presenting the award to Coppola, George Lucas pointed out that Coppola was one of the first to embrace the whole digital change, which Lucas now called a revolution. He characterized Coppola as "truly the godfather of a generation who changed the course of motion picture history" and described him as an "innovator, artist, icon, and, most importantly, a rebel."[4]

The influence of Coppola on the art and craft of cinema is incalculable. His watch words have held him in good stead and ensured his legacy. Coppola has said that "the things you get fired for when you're young—the things that run against the grain, that are not common or logical, that don't fit into a standard approach—are the exact same things that you win lifetime achievement awards for when you're old."[5] In his 70s, one senses that Francis Coppola is at peace with himself. He wrote an entry in his journal on March 10, 1991, that seems to sum up his life view:

> Sunday afternoon in Rutherford, Napa Valley
>
> The sun shines on the green of my place,
> The lawn slopes,
> And the trees blow with blossoms . . .
>
> This is my home,
> And yet it is so perfect.
> How can I have something like this?
> Without worry
> Without fear of loss.
> It surprises me
> that my life is so lovely.[6]

Filmography

FRANCIS FORD COPPOLA

The Bellboy and the Playgirls (1962)

Defin Film, Rapid Film, Screen Rite Picture Company. Running time: 85 minutes. Director: Francis Ford Coppola. Screenplay: Francis Ford Coppola, Dieter Hildebrandt, Margh Malina. Producers: Wolf C. Hartwig, Harry Ross. Director of Photography: Paul Grupp. Editor: Jack Hill. Music: Klaus Ogermann. Cast: June Wilkinson, Don Kenney, Karin Dor, Willy Fritsch, Michael Cramer, Louise Lawson, Laura Cummings, Gigi Martine, Ann Perry, Jan Davidson, Loria Shea.

Tonight For Sure (1962)

Premier Pictures Company. Running time: 69 minutes. Director: Francis Ford Coppola. Screenplay: Francis Ford Coppola, Jerry Shaffer. Producers: Ray S. Adiel, Francis Ford Coppola. Director of Photography: Jack Hill. Editor: Ronald Waller. Sound: Gerry McKibben. Music: Carmine Coppola. Cast: Karl Schanzer (Benjamin Jabowski), Donald Kenney (Samuel Hill), Marli Renfor, Virginia Gordon, Barbara Martin, Linda Gibson, Sandy Silver, Pat Brooks, Electra, Exotica, Laura Cornell, Karen Lee, Sue Martin, Marcelino Espinose, Anita Danchick.

Dementia 13 (1963)

Filmgroup Productions. Running time: 75 minutes. Director: Francis Coppola. Screenplay: Francis Coppola. Producers: Roger Corman, Marianne Wood. Director of Photography: Charles Hanawalt. Art Direction: Albert Locatelli. Editors: Stuart O'Brien, Mort Tubor. Sound: Joseph Gross, Liam Saurin. Music: Ronald Stein. Cast: William Cambpell (Richard Haloran), Luana Anders (Louise Haloran), Bart Patton (Billy Haloran), Mary Mitchel

(Kane), Patrick Magee (Justin Caleb), Ethne Dunne (Lady Haloran), Peter Read (John Haloran), Karl Schanzer (Simon), Ron Perry (Arthur), Derry O'Donavan (Lilly), Barbara Dowling (Kathleen).

You're a Big Boy Now (1966)

Seven Art Productions. Running time: 96 minutes. Director: Francis Ford Coppola. Screenplay: Francis Ford Coppola based on the novel by David Benedictus. Producer: Phil Feldman. Director of Photography: Andrew Laslo. Art Direction: Vassele Fotopoulos. Editor: Aram Avakian. Costume Design: Theoni V. Aldredge. Sound Editor: Jean Begley. Sound Mixer: Jack Jacobsen. Sound Editor: Sanford Racklow. Sound Remixer: Dick Vorisek. Music: Robert Prince. Cast: Elizabeth Hartman (Barbara Darling), Geraldine Page (Margery Chanticleer), Peter Kastner (Bernard Chanticleer), Rip Torn (I. H. Chanticleer), Michael Dunn (Richard Mudd), Tony Bill (Raef del Grado), Julie Harris (Miss Nora Thing), Karen Black (Amy Partlett).

Finian's Rainbow (1968)

Warner Bros. Running time: 141 minutes. Director: Francis Ford Coppola. Screenplay and book: E. Y. Harburg, Fred Saidy. Producers: Joel Freeman, Joseph Landon. Director of Photography: Philip Lathrop. Production Design: Hilyard M. Brown. Editor: Melvin Shapiro. Costumes: Dorothy Jeakins. Sound: M. A. Merrick, Dan Wallin. Cast: Fred Astaire (Finian McLonergan), Petula Clark (Sharon McLonergan), Tommy Steele ("Og" the Leprechaun), Don Francks (Woody Mahoney), Keenan Wynn (Senator Billboard Rawkins), Barbara Hancock (Susan the Silent), Al Freeman Jr. (Howard), Ronald Colby (Buzz Collins), Dolph Sweet (Sheriff), Wright King (District Attorney), Louil Silas (Henry).

The Rain People (1969)

Warner Brothers/Seven Arts. Running time: 101 minutes. Director: Francis Ford Coppola. Screenplay: Francis Ford Coppola. Producers: Ronald Colby, George Lucas, Bart Patton, Mona Skager. Director of Photography: Bill Butler (Wilmer). Art Direction: Leon Erickson. Editor: Barry Malkin (Blackie). Sound: Nathan Boxer, Walter Murch, James Sabat. Music: Ronald Stein. Cast: James Caan (Jimmy Killgannon), Shirley Knight (Natalie Ravenna), Robert Duvall (Gordon), Mayra Zimmet (Rosalie), Tom Aldredge (Mr. Alfred), Laura Crews (Ellen), Andrew Duncan (Artie), Margaret Fairchild (Marion), Sally Gracie (Beth), Alan Manson (Lou), Robert Modica (Vinny Ravenna).

The Godfather (1972)

Paramount Pictures. Running time: 175 minutes Director: Francis Ford Coppola. Screenplay: Mario Puzo, Francis Ford Coppola from the novel by Mario Puzo. Producers: Gray Frederickson, Albert S. Ruddy, Robert Evans. Director of Photography: Gordon Willis. Production Design: Dean Tavoularis. Editor: William Reynolds, Peter Zinner. Costumes: Anna Hill Johnstone. Sound: Bud Grenzbach, Christopher Newman, Richard Portman. Music: Nino Rota. Cast: Marlon Brando (Don Vito Corleone), Al Pacino (Michael), James Caan (Sonny), Richard Castellano (Clemenza), Robert Duvall (Tom Hagen), Sterling Hayden (Capt. McCluskey), John Marley (Jack Woltz), Richard Conte (Barzini), Al Lettieri (Solozzo), Diane Keaton (Kay Adams), Abe Vigoda (Tessio), Talia Shire (Connie Corleone), Gianni Russo (Carlo), John Cazale (Fredo), Rudy Bond (Cuneo).

The Conversation (1974)

The Directors Company, The Coppola Company, American Zoetrope. Running time: 113 minutes. Director: Francis Ford Coppola. Screenplay: Francis Ford Coppola. Producers: Francis Ford Coppola, Fred Roos. Director of Photography: Bill Butler. Production Design: Dean Tavoularis. Costumes: Aggie Guerard Rodgers. Supervising Editor: Water Murch. Editor: Richard Chew. Sound Montage and Rerecording: Walter Murch. Music: David Shire. Cast: Gene Hackman (Harry Caul), John Cazale (Stan), Allen Garfield (Bernie Moran), Frederic Forrest (Mark), Cindy Williams (Ann), Michael Higgins (Paul), Elizabeth MacRae (Meredith), Teri Garr (Amy), Harrison Ford (Martin Stett), Mark Wheeler (Receptionist), Robert Shields (Mime), Phoebe Alexander (Lurleen).

The Godfather Part II (1974)

Paramount Pictures, The Coppola Company. Running time: 200 minutes. Director: Francis Ford Coppola. Screenplay: Francis Ford Coppola, Mario Puzo. Producer: Francis Ford Coppola. Director of Photography: Gordon Willis. Production Design: Dean Tavoularis. Costumes: Theodora Van Runkle. Editors: Richard Marks, Barry Malkin, Peter Zinner. Music: Nino Rota. Cast: Al Pacino (Michael), Robert Duvall (Tom Hagen), Diane Keaton (Kay), Robert De Niro (Vito Corleone), John Cazale (Fredo), Talia Shire (Connie Corleone), Lee Strasberg (Hyman Roth), Michael V. Gazzo (Frankie Pentangeli), G. D. Spradlin (Senator Pat Geary), Richard Bright (Al Neri), Gastone Moschin (Fanucci), Tom Rosqui (Rocco Lampone), Bruno Kirby (Young Clemenza), Frank Sivero (Genco), Francesca De Sapio (Young Mama Corleone).

Apocalypse Now (1979)

Zoetrope Studios. Running time: 153 minutes. Director: Francis Ford Coppola. Screenplay: Francis Ford Coppola, John Milius based on the novel *Heart of Darkness* by Joseph Conrad. Producers: Kim Aubry, Francis Coppola, Gray Frederickson. Director of Photography: Vittorio Storaro. Production Design: Dean Tavoularis. Editors: Lisa Fruchtman, Gerald B. Greenberg, Walter Murch. Music: Carmine Coppola, Francis Coppola. Cast: Marlon Brando (Col Walter E. Kurtz), Martin Sheen (Capt. Benjamin L. Willard), Robert Duvall (Lieutenant Col. Bill Kilgore), Frederic Forrest (Jay "Chef" Hicks), Sam Bottoms (Lance B. Johnson), Laurence Fishburne (Tyrone "Clean" Miller), Albert Hall (Chief Phillips), Harrison Ford (Col. Lucas), Dennis Hopper (Photojournalist), G. D. Spradlin (General Corman), Jerry Zeismer (Jerry, Civilian), Scott Glenn (Lieutenant Richard M. Colby), Bo Byers (MP Sgt #1), James Keane (Kilgore's Gunner), Kerry Rossall (Mike from San Diego).

One From the Heart (1982)

Zoetrope Studios. Running time 107 minutes. Director: Francis Ford Coppola. Screenplay: Armyan Bernstein, Francis Ford Coppola. Story: Armyan Bernstein. Producers: Kim Aubry, Armyan Bernstein, Francis Ford Coppola, Gray Frederickson, Fred Roos, Mona Skager. Director of Photography: Ronald V Garcia, Vittorio Storaro. Production Design: Dean Tavoularis. Editors: Rudi Fehr, Anne Goursaud, Randy Roberts. Costumes: Ruth Morley. Sound: Chris McLaughlin. Sound Design: Richard Beggs. Music: Tom Waits. Cast: Frederic Forrest (Hank), Teri Garr (Frannie), Raul Julia (Ray), Nastassia Kinski (Lella), Lannie Kazan (Maggie), Harry Dean Stanton (Moe), Allen Garfield (Restaurant Owner), Jeff Hamlin (Airline Ticket Agent), Italia Coppola (Couple in Elevator), Carmine Coppola (Couple in Elevator), Edward Blackoff (Understudy), James Dean (Understudy), Rebecca De Mornay (Understudy), Javier Grajeda (Understudy).

The Outsiders (1983)

Zoetrope Studios. Running time: 91 minutes. Director: Francis Ford Coppola. Screenplay: Kathleen Knutson Rowell based on the novel by S. E. Hinton. Producers: Kim Aubry, Gian-Carlo Coppola, Gray Frederickson, Fred Roos. Director of Photography: Stephan Burum. Production Design: Dean Tavoularis. Editor: Anne Goursand. Sound: Jim Webb. Sound Design: Richard Beggs. Music: Carmine Coppola. Cast: C. Thomas Howell (Ponyboy Curtis), Matt Dillon (Dallas Winston), Ralph Macchio (Johnny Cade), Patrick Swayze (Darrel Curtis), Rob Lowe (Sodapop Curtis), Emilio Estevez (Two-Bit Matthews), Tom Cruise (Steve Randle), Glenn Withrow

(Tim Shepard), Diane Lane (Cherry Valance), Leif Garrett (Bob Sheldon), Darren Dalton (Randy Anderson), Michelle Meyrink (Marcia).

Rumble Fish (1983)

Zoetrope Studios. Running time: 94 minutes. Director: Francis Ford Coppola. Screenplay: Francis Ford Coppola, S. E. Hinton based on her novel *Rumble Fish*. Producers: Doug Claybourne, Francis Ford Coppola, Gian-Carlo Coppola, Roman Coppola, Fred Roos. Director of Photography: Stephen H. Burum. Production Design: Dean Tavoularis. Editor: Barry Malkin. Costumes: Marjorie Bowers. Sound: David Parker. Sound Designer: Richard Beggs. Music: Stewart Copeland. Cast: Matt Dillon (Rusty James), Mickey Rourke (The Motorcycle Boy), Diane Lane (Patty), Dennis Hopper (Father), Daiana Scarwid (Cassandra, Vincent Spano (Steve), Nicholas Cage (Smokey), Chris Penn (B. J. Jackson), Laurence Fishburne (Midget), William Smith (Patterson the Cop), Michael Higgins (Mr. Harrigan), Glenn Withrow (Bill Wilcox), Tom Waits (Benny), Sofia Coppola (Donna), Gian-Carlo Coppola (Cousin James), S. E. Hinton (Hooker on Strip).

The Cotton Club (1984)

Zoetrope Studios. Running time: 127 minutes. Director: Francis Coppola. Screenplay: William Kennedy, Francis Coppola, Mario Puzo from a novel by James Haskins. Producers: Robert Evans, Dyson Lovell. Director of Photography: Stephen Goldblatt. Production Design: Richard Sylbert. Costumes: Milena Canonero. Editors: Robert Q. Lovett, Barry Malkin. Sound: Richard Beggs, Edward Byers. Music: John Barry. Cast: Richard Gere (Dixie Dwyer), Gregory Hines (Sandman Williams), Diane Lane (Vera Cicero), Lonette McKee (Lila Rose Oliver), Bob Hoskins (Owney Madden), James Remar (Dutch Schultz), Nicolas Cage (Vincent Dwyer), Allen Garfield (Abbadabba Berman), Fred Gwynne (Frenchy Demange), Gwen Verdon (Tish Dwyer), Lisa Jane Persky (Frances Flegenheimer), Maurice Hines (Clay Williams), Julian Beck (Sol Weinstein), Novella Nelson (Madame St. Clair), Laurence Fishburne (Bumpy Rhodes), John P. Ryan (Joe Flynn), Tom Waits (Irving Stark), Ron Karabatsos (Mike Best), Glenn Withrow (Ed Popke), Jennifer Grey (Patsy Dwyer).

Peggy Sue Got Married (1986)

TriStar Pictures, Rastar Pictures, Zoetrope Studios. Running time: 103 minutes. Director: Francis Ford Coppola. Screenplay: Jerry Lelchling, Arlene Sarner. Producers: Paul R Gurian, Barrie M. Osborne. Director of Photography: Jordan Cronenweth. Production Design: Dean Tavoularis. Costumes: Theodora Van Runkle. Editor: Barry Malkin. Sound: Richard Bryce Goodman. Music: John Barry. Cast: Kathleen Turner (Peggy Sue),

Nicolas Cage (Charlie Bodell), Barry Miller (Richard Norvik), Catherine Hicks (Carol Heath), Joan Allen (Maddy Nagle), Kevin J. O'Connor (Michael Fitzsimmons), Jim Carrey (Walter Getz), Lisa Jane Persky (Delores Dodge), Lucinda Jenney (Rosalie Testa), Wil Shriner (Arthur Nagle), Barbara Harris (Evelyn Kelcher), Don Murray (Jack Kelcher), Sofia Coppola (Nancy Kelcher), Maureen O'Sullivan (Elizabeth Alvorg).

Gardens of Stone (1987)

TriStar Pictures, Zoetrope Studios. Running time: 111 minutes. Director: Francis Ford Coppola. Screenplay: Ronald Bass based on the novel by Nicholas Profitt. Producers: Francis Ford Coppola, Jay Emmett, Michael l. Levy, Fred Roos, David Valdes, Stan Weston. Director of Photography: Jordan Cronenweth. Production Design: Dean Tavoularis. Costumes: Willa Kim, Judianne Makovsky. Editor: Barry Malkin. Sound: Thomas Causey. Sound Design: Richard Beggs. Music: Carmine Coppola. Cast: James Caan (Sgt. Clell Hazard), Anjelica Huston (Samantha Davis), James Earl Jones (Sgt. Maj. "Goody" Nelson), D. B. Sweeney (Jackie Willow), Dean Stockwell (Capt. Homer Thomas), Mary Stuart Masterson (Rachel Feld), Dick Anthony Williams (Slasher Williams), Lonette McKee (Betty Rae), Sam Bottoms (Lt. Webber), Elias Koteas (Pete Deveber), Laurence Fishburne (Sgt. Flanagan), Casey Siemaszho (Wildman), Peter Masterson (Col. Feld), Carlin Glynn (Mrs. Feld).

Tucker: The Man and His Dream (1988)

Lucasfilm. Running time: 110 minutes. Director: Francis Ford Coppola. Screenplay: Arnold Schulman, David Seidler. Producers: George Lucas, Fred Roos, Fred Fuchs. Director of Photography: Vittorio Storaro. Production Design: Dean Tavoularis. Costumes: Milena Canonero. Editor: Priscilla Nedd-Friendly. Sound: Gloria S. Borders, Richard Beggs. Music: Joe Jackson. Cast: Jeff Bridges (Preston Tucker), Joan Allen (Vera Tucker), Martin Landau (Abe), Frederic Forrest (Eddie), Mako (Jimmy), Elias Koteas (Alex Tremulis), Christian Slater (Junior), Nina Siemaszko (Marilyn Lee), Anders Johnson (Johnny), Corin Nemec (Noble Tucker), Marshall Bell (Frank), Jay O. Sanders (Kirby), Peter Doant (Otto Kemer), Dean Goodman (Bennington), John X. Heart (Ferguson's Agent), Don Novello (Stan), Patti Austin (Millie), Sandy Bull (Stan's Assistant), Joe Miksak (Judge Igoe), Scott Beach (Floyd Cerf), Roland Scrivner (Oscar Beasley), Dean Stockwell (Howard Hughes), Bob Stafford (Narrator).

New York Stories: Segment: Life without Zoe (1989)

Touchstone Pictures. Director: Francis Ford Coppola. Screenplay: Francis Ford Coppola, Sofia Coppola. Producer: Fred Fuchs, Fred Roos. Director of

Photography: Vittorio Storaro. Production Design: Dean Tavoularis. Costumes: Sofia Coppola. Sound: Dan Sable, Lee Dichter, Michael Kirschberger. Editor: Barry Malkin. Music: Carmine Coppola. Cast: Paul Herman (Doorman), Heather McComb (Zoe), Talia Shire (Charlotte), Gia Coppola (Baby Zoe), Giancarlo Giannini (Claudio), James Keane (Jimmy), Don Novello (Hector), Bill Moor (Mr. Lily), Tom Mardirsian (Hasid), Jenny Nichols (Lundy), Gina Scianni (Devo), Diane Lin Cosman (Margit), Selim Tilli (Abu), Robin Wood-Chapelle (Gel), Celia Nestelle (Hillary), Alexandra Becker (Andrea), Adrien Brody (Mel), Michael Higgins (Robber), Chris Elliott (Robber), Thelma Carpenter (Maid), Carmine Coppola (Street Musician), Carole Bouquet (Princess Saroya), Jo Jo Starbuck (Ice Skater).

The Godfather Part III (1990)

Paramount Pictures, Zoetrope Studios. Running time: 162 minutes. Director: Francis Ford Coppola. Screenplay: Mario Puzo, Francis Ford Coppola. Producers: Francis Ford Coppola, Gray Frederickson, Fred Fuchs, Nicholas Gage, Marina Gefter, Charles Mulvehill, Fred Roos. Director of Photography: Gordon Willis. Production Design: Dean Tavoularis. Editors: Lisa Fruchtman, Barry Malkin, Walter Murch. Costumes: Milena Canonero. Sound Design: Richard Beggs. Music: Carmine Coppola. Cast: Al Pacino (Don Michael Corleone), Diane Keaton (Kay Adams Michelson), Talia Shire (Connie Corleone Rizzi), Andy Garcia (Vincent Mancini), Eli Wallach (Don Altobello), Joe Mantegna (Joey Zaza), George Hamilton (B. J. Harrison), Bridget Fonda (Grace Hamilton), Sofia Coppola (Mary Corleone).

Bram Stoker's Dracula (1992)

American Zoetrope, Columbia Pictures. Running time: 128 minutes. Director: Francis Ford Coppola. Screenplay: James V. Hart based on the novel *Dracula* by Bram Stoker. Producers: Michael Apted, Francis Ford Coppola, Susie Landau, Fred Fuchs, James V. Hart, Charles Mulvehill, Robert O'Connor, John Veitch. Director of Photography: Michael Ballhaus. Production Design: Thomas Sanders. Editors: Anne Goursaud, Glen Scantlebury, Nicholas C. Smith. Costumes: Eiko Ishioka. Sound: Robert Janiger. Sound Design: Lelie Shatz. Music: Wojciech Kilar. Cast: Gary Oldman (Dracula), Winona Ryder (Mina Murray/Elisabeta), Anthony Hopkins (Professor Abraham Van Helsing), Keanu Reeves (Jonathan Harker), Richard E. Grant (Dr. Jack Seward), Cary Elwes (Lord Arthur Holmwood), Billy Cambell (Quincy P. Morris), Sadie Frost (Lucy Westenra), Tom Waits (R. M. Renfield), Monica Bellucci (Dracula's Bride), Michaela Bercu (Dracula's Bride), Florina Kendrick (Dracula's Bride).

Jack (1996)

American Zoetrope, Hollywood Pictures. Running time: 113 minutes. Director: Francis Ford Coppola. Screenplay: James DeMonaco, Gary Nadeau. Producers: Doug Claybourne, Francis Ford Coppola, Fred Fuchs, Ricardo Mestres. Director of Photography: John Toll. Production Design: Dean Tavoularis. Editor: Barry Malkin. Costumes: Aggie Guerard Rodgers. Sound: Agamemmnon Andrianos. Music: Michael Kamen. Cast: Robin Williams (Jack Powell), Diane Lane (Karen Powell), Brian Kerwin (Brian Powell), Jennifer Lopez (Miss Marquez), Bill Cosby (Lawrence Woodruff), Fran Drescher (Delores "D.D." Durante), Adam Zolotin (Louis "Louie" Durante), Todd Bosley (Eddie), Seth Smith (John John), Mario Yedidia (George), Jeremy Lelliott (Johnny duffer).

The Rainmaker (1997)

Constellation Entertainment, Douglas/Reuther Productions, American Zoetrope. Running time: 135 minutes. Director: Francis Ford Coppola. Screenplay: Francis Ford Coppola based on the novel by John Grisham. Narration: Michael Herr. Producers: Michael Douglas, Fred Fuchs, Gerogia Kacandes, Gary Scott Marcus, Steven Reuther. Director of Photography: John Toll. Production Design: Howard Cumnmings. Editors: Melissa Kent, Barry Malkin. Costumes: Aggie Guerard Rodgers. Music: Elmer Bernstein. Cast: Matt Damon (Rudy Baylor), Danny DeVito (Deck Shifflet), Claire Danes (Kelly Riker), Jon Voight (Leo F. Drummond), Mary Kay Place (Dot Black), Dean Stockwell (Judge Harvey Hale), Teresa Wright (Colleen "Miss Birdie" Birdsong), Virginia Madsen (Jackie Lemancyzk), Mickey Rourke (Bruiser Stone), Andrew Shue (Cliff Riker), Red West (Buddy Black), Johnny Whitworth (Donny Ray Black).

Youth without Youth (2007)

American Zoetrope. Running time: 124 minutes. Director: Francis Ford Coppola. Screenplay: Francis Ford Coppola based on the novella by Mircea Eliade. Producers: Francis Ford Coppola, Anahid Nazarian, Fred Roos, Masa Tsuyuki. Director of Photography: Mihai Malaimare Jr. Production Design: Calin Papura. Editor: Walter Murch. Costumes: Gloria Papura. Music: Osvaldo Golijoy. Cast: Tim Roth (Dominic), Alexandra Maria Lara (Vernonic/Laura), Bruno Ganz (Professor Standlulescu), Andre Hennicke (Josef Rudolf), Marcel Jures (Pro. Giuseppe Tucci), Adrian Pintea (Pandit), Alexandra Pirici (Woman in Room 6), Florin Piersic Jr. (Dr. Gavrla), Zoltan Butuc (Dr. Chrila).

Tetro (2009)

American Zoetrope. Running time: 127 minutes. Director: Francis Ford Coppola. Screenplay: Francis Ford Coppola based on *Versa Fausta* by Mauricio Kartun. Producers: Marlela Besuievsky, Francis Ford Coppola, Valerio Di Paolis, Gerardo Heirero, Anahid Nazarian, Fred Roos, Masa Tsuyuki. Director of Photography: Mihai Malaimare Jr. Production Design: Sebastain Orgambide. Editor: Walter Murch. Costumes: Cecila Monti. Sound: Leandro de Loredo. Music: Osvaldo Goljoy. Cast: Vincent Gallo (Angelo "Tetro" Tetrocini), Alden Ehrenreich (Bennie), Maribel Verdú (Miranda), Silvia Perez (Silvana), Rodrigo De la Serna (Jose), Erica Rivas (Ana), Mike Amigorena (Abelardo), Lucas Di Conza (Young Tetro), Adriana Mastrangelo (Angela), Klaus Maria Brandauer (Carlo/Alfie Tetrocini), Sofia Gala (Maria Luisa), Jean-Francois Cassanovas (Enrique), Carmen Maura (Alone), Francesca De Sapio (Amalia).

Twixt (2011)

American Zoetrope. Running time: 90 minutes. Director: Francis Ford Coppola. Screenplay: Francis Ford Coppola. Producers: Francis Ford Coppola, Josh Griffith, Jim Hays, Anahid Nazarian, Fred Roos, Masa Tsuyuki. Director of Photography: Mihai Malaimare Jr. Editors: Kevin Bailey, Glen Scantlebury, Robert Schafer. Costumes: Marjorie Bowers. Sound Design: Richard Beggs. Music: Dan Deacon, Osvaldo Golijov. Cast: Val Kilmer (Hall Baltimore), Bruce Dern (Bobby LaGrange), Ben Chaplin (Edgar Allan Poe), Elle Fanning (V), Joanne Whalley (Denise), David Paymer (Sam Malkin), Alden Ehrenreich (Flamingo), Anthony Fusco (Pastor Allan Floyd), Don Novello (Melvin), Ryan Simpkins (Carolyne).

SOFIA COPPOLA

The Virgin Suicides (2000)

American Zoetrope. Running time: 97 minutes. Director: Sofia Coppola. Screenplay: Sofia Coppola based on the novel by Jeffrey Eugenides. Producers: Willi Baer, Suzanne Colvin, Francis Ford Coppola, Julie Costanzo, Fred Fuchs, Jordan Gertner, Dan Halsted, Chris Hanley, Gary Marcus, Fred Roos. Director of Photography: Edward Lachman. Production Design: Jasna Stefanovic. Editors: Melissa Kent, James Lyons. Costumes: Nancy Steiner. Sound: Felipe Borreto. Sound Design: Richard Beggs. Music: Air. Cast: James Woods (Ronald Lisbon), Kathleen Turner (Mrs. Lisbon), Kirsten Dunst (Lux Lisbon), Josh Harnett (Trip Fontaine), Michael Pare (Adult Trip Fontaine), Scott Glenn (Father Moody), Danny DeVito (Dr. Horniker), A. J. Cook (Mary Lisbon), Hanna Hall (Cecilia Lisbon), Leslie

Hayman (Therese Lisbon), Chelse Swain (Bonnie Lisbon), Anthony Desimone (Chase Buell), Lee Kagan (David Barker), Robert Schwartzman (Paul Baldino), Noah Shebib (Parkie Denton), Giovanni Ribisi (Narrator).

Lost in Translation (2003)

Focus Features, Tohokashinsha Film Company, American Zoetrope. Running time: 104 minutes. Director: Sofia Coppola. Screenplay: Sofia Coppola. Producers: Francis Ford Coppola, Mitch Glazer, Callum Green, Kiyoshi Inoue, Ross Katz, Fred Roos, Stephen Schible. Director of Photography: Lance Acord. Production Design: K. K. Barrett, Anne Ross. Editor: Sarah Flack. Costumes: Nancy Steiner. Sound: Drew Kunin. Sound Design: Richard Beggs. Music: Kevin Shields. Cast: Scarlett Johansson (Charlotte), Bill Murray (Bob Harris), Akiko Takeshita (Ms. Kawasaki), Kazuyoshi Minamimagoe (Press Agent), Kazuko Shibata (Press Agent), Take (Press Agent), Ryuichiro Baba (Concierge), Akira Yamaguchi (Bellboy), Catherine Lambert (Jazz Singer), Francois du Bois (Sausalito Piano), Tim Leffman (Sausalito Guitar), Gregory Pekar (American Businessman #1), Richard Allen (American Businessman #2), Giovanni Ribisi (John), Yutaka Tadokoro (Commercial Director).

Marie Antoinette (2006)

Columbia, American Zoetrope. Running time: 123 minutes. Director: Sofia Coppola. Screenplay: Sofia Coppola. Producers: Francis Ford Coppola, Sofia Coppola, Callum Greene, Ross Katz, Christine Raspillere, Paull Rassam, Fred Roos. Director of Photography: Lance Acord. Production Design: K. K. Barrett. Editor: Sarah Flack. Costumes: Milena Canonero. Sound: Stuart Wilson. Sound Design: Richard Beggs. Cast: Kirsten Dunst (Marie Antoinette), Jason Schwartzman (Louis XVI), Judy Davis (Comtesse de Noailles), Rip Torn (Louis XV), Rose Byrne (Duchessa de Polignac), Asia Argento (Comtessa du Barry), Molly Shannon (Aunt Victoire), Shirley Henderson (Aunt Sophie), Danny Huston (Emperor Joseph II), Marianne Faithfull (Empress Maria Thersea), Mary Nighy (Princess Lamballe), Sebastian Armesto (Comte Louis de Provence), Jamie Doman (Count Axel Fersen), Aurore Clemente (Duchesse de Char), Guillaume Gallienne (Vergennes).

Somewhere (2010)

Focus Features, American Zoetrope. Running time: 97 minutes. Director: Sofia Coppola. Screenplay: Sofia Coppola. Producers: Michele Anzalone, G. Mac Brown, Francis Ford Coppola, Roman Coppola, Sofia Coppola, Youree Henley, Paul Rassam, Fred Roos, Roberta Senesi, Jordan Stone. Director of

Photography: Harris Savides. Production Design: Anne Ross. Editor: Sarah Flack. Costumes: Stacey Battat. Sound: Susumu Tokunow. Sound Design: Richard Beggs. Music: Phoenix. Cast: Stephen Dorff (Johnny Marco), Chris Pontius (Sammy), Erin Wasson (Party Girl #1), Alexandra Williams (Party Girl # 2), Nathalie Fay (Party Girl #3), Kristina Shannon (Bambi), Karissa Shannon (Cindy), John Prudhont (Chateau Patio Waiter), Ruby Copley (Chateau Patio Girl), Angela Lindvall (Blonde in Mercedes), Meryna Linchuck (Vampire Model), Meghan Collison (Vampire Model), Jessica Miller (Vampire Model), Elle Fanning (Cleo), Lala Sloatman (Layla).

Notes

CHAPTER 1

1. Francis Coppola's maternal grandfather was Francesco Pennino (his namesake).
2. *Academy of Achievement*, June 17, 1994. www.achievement.org.
3. Peter Cowie, *Coppola* (New York: Da Capo Press, 1994), 18.
4. Ibid., 22.

CHAPTER 2

1. Vincent LoBrutto, *By Design: Interviews with Film Production Designers* (Westport, CT: Praeger, 1992), 261.
2. The novel was written by David Benedictus in 1963 and optioned by Coppola.
3. Michael Goodwin and Naomi Wise, *On the Edge: The Life & Times of Francis Coppola* (New York: Morrow, 1989), 64.
4. Ibid., 69.
5. Ibid., 67.
6. Michael Schumacher, *Francis Ford Coppola: A Filmmaker's Life* (New York: Crown, 1999), 47.

CHAPTER 3

1. Peter Cowie, *Coppola* (New York: Da Capo Press, 1994), 39.
2. The aspect ratio is a measurement of the camera film frame or the projected image stated as ratio of horizontal to vertical.
3. LeRoi Jones (1934–), now known as Amiri Baraka. American poet, teacher, and activist.
4. Sanford Meisner (1905–1997), American actor and acting teacher. Developed a form of method acting known as the Meisner Technique.
5. Dennis Schaefer and Larry Salvato, *Masters of Light: Conversations with Contemporary Cinematographers* (Berkeley: University of California Press, 1984), 88.
6. Michael Goodwin and Naomi Wise, *On the Edge: The Life & Times of Francis Coppola* (New York: William Morrow and Company, 1989).

CHAPTER 4

1. Michael Schumacher, *Francis Ford Coppola: A Filmmaker's Life* (New York: Crown, 1999), 80.
2. Michael Goodwin and Naomi Wise, *On the Edge: The Life & Times of Francis Coppola* (New York: William Morrow and Company, 1989), 114.
3. Schumacher, 97.
4. Patricia Bosworth, *Marlon Brando* (New York: Penguin, Lipper/Viking, 2001), 172.
5. Vincent LoBrutto, *Principal Photography: Interviews with Feature Film Cinematographers* (Westport, CT: Praeger, 1994), 88–89.
6. Vincent LoBrutto, *Selected Takes: Film Editors on Editing* (Westport, CT: Praeger, 1991), 21.
7. Alex Simon, "Talia Shire Remembers the Family Business," *The Hollywood Interview*, September 22, 2008.
8. Michael Goodwin and Naomi Wise, *On the Edge: The Life & Times of Francis Coppola* (New York: William Morrow and Company, 1989), 143.
9. Gerald Peary, *American Movie Classics Magazine*. Fall 2000.
10. Vincent LoBrutto, *Sound on Film: Interviews with the Creators of Film Sound* (Westport, CT: Praeger, 1994), 90.
11. Ibid., 90.
12. Stephen Randall and the editors of *Playboy Magazine*, eds. *The Playboy Interviews: The Directors* (Milwaukee WI: M Press, 2006), 86.
13. Stephen Randall and the editors of *Playboy Magazine*, eds. *The Playboy Interviews: The Directors* (Milwaukee, WI: M Press, 2006), 84.
14. Alex Simon, "Talia Shire Remembers the Family Business," *The Hollywood Interview*, September 22, 2008.
15. Stephen Randall and the editors of *Playboy Magazine*, eds. *The Playboy Interviews: The Directors* (Milwaukee, WI: M Press, 2006), 84.
16. Vincent LoBrutto, *Principal Photography: Interviews with Feature Film Cinematographers* (Westport, CT: Praeger, 1994), 26–27.
17. Ibid.
18. Ibid.
19. As quoted in "The Only One Here, Robert De Niro's Unforgettable Characters: *The Godfather Part II* (1974)," Focus Features, February 13, 2012. www.focusfeatures.com.
20. Academy Award ceremony, 1975. Francis Coppola, accepting Best Supporting Actor Oscar for *The Godfather Part II* on Robert De Niro's behalf.
21. David Thompson, *Have You Seen?* (New York: Knopf, 2008), 328.

CHAPTER 5

1. Michael Goodwin and Naomi Wise, *On The Edge: The Life and Times of Francis Coppola* (New York: William Morrow and Company, 1989), 200.
2. Stephen Farber and Marc Green, *Hollywood Dynasties* (New York: Fawcett Crest, 1984). 337.
3. Ibid., 360.
4. Ibid., 361.

5. Peter Cowie, *The Apocalypse Now Book* (New York: Da Capo, 2001), 11–12.
6. Ibid., 15.
7. John Boorman and Walter Donohue, eds. *Projections 6: A Journey into Light* (London: Faber and Faber, 1996), 255.
8. Michael Herr is the author of *Dispatches*, concerning his experiences during the Vietnam War. He was involved in writing Willard's voiceover in *Apocalypse Now*. He later collaborated with director Stanley Kubrick on the Vietnam film *Full Metal Jacket*.
9. Vincent LoBrutto, *Selected Takes: Film Editors on Editing* (Westport, CT: Praeger, 1991), 184.
10. "*Apocalypse Now* (1979)," www.imdbpro.com.
11. Milton Glaser: Francis Ford Coppola commissioned renowned graphic designer Milton Glaser to design a "theater-like" playbill so *Apocalypse Now* could, in its initial presentation, be run without head or tail credits.
12. *Apocalypse Now* playbill including Francis Ford Coppola statement. Authors attended screening in August 1979 where playbills were distributed.

CHAPTER 6

1. Neal Gabler, *An Empire of Their Own: How the Jews Invented Hollywood* (New York: Anchor Books, 1989).
2. Cameron Bailey, "A Conversation with Francis Ford Coppola 2011," Toronto International Festival, September 10, 2001.
3. Italian Neorealism: A post–World War II film movement active in Italy from 1944 through 1953 with a moral and stylistic commitment to realism.
4. Thomas Schatz, *The Genius of the System: Hollywood Filmmaking in the Studio Era* (New York: Pantheon Books, 1988).
5. Carmine Coppola, page 3 from *Napoleon* playbill, 1981.
6. Triptych: three separate motion picture screened aligned and attached to create a wide screen image.
7. Tom Luddy is a San Francisco film curator and archivist who screened hard-to-see films for public view. One of the original partners of the Telluride Film Festival.
8. Michael Schumacher, *Francis Ford Coppola: A Filmmaker's Life* (New York: Crown Publishers, 1999), 183.
9. Jon Lewis, *Whom God Wishes to Destroy: Francis Coppola and the New Hollywood* (Durham, NC: Duke University Press, 1997), 52–54.
10. Peter Cowie, *Coppola* (New York: Da Capo Press, 1994), 148.
11. Jon Lewis, *Whom God Wishes...*, 40.
12. imdbpro.com, "*One From the Heart* Budget (estimated)."
13. "The Conversation: Francis Coppola & Gay Talese," *Esquire*, July 1981, 78.

CHAPTER 7

1. Vincent LoBrutto, *Selected Takes: Film Editors on Editing* (Westport, CT: Praeger, 1991), 35.
2. Michael Goodwin and Naomi Wise, *On the Edge: The Life & Times of Francis Coppola* (New York: William Morrow and Company, 1989), 276.

3. Edward Lewis, "Wim Wenders Discusses Painful 'Hammett' Collaboration with Coppola." *The Playlist*, October 22, 2011.
4. Aljean Harmetz, "Making 'The Outsiders': A Librarian's Dream," *New York Times*, March 23, 1983.
5. Manohla Dargis, "Coppola Pays a Return Visit to His *Gone with the Wind* for Teenagers," *New York Times*, September 9, 2005.
6. David Denby, *New York Magazine*, 1983.
7. Robert Sellers, *Hollywood Hellraisers* (New York: Skyhorse Publishing), 219.

CHAPTER 8

1. Michael Schumacher, *Francis Ford Coppola: A Filmmaker's Life* (New York: Crown Publishers, 1999). 339.
2. David Thomson and Lucy Gray, "Idols of the King," *Film Comment* 19 (September–October 1983), reprinted in Gene D. Phillips and Rodney Hill (eds.), *Francis Ford Coppola Interviews* (Jackson: University of Mississippi Press, 2004).
3. Vincent LoBrutto, *Principal Photography: Interviews with Feature Film Cinematographers* (Westport, CT: Praeger, 1999), 23.
4. Schumacher, 349.
5. Alex Simon, "Interview Robert Evans," *The Hollywood Interview*, January 6, 2008, http://thehollywoodinterview.blogspot.com/2008/01/robert-evans-hollywood-interview.html.
6. Schumacher, 372.
7. Peter Cowie, *Coppola* (New York: Da Capo Press, 1994), 196–97.
8. Alex Simon, "Nicolas Cage: Bad to the Bone," *The Hollywood Interview*, December 1, 2009.
9. Ibid.
10. Schumacher, 377.
11. Schumacher, 387.
12. William Plummer, "Two Months after Boating Accident Griffin O'Neal Is Indicted in the Death of Friend Gio Coppola," *People* 26, no. 6 (August 11, 1986).
13. "Behind the Scenes with America's Great Filmmaking Clan," *The Independent*, August 10, 2008; Eleanor Coppola, *Notes* entry, May 29, 1986.
14. Peter Keough, "Coppola Carves a Cinematic Elegy: *Gardens of Stone*," *Chicago Sun Times*, May 10, 1987.
15. Dave Kehr, "Coppola's 'Garden' Too Solemn to Grow on You," *Chicago Tribune*, May 6, 1987.
16. Harlan Jacobson, "Vintage Coppola." *Film Comment*, January/February 2008, 21.

CHAPTER 9

1. Michael Goodwin and Naomi Wise, *On the Edge: The Life & Times of Francis Coppola* (New York: William Morrow and Company, 1989), 418.
2. Robert Lindsey, *New York Times Magazine*, July 24, 1988, 139.
3. Michael Schumacher, *Francis Ford Coppola: A Filmmaker's Life* (New York: Crown Publishers, 1999), 398.

4. Peter Travers, "Picks and Pans Review: Tucker," *People* 30, no. 8 (August 22, 1988).

5. Robert Lindsey, *New York Times Magazine*, July 24, 1988, 139.

6. John Boorman and Walter Donohue (eds.), "Martin Scorsese," in *Projections 11: Film-makers on Film-Making* (London: Faber & Faber, 2000), 60.

7. Guy Garcia, "The Next Don?" *American Film*, December 1990, 28.

8. John Boorman and Walter Donohue (eds.), *Projections 6: Film-makers on Film-Making* (London: Faber & Faber, 1996), 50.

9. Lynn Hirschberg, "The Coppola Smart Mob," *New York Times,* August 31, 2003.

10. John Boorman and Walter Donohue (eds.), *Projections 6: Film-makers on Film-Making* (London: Faber & Faber, 1996), 61.

11. imdbpro.com, "*The Godfather Part III* Business: Gross Worldwide Copyright 1990–2012."

12. "Coppola Files for Bankruptcy," *New York Times*, July 2, 1992.

13. John Boorman and Walter Donohue (eds.), *Projections 3: Film-makers on Film-Making* (London: Faber & Faber, 1994), 10.

14. Ibid., 17.

15. Michael Feeney Callan, *Anthony Hopkins: The Unauthorized Biography* (New York: Charles Scribner's, 1993), 320.

16. John Boorman and Walter Donohue (eds.), *Projections 6: Film-makers on Film-Making* (London: Faber & Faber, 1996), 60.

17. John Boorman and Walter Donohue (eds.), *Projections 3: Film-makers on Film-Making* (London: Faber & Faber, 1994), 38.

18. www.imdbpro.com, "*Bram Stoker's Dracula* 1993 Worldwide."

CHAPTER 10

1. Stephen Farber and Marc Green, *Hollywood Dynasties* (New York: Fawcett Crest, 1984), 373.

2. Patrick Goldstein, "Great Harlot's Ghost!: 1,334 Pages Too Much? Mailer's CIA Novel Is Coppola's Movie by Milius," *Los Angeles Times*, December 15, 1991.

3. Michael Schumacher, *Francis Ford Coppola: A Filmmaker's Life* (New York: Three Rivers Press, 2001), 462–63.

4. Ibid., 470.

5. John Boorman and Walter Donohue (eds.), *Projections 3: Film-makers on Film-Making* (London: Faber & Faber, 1994).

CHAPTER 11

1. "Storytelling—All Story," *Zoetrope: All-Story*, n.d. http://www.all-story.com/.

2. Thane Peterson, "A Conversation with Francis Ford Coppola." *Bloomberg Businessweek*, September 12, 2000.

3. Andrew Durham is a successful photographer working in commercial advertising for such accounts as *Details* magazine, *Elle*, *Interview*, *The New York Times*, *Time Out*, and Louis Vuitton.

4. As quoted in "Milkfed," *I Want to Be a Coppola*, August, 13, 2011, http://www.iwanttobeacoppola.com/sofia-coppola-favorites.

5. *The Jon Stewart Show*, February 2, 2005.
6. Sarah Cristobal, "A monthly look at the faces that have made history: Sofia Coppola," Style.com.
7. "Reviews: *Being John Malkovich*," *Film Quarterly* 56, no. 1 (Fall 2002).
8. Ethan Smith, "Spike Jonze Unmasked," *New York Magazine–Metro*, http:// nymag.com/nymetro/movies/features/1267/.
9. Eleanor Coppola, *Virgin Suicides*, DVD documentary/featurette.

CHAPTER 12

1. Sofia Coppola was born during the making of *The Godfather* and just weeks after was shown as Connie's newborn baby boy in the pivotal baptism scene.
2. John Boorman and Walter Donohue (eds.), *Projections 6: Film-makers on Film-Making* (London: Faber & Faber, 1996), 61.
3. Karen Valby, "Fresh Heir: By Following in Her Father's Footsteps, a Young Filmmaker Finds Her Own Way," *Entertainment Weekly*, October 3, 2003, 51.
4. Stephanie Hayman, a close friend from high school, cowrote the short.
5. The themes were similar, involving high school girls being bullied.
6. Bill Owens, California photographer; born 1938; received Guggenheim fellowship and NEA grants; known for photographs of domestic scenes.
7. "Q & A Cinematographer Ed Lachman," *AMC Film Critic*, May 2008, www .filmcritic.com.
8. "*The Virgin Suicides*: Production Notes," *Cinema Review*, www.cinemareview .com.
9. James Lyons (1960–2007), film editor known for Todd Haynes's films *Far from Heaven* and *Safe*.
10. "*The Virgin Suicides*: The Music," *Cinema Review*, www.cinemareview.com.
11. *The Virgin Suicides*, DVD featurette.
12. Ibid.
13. Sofia played Nancy, a bratty sister in *Peggy Sue Got Married*, directed by her father and starring Kathleen Turner and her cousin Nicolas Cage.
14. "*The Virgin Suicides*: The Cast," *Cinema Review*, www.cinemareview.com.
15. Ibid.

CHAPTER 13

1. John Boorman and Walter Donohue (eds.), *Projections 6: Film-makers on Film-Making* (London: Faber & Faber, 1996), 53.
2. J. J. Martin, "A Fashionable Life: Jacqui Getty," *Harper's Bazaar*, May 1, 2007, harpersbazaar.com.
3. Frank Bruni, "The Way We Live Now: Family Album: In the Name of the Father," *New York Times*, May 19, 2002, 2.
4. "What I've Learned—Francis Ford Coppola Interview," *Esquire*, August 2009, www.esquire.com.
5. www.film4.com, "Producer Kim Aubry: *Apocalypse Now Redux*: film4 Interview."
6. Rhett Butler's closing line to Scarlett O'Hara in the motion picture *Gone with the Wind*.

7. www.film4.com, "Producer Kim Aubry: *Apocalypse Now Redux*: film4 Interview.", 5.
8. David Thomson, "Summer Films: Apocalypse Then, and Now," *New York Times*, May 13, 2001.
9. Walter Murch, *In the Blink of an Eye: A Perspective on Film Editing*, 2nd ed. (Los Angeles: Silman-James Press, 2001), front cover.
10. Nathan Forrest Winters, "Victor Salva's Horror Stories," *Los Angeles Times*, June 11, 2006, latimes.com.

CHAPTER 14

1. Lynn Hirschberg, "The Coppola Smart Mob," *New York Times*, August 31, 2003, 11.
2. Ibid., 11.
3. Ibid., 2.
4. Ibid.
5. Alexander Ballinger, *New Cinematographers* (New York: Collins Design, 2004), 36–39.
6. Bumble Ward (Coppola's publicist), in "Sofia Coppola, Spike Jonze to Divorce," *USA Today*, December 9, 2001, http://www.usatoday.com/life/2003-12-09-coppola-divorce_x.htm.

CHAPTER 15

1. Steven Kolpan, *A Sense of Place: An Intimate Portrait of the Niebaum–Coppola Winery and the Napa Valley* (New York: Routledge, 1999), 86–88.
2. "Our Wines: Discover Our Wines," Francis Ford Coppola Winery, http://www.franciscoppolawinery.com.
3. "Obituary," *Los Angeles Times*, January 24, 2004.

CHAPTER 16

1. Colleen Claes, "Why You Hate Sofia Coppola's 'Marie Antoinette,'" *Open Salon*, January 11, 2010, http://open.salon.com/blog/colleenclaes/2010/01/11/why_you_hate_sofia_coppolas_marie_antoinette.
2. The death of Marie Antoinette is not depicted in the film. The film ends with Marie and Louis being forced out of Versailles.
3. Francis Ford Coppola, commentary on featurette of *Marie Antoinette* DVD.
4. Rebecca Murray, "Hollywood Movies: Writer/Director Sofia Coppola Talks about *Marie Antoinette*," About.com.

CHAPTER 17

1. Francis Ford Coppola, Foreword, in Mircea Eliade, *Youth without Youth* (Chicago: University of Chicago, 2007), vi, vii.
2. Alex Simon, "Francis Ford Coppola Interview," *The Hollywood Interview*, January 7, 2008, http://www.the hollywoodinterview.com.
3. Ibid.

CHAPTER 18

1. Ladane Nasseri, "Francis Ford Coppola Sees Cinema World Falling Apart," *Bloomberg*, October 11, 2009, http://www.bloomberg.com.
2. "Mihai Malaimare Jr." *Internet Encyclopedia of Cinematographers*, http://www.cinematographers.nl.
3. Larry Rohter, "With *Tetro* Francis Ford Coppola Is Making His Own Kind of Film," *New York Times*, June 3, 2009, AR18.
4. Kaleem Afbab, "Francis Ford Coppola—It's All about the Family Business," *The Independent*, June 11, 2010.
5. Larry Rohter, "With Tetro Francis Ford Coppola Is Making His Own Kind of Film," *New York Times*, June 3, 2009.
6. Nanette Asimov, "August Coppola, Arts Educator Dies at 75," *SFGate*, November 4, 2009.
7. "Obituaries August Coppola," *LATimes.com*, October 30, 2009.

CHAPTER 19

1. Frank Bruni, "Elle Fanning, The Next Golden Child Phenomenon," *New York Times*, December 8, 2010.

CHAPTER 20

1. David Gritten, "On the Road to Nowhere," *The Telegraph*, April 16, 2004.

CHAPTER 21

1. Joelle Diderich, "Sofia Coppola Directs Marni for H&M Campaign," *Women's Wear Daily*, December 14, 2011.

CHAPTER 22

1. The Catiline Conspiracy was a conspiracy against ancient Rome during the time of Caesar and Cicero with the objective of destroying the Roman Republic.
2. Jill Kearney, "Francis Ford Coppola: His Latest Hero Dreamed of Producing a New Automobile. Francis Ford Coppola Simply Wants to Create a Whole New Art Form," *Mother Jones*, September 1988.
3. "Coppola Eyes All-Star Cast for Megalopolis," *ABC News*, July 19, 2001.
4. "Coppola's Megalopolis," *IGN Movies*, May 15, 2001, http://movies.ign.com.
5. Statement released by Warner Bros. in *Daily Variety*, February 26, 1992.
6. Stu Koback, "Kim Aubry: Transferring Zoetrope's Vision," *Film on Disc*, n.d., http://www.filmsondisc.com/features/Kim_Aubry.

CHAPTER 23

1. Ariston Anderson, "Francis Ford Coppola: On Risk, Money, Craft & Collaboration," the99percent.com, http://the99percent.com/articles/6973/ Francis-Ford-Coppola-On-Risk-Money-Craft-Collaboration. (Interview after *Twixt*).

2. Eleanor Coppola, *Notes on a Life* (New York: Knopf Doubleday, 2008).

3. Steve Rose, "How Godfather Don Francis Ford Coppola Keeps Film-making in the Family," *The Guardian*, June 11, 2010.

4. Presentation of 2010 Irving Thalberg Life Achievement Award to Francis Ford Coppola, speech by George Lucas, Motion Picture Academy of Arts and Sciences.

5. Alison Beard, "An Interview with Francis Ford Coppola," *Harvard Business Review*, October 2011.

6. "Francis Coppola's Journals," in John Boorman and Walter Donohue (eds.), *Projections 3: Film-makers on Film-Making* (London: Faber & Faber, 1994), 12.

Bibliography

Andrew, Geoff, ed. *Film: The Critics' Choice: 150 Masterpieces of World Cinema Selected and Defined by the Experts*. New York: Billboard Books, 2001.

Bach, Stephen. *Final Cut: Dreams and Disaster in the Making of Heaven's Gate*. New York: Morrow, 1985.

Ballinger, Alexander. *New Cinematographers*. New York: HarperCollins, 2004.

Biskind, Peter. *Easy Riders, Raging Bulls: How the Sex-Drugs-and-Rock 'n' Roll Generation Saved Hollywood*. New York: Simon & Schuster, 1998.

Boorman, John, and Walter Donohue, eds. *Projections 6: Filmmakers on Film-making*. London: Faber and Faber, 1996

Boorman, John, and Walter Donohue, eds. *Projections 7: Filmmakers on Film-making*. London: Faber and Faber, 1997.

Bosworth, Patricia. *Marlon Brando*. New York: Lipper/Viking, 2001.

Brando, Marlon, with Robert Lindsey. *Brando: Songs My Mother Taught Me*. New York: Random House, 1994.

Brownlow, Kevin. *The Parade's Gone By . . .* New York: Knopf, 1968.

Callan, Michael Feeney. *Anthony Hopkins: The Unauthorized Biography*. New York: Charles Scribner's Sons, 1993.

Chaillet, Jean-Paul, and Elizabeth Vincent. *Francis Ford Coppola*. New York: St. Martin's Press, 1984.

Clarens, Carlos. *Crime Movies*. New York: Da Capo Press, 1997.

Cook, David A. *History of the American Cinema, Volume 9 1970–1979: Lost Illusions: American Cinema in the Shadow of Watergate and Vietnam*. Berkeley: University of California Press, 2000.

Coppola, Eleanor. *Notes*. New York: Simon and Schuster, 1979.

Cowie, Peter. *The Apocalypse Now Book*. New York: Da Capo Press, 2000, 2001.

Cowie, Peter. *Coppola*. New York: Da Capo Press, 1994.

Dearborn, Mary V. *Mailer*. Boston: Houghton Mifflin Company, 1999.

Delorme, Stéphane. *Cahiers du Cinema: Masters of Cinema: Francis Ford Coppola*. Paris: Cahiers du cinéma Sarl, 2010.

Dougan, Andy. *Untouchable: A Biography of Robert De Niro*, 2nd ed. New York: Thunder's Mouth Press. 1996.

Ebert, Roger. *The Great Movies*. New York: Broadway Books, 2002.

Faber, Stephen, and Marc Green. *Hollywood Dynasties*. New York: Fawcett Crest, 1984.

Gabler, Neal. *An Empire of Their Own: How the Jews Invented Hollywood*. New York: Crown, 1988.

Goodwin, Michael, and Naomi Wise. *On the Edge: The Life and Times of Francis Coppola*. New York: William Morrow and Company, Inc., 1989.

Kennedy, William, Francis Coppola, and Mario Puzo. *The Cotton Club: The Complete Script in Its Original Form*. New York: St. Martin's Press, 1986.

Lebo, Harlan. *The Godfather Legacy*. New York: Fireside, 1997.

Lewis, Jon. *Whom God Wishes to Destroy . . . : Francis Coppola and the New Hollywood*. Durham, NC, and London: Duke University Press, 1995.

LoBrutto, Vincent. *Becoming Film Literate: The Art and Craft of Motion Pictures*. Westport, CT: Praeger, 2005.

LoBrutto, Vincent. *Principal Photography: Interviews with Feature Film Cinematographers*. Westport, CT: Praeger, 1992.

LoBrutto, Vincent. *Selected Takes: Film Editors on Editing*. New York: Praeger, 1991.

LoBrutto, Vincent. *Sound-on-Film: Interviews with Creators of Film Sound*. Westport, CT: Praeger, 1994.

Manso, Peter. *Brando: The Biography*. New York: Hyperion, 1994.

McKay, Keith. *Robert De Niro: The Hero behind the Masks*. New York: St. Martin's Press, 1986.

Monaco, James. *American Film Now: The People, The Power, The Money, The Movies*. New York: Oxford University Press, 1979.

Mordden, Ethan. *The Hollywood Studios: House Style in the Golden Age of the Movies*. New York: Simon & Schuster, 1989.

Ondaatje, Michael. *The Conversations: Walter Murch and the Art of Editing Film*. New York: Knopf, 2002.

Phillips, Gene D. *Godfather: The Intimate Francis Ford Coppola*. Lexington: The University Press of Kentucky, 2004.

Phillips, Gene D., and Rodney Hill, eds. *Francis Ford Coppola Interviews*. Jackson: University Press of Mississippi, 2004.

Puzo, Mario. *The Godfather*. New York: New American Library, 2002.

Randall, Stephen, and the editors of *Playboy Magazine*, eds. *The Playboy Interviews*. Milwaukee, WI: M Press, 2006.

Schaefer, Dennis, and Larry Salvato. *Masters of Light: Conversations with Contemporary Cinematographers*. Berkeley: University of California Press, 1984.

Schatz, Thomas. *The Genius of the System: Hollywood Filmmaking in the Studio Era*. New York: Pantheon, 1988.

Schumacher, Michael. *Francis Ford Coppola: A Filmmaker's Life*. New York: Crown Publishers, 1999.

Stempel, Tom. *Framework: A History of Screenwriting in the American Film*. New York: Continuum, 1988.

Thomson, David. *"Have You Seen . . . ?": A Personal Introduction to 1,000 Films*. New York: Knopf, 2008.

Waxman, Sharon. *Rebels on the Backlot: Six Maverick Directors and How They Conquered the Hollywood Studio System*. New York: HarperEntertainment, 2005.

Index

About the Authors

VINCENT LOBRUTTO is a film instructor in the Department of Film, Video and Animation at the School of Visual Arts in Manhattan. He is the author of numerous books on filmmaking and received the 2011 Robert Wise Award for journalistic excellence from the American Cinema Editors Society. LoBrutto has written biographies of filmmakers Stanley Kubrick, Martin Scorsese, and Gus Van Sant.

HARRIET R. MORRISON is a graduate of the Masters of Fine Arts program at Sarah Lawrence College in Bronxville, New York. She has written film criticism and profiles about outstanding women in the workplace for women's publications. Morrison is a management consultant dealing with issues of work equity for women.